Yemen Chronicle

ALSO BY STEVEN C. CATON

Lawrence of Arabia: A Film's Anthropology
"Peaks of Yemen I Summon": Poetry as Cultural Practice in a North Yemeni Tribe

YEMEN

CHRONICLE

An Anthropology of War and Mediation

STEVEN C. CATON

HILL AND WANG

A division of Farrar, Straus and Giroux

New York

Hill and Wang
A division of Farrar, Straus and Giroux
120 Broadway, New York 10271

First edition, 2005

Library of Congress Cataloging-in-Publication Data
Caton, Steven Charles, 1950–
    Yemen chronicle : an anthropology of war and mediation / Steven C. Caton.
    p.   cm.
    ISBN: 978-0-8090-9882-8

    1. Yemen—Social life and customs. 2. Caton, Steven Charles, 1950–
3. Anthropologists—United States—Biography.   I. Title.
DS247.Y44C38 2005
953.05′2—dc22

                                                      2005041978

Designed by Debbie Glasserman

Maps designed by Jeffrey L. Ward

www.fsgbooks.com

P1

For Don

Contents

Maps can be found on pages 11, 34, and 88.

Yemen Chronicle

Prologue

∽

GRAVESIDE

Wadi Maswar, Republic of Yemen   July 1, 2001
"You wanted to see where my father is buried, Mr. Steven."

At my feet there was only a simple necklace of pebbles to mark the perimeter of the grave. Had Ahmed not pointed it out to me, I might have blithely walked over it. As is the manner in northern Yemen, the headstone of this grave was small and plain, with not even a name or date inscribed on it. And it was shocking to see shards of pottery scattered over the graves until one learned that broken clay vessels were strewn about not out of callous disrespect of the dead but as a reminder of the fragility of life.

"Every soul shall taste death," it says in the Qur'an. "We shall test you with good and evil. To Us you will return."

Scraps of paper and plastic bags scuttled across the graveyard in the wind. Refuse was an almost insurmountable problem all over Yemen, thanks to western manufactured goods. There was no easy way to dispose of the trash they created in a society that was used to throwing refuse out the window and leaving it to degrade naturally. I winced at a squashed can of Nido powdered milk wedged in the middle of Muhammad's grave. I wanted to pick it up and throw it away, and the absurdity of it made me laugh. *Yes, Muhammad, you would have appreciated the perverse irony of it.*

He was buried next to his mother and father. They had passed away in quick succession soon after their son's death. Died of broken hearts, it was said. Their graves were similarly anonymous and nondescript.

"In the name of God, Most Gracious, Most Merciful," I whispered. Ahmed and the other young men intoned the opening of the Qur'an with me.

> *Praise be to God, the Lord of the world.*
> *Most Gracious, Most Merciful, Master of the Day of Judgment.*
> *Thee do we worship and to Thee we turn in supplication.*
> *Show us the right path, the way of those on whom Thou hast bestowed Thy Grace,*
> *Those whose lot is not [Thy] wrath and who do not go astray.*
>
> *Amen.*

If any lives tested a faith, my companions' certainly had. And faith was all that was left to them. It was all the more unforgivable that I— who came from a country about which one older Yemeni exclaimed in helpless amazement but with no bitterness, "Ah, America, it seems as though God has showered all His Blessings on thee"—should have wavered in mine. After what had happened to this country, to this part of the world, not to speak of my friend Muhammad and his family, it was hard to believe in God's mercy.

I knelt and reached out to touch a stone on the grave. *I'm sorry, Muhammad, that I never made it back to Yemen to see you again. Sorry that I didn't try harder to stay in touch with you or to get you into the United States.*

"Don't cry, Mr. Steven." I felt Ahmed's hand resting gently on my shoulder. "It's the way things are."

1

∽

SANCTUARY

Khawlan al-Tiyal, Yemen Arab Republic. November 25, 1979
I had finally arrived at the place where I was to begin my fieldwork, a village whose inhabitants claimed descent from the Prophet Muhammad. Called in Yemeni Arabic a *hijra*, or sanctuary, it was a settlement where the surrounding tribes of this eastern region of Yemen, known as Khawlan al-Tiyal, could pray in the mosque and trade in the souk without fear of being attacked by enemies. As a stranger in this strange land, I needed to live under protection, and if it was not to be that of a powerful sheikh, then I hoped it would be the sanctuary's.

Jon Mandaville, Director of the American Institute for Yemeni Studies, had just left in his jeep, and the many cartons that held my belongings, which he had helped me to transport from Sana'a, the capital, lay scattered at my feet. They caught the attention of village youngsters playing outside my door, who later called me "Mr. Karatis," or Mr. Cartons, because of them. This would be the least embarrassing of my nicknames.

A tall, very erect gentleman, every inch a stern Old Testament prophet, strode up to the courtyard to see why the children were making such a commotion. After the proper salutations to me, he inquired, "Are you a doctor?" The house into which I was moving had been formerly occupied by a Peace Corps couple, the wife of whom had been a nurse. He indicated that her ministrations were sorely missed. No, I reluctantly conceded, I was not a doctor.

"Ah, of course." He smiled knowingly. "You must be our new English teacher," for an English teacher was what the husband of the Peace Corps nurse had been. "We need an English teacher almost as badly as we do a doctor."

"No, neither doctor nor English teacher. I'm an anthropologist."

"Fine," he said, either not understanding what I had said or choosing to ignore it. "We'll take you to the school in the morning to teach the children English. Where did you learn to speak Arabic?"

"In the United States and in Saudi Arabia."

"Oh, you taught English there, too, no doubt."

"No, I've never taught English in my life. In Saudi Arabia I worked for the Ministry of Education, in their Department of Antiquities."

He looked at me as though I were finally beginning to make sense. "Aha! You've come to dig up our ancient treasures. Khawlan is full of them, you know, going all the way back to the Sabaeans."

"Actually, I want to collect your poetry."

His expression was blank. The reason for my being in the village was obscure once more. After a pause, he tried another tack. "What's your name?"

I had long ago learned to arabize my American name so that it could be pronounced more easily by my Yemeni friends. "I-S-T-I-F-A-N."

Silence. The unflappable children were momentarily aghast.

"*What's* your name?" the old man inquired incredulously. I repeated it, much to the delight now of the boys and girls. "Change your name!" the old man snapped. The children began to snigger.

I'd been in the village less than an hour and already felt like taking flight. But curiosity got the better of embarrassment, and I asked to know why.

"Believe me, I'm your friend. Just change your name!"

"Well, what's *your* name?"

"Ali."

"Well, Sayyid Ali, I'll change my name, but if you're my friend, you must tell me why."

Now it was his turn to be flustered. "No, no, I can't," he stammered. "At least not with the children present."

"Your discretion is already lost on them." I pointed to their grinning faces. "I'm the only one who's still in the dark."

"Well, I don't want to hurt your feelings, but you do know what *fann* means, don't you?"

"Why, yes, a work of art." By this time, the kids were howling with laughter.

"You mean you still don't get it?" The old man looked at me as though I were a congenital idiot. "*Ist-i-fann*. My *ist* is a work of art. *Ist-i-fann*. My *ist* is a work of art."

I kept repeating the sentence to myself, wondering what its meaning could be. I gave the man a puzzled look.

"I'll tell you some other time," he said and made ready to beat a hasty retreat.

"No, no, you must tell me now," I insisted. He bit his lip and tried to point to his backside without the children noticing.

I now realized what I'd been saying. The whole year I'd been in Yemen, I'd been introducing myself to people as "Hello, my ass is a work of art."

I couldn't help laughing. "You're right, Ali. You *are* my friend. As you say, I must change my name."

"Do you like Seif?" he suggested encouragingly. "Seif al-Islam: that was the name of the imam's son, you know, in the olden days of the monarchy."

In Arabic, *seif* also means "sword," and that was certainly more flattering to my masculine ego than "ass." But I wasn't sure I wanted to be identified quite so closely with the ancien régime, so I offered an alternative. "Or Seif bin Dhi Yazan." This Yemeni folk hero, an actual historical personage, was thought to have beaten back invading Ethiopian Christian forces a century before the advent of Islam.

"Good, good," the old man exclaimed, obviously pleased by this diplomatic solution. "From now on, we'll call you Seif."

The children demurred, for they were having far too much fun with *Ist-i-fann*. For weeks afterward, whenever I would leave my house with them trailing behind me, I would hear "Whatsyourname? Whatsyour-name? Whatsyourname?"

"Seif."

"*No-o-o*. What's your *real* name? What's your *American* name?"

And then they would skip away, clucking in tones of mock dismay, "Imagine! For a whole year, he called himself I-S-T-I-F-A-N-N."

It was a consolation to learn later on that nearly everyone in the sanctuary, even its most respected members, had a nickname, such as "the poor one" or "the hunchback" or "the blind one" or "the beltmaker" or "the agent" (who looked after my house when the landlord was away). I had not only arrived but been accepted, in an ambivalent sort of way. My American name had become my nickname, as I learned had happened also with the beloved nurse, for I would be slyly asked why she was called Jeannie when everyone knew that *jinni* means "evil spirit."

It was stipulated in the contract I signed with my landlord that I had to "juss" my lodgings, the first floor of a large stone house, at either the beginning or the end of the period of my lease. *Juss* is a whitewash, a mixture of water and finely ground limestone applied mainly to the inside walls of a house. I thought it would be to my advantage to enjoy the benefits of whitewashed walls sooner rather than later, so I decided to do it right away. It would be a sign of having taken possession, like applying a fresh coat of paint to a newly purchased home.

It was a simple job, but transporting the *juss* from Sana'a was a headache, as I explained in a letter to my mother.

January 5, 1980

Dear Hanni:

. . . I've hired a man [my upstairs neighbor, Ahmed] to do a job called "jussing" which is whitewashing the inside of my apartment. I carted the plaster back from Sana'a myself. What a trip that was! The road is extremely bumpy, being unpaved and traversing mountainous terrain. That plaster, which comes in a very fine white powder, is packed in burlap sacks which are slightly porous. Naturally, the pow-der escaped through the small holes in the burlap weave while the car was careening and bouncing on its way, with the result that we soon found ourselves enveloped in a fine cloud of the stuff. Because it consists of lime, it irritates the skin and eyes, so we were scratching, rubbing, and sneezing, until finally we had to stop the car and figure out a way to transport it without being covered in it. I was all for dumping it and starting all over again, but my friend [Muhammad the Window Maker, Ahmed's older brother] was more patient and prevailed on me to consider less wasteful alternatives. Eventually we went back to Sana'a to get large plastic trash bags in which we dropped the sacks of plaster and then completed the journey.

The situation in Sana'a is still very peaceful, and [the sanctuary], of course, is completely safe. I do wish that you and Dad might be able to visit me in Yemen sometime in the spring or fall . . .

In the courtyard of my house, Muhammad the Window Maker (not the same Muhammad whose grave I visited in 2001) carefully prepared the mixture in wheelbarrows, stirring it until it looked like a vanilla milk shake. He then poured the thick liquid into buckets that Ahmed carried into the house.

Ahmed showed me how to apply the whitewash. Dipping strips of white cloth in the mixture, he swatted them against the wall. Smack, smack, smack. You had to squint or look away to avoid getting stung in the eyes by the vile stuff, all the while trying to aim at a bare spot. In the process we both ended up looking like Casper the Friendly Ghost. I questioned the efficiency of this obviously slapdash method of application but was assured by Ahmed that it was preferable over, say, the use of a brush or sponge. Though I had my doubts on that score, even I had to admire the uniformity of the finish when we were done. No streaks, no blotches, only a smooth, slightly crystalline surface that glistened like the icing on a cake.

Beans and freshly baked bread had been prepared for lunch by Ahmed's wife, Fatimah. I could not tell what she looked like under her veil, a cloth tie-dyed in red, blue, and black that was pulled far in front of her face, but she had a beautiful voice—clarion and soothingly melodious. The three of us chatted amicably while taking turns cuddling the couple's two-year-old son, Ahmed bin Ahmed, or Junior, as I called him. In just a few hours the whitewash was dry. Ahmed helped me put my furnishings back inside the house, and my apartment was ready for occupancy.

I was happy and relieved for the first time since my arrival in Yemen ten months earlier. There had been so many obstacles and delays that I had begun to doubt I would ever get to settle down. The act of moving into a place of my own symbolized the stability I craved, which had been eluding me. To understand why until then my fieldwork had been such a maddening combination of false starts and missteps, one has to know something of the drastic political situation in Yemen in 1979, and so I must say something of the earlier political history of the Arabian Peninsula.

What is now known as the Republic of Yemen was in 1979 two separate countries, informally referred to as North and South Yemen, or the Yemen Arab Republic and the People's Democratic Republic of Yemen, respectively. As a result of the geopolitics of the Arabian Peninsula during the cold war and the different political systems that emerged in the shadow of Soviet-American rivalry—a republican government in North Yemen under the sway of Saudi Arabia and, by extension, the United States; a regime in South Yemen that was a staunch communist ally of the Soviet Union—hostilities between the two had been more or less constant since their founding. North Yemen was the first to emerge from its cocoon, in 1962, when the thousand-year-old monarchy there (actually more like a theocracy, headed by an imam) was overthrown in favor of a constitutional republic. A protracted and bloody civil war followed between royalists and adherents to the imam, who were supported by Saudi Arabia, and republican loyalists, allied with Egypt; it ended in 1974. Though the republic emerged victorious, the bitter struggle left its infrastructure and economy in tatters. Saudi Arabia and Kuwait, along with the United States and various European nations, came to its aid, but most of the income for reconstruction was from remittance payments of Yemenis working in the Gulf States. Meanwhile, South Yemen, shortly after receiving independence from Great Britain in 1967, became a powerful Marxist state. By con-

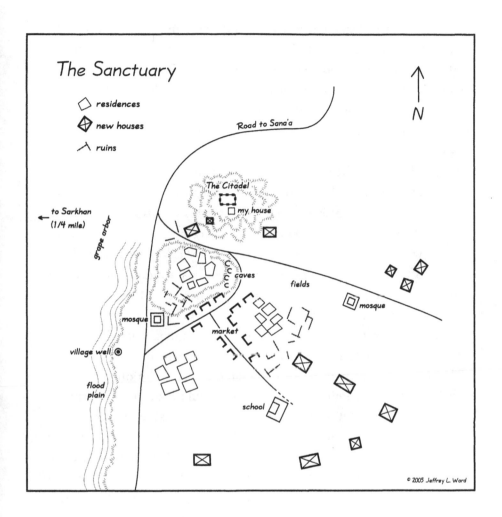

The Sanctuary

◇ residences
◈ new houses
⅄ ruins

Road to Sana'a

The Citadel
□ my house

to Sarkhan
(1/4 mile)

grape arbor

caves

fields

mosque

market

mosque

village well ◉

flood
plain

school

N

© 2005 Jeffrey L. Ward

trast with North Yemen, it managed to develop in relative peace, with aid from the Soviet Union. Its educational system was sound, and its military well-armed and well-organized. Given the global political alliances of the time, it was inevitable that North and South Yemen were at odds with each other, and the North regularly accused the South of trying to destabilize its regime by arming and mobilizing insurgents on its borders.

In early 1979, when I came to North Yemen for the first time, the simmering hostilities between the two states rose to a boil as South Yemen invaded its northern neighbor. American newspapers were full of the story, which was somewhat surprising because Yemen, a poor nation with what political scientists frequently call a "weak state," was all too often considered a backwater, its political troubles too minor to affect events in the Middle East, let alone the rest of the world. But Yemen was not the only trouble spot in the Middle East that year, and the question in the back of many American minds was whether the conflict between North and South Yemen was part of a larger pattern. The Soviet Union had invaded Afghanistan; a revolution against the Shah of Iran was gaining momentum—it would lead to his overthrow in November—and it was not clear whether Marxist revolutionaries or their Islamic allies would gain the upper hand in the ensuing struggle to take over the reins of government. The U.S. Department of State did not consider that a communist aggression on the Arabian Peninsula threatening not only North Yemen but also its oil-rich neighbor Saudi Arabia was a mere local conflict, but looked on it as part of a potentially more ominous geopolitical trend.

In the middle of March, I received a worried telegram from my sister.

FAMILY IS CONCERNED ABOUT PENDING WAR IN YEMEN STOP SUG-
GESTING THAT YOU CONSIDER RETURNING TO US STOP PLEASE
CALL OR WRITE

I wasn't sure if "US" was "U.S." or "us," but then the ambiguity was apt in this overheated moment. I replied:

SITUATION NOT CRITICAL DESPITE US NEWS REPORTS STOP LETTER FOLLOWS

This was not just a sop intended to quiet my family's fears (as the last two sentences of reassurance in the letter I wrote to my mother were), for there was a history to this conflict that American news media generally didn't cover. When events are seen as significant in the perspective of some global vision, other parts of the story that are important locally may be overlooked. As it was put to me sanguinely by someone whom I respected and who had lived in Yemen for nearly two decades, "We've seen this all before. Every seven years, in fact! The two sides decide to fight, then make peace, and then go about their business again."

But the fighting between the two Yemens had made it difficult to travel, so I had to bide my time to relocate to what I hoped would be a more desirable research site than Sana'a, the capital, once the security situation had improved. Several Yemenis told told me about a region due east of the capital that was renowned for its tribal poets. I was itching to get there and meet some of them.

I assumed at the time that there was such a thing as an "authentic" tribal poetry, whose heart beat in a rural and seemingly remote setting such as Khawlan al-Tiyal and not in a complex urban setting such as Sana'a (where later in fact I would study the works of many tribal poets, who had migrated from Yemen's drought-stricken countryside to enlist in the army or become taxi drivers or private security guards). But after only six months, I realized how simplistic that assumption was. The urban-rural dichotomy and the cultural dichotomy of tribal–nontribal, not to speak of the political one of state-nonstate, were, if not exactly wrong, then misleading. They certainly could not be neatly correlated. For example, the "hottest" tribal poet in Yemen in 1979, Muhammad al-Gharsi, whose cassette tapes sold out before everyone else's in the stereo stores, had his main residence in Sana'a, where he was in the army. Because of his poetic gifts but no less because of his connections to the president, Ali Abdullah Salih, he became an eloquent spokesman for the republican regime. But staying in the capital to study tribal poetry was in my view a fall-back position, in the event that I could not get to Khawlan. The allure of Khawlan for me was like that of the wild frontier in the imaginations of nineteenth-century Americans who journeyed to the Old West.

Had I known how difficult settling in Khawlan would be, I might not have even tried it. My hope was to live in a proper "tribal" village with "tribal" poets, but that required the permission of a local sheikh, and I could not persuade a single one to give it and grant me his protection besides. And why should he, when I had nothing to offer in return except inconvenience and possibly trouble? I had gone so far as to be interviewed on prime-time national television by one of its female stars, who put in a kind word on my behalf at the end of the program. But even the intervention of this beloved pop-culture icon was to no avail. Calls offering to adopt me did not come flooding in, and once again I found myself having to revert to Plan B—studying the poets in Sana'a. Then, in the late spring, someone told me of a Peace Corps couple living in a small village in Khawlan that was a sanctuary protected by the local tribes. As they were about to be reassigned, their premises would be vacant soon, and perhaps their landlord would agree to rent it to me. Though grateful for this small crumb, I was not enthusiastic about the prospect of living in a such a place. It was not a "tribal" village—few tribesmen, in fact, lived in it—even though it was located in the heart of an important tribal region. It was the home principally of the highborn descendants of the Prophet, known as *sada*, who were the religious elite in Yemen and subscribed to a rather different cultural ethos than that of the tribes, with their love of spontaneously created oral poetry. To make matters worse, I would be associated with the politically suspect Peace Corps, and I conveniently forgot that the reputation of anthropologists was hardly better.

In spite of these reservations, I visited the *bijra*. After the tumultuous and anxious months I had spent waiting out the war in the capital, it seemed to provide the safety and tranquillity I yearned for. A village of no more than five hundred people, it was nestled in a starkly beautiful landscape of cone-shaped volcanic hills and meandering watercourses. I was somewhat dismayed by its lack of basic amenities, but in those days few places in Yemen outside Sana'a had electricity or running water. To my relief, the Peace Corps couple's house was clean, light, and in good repair. More important was the goodwill toward Americans that they had inspired and of which I hoped to be the beneficiary. I decided to move to the sanctuary and into the couple's apartment in spite of the landlord's exorbitant rent. In truth, I had little choice. I had to settle into a field site soon or I would run out of fellowship money.

A welcoming committee of sorts came when the *juss* job was done. A neighbor boy, Ali the Bird, shyly poked his head in the door to pay his respects. This was the first time we had met. I asked him to take a photograph of Ahmed and me with my camera, since my hands were still covered in plaster. There we were, standing in the wind, my arm tightly gripped around Ahmed's shoulder as though I were trying to squeeze the life out of him.

A door in the hall of my quarters opened onto a stairway that led to the upstairs apartment, where Ahmed lived with his wife and young son. It could not be opened from my side. Of course, it was entirely right that I should not have access to their abode, for the simple reason that Fatimah was alone in it for much of the day, but I did not like the fact that I could not prevent their entry into my place. No doubt our landlord thought that Ahmed, who looked after the house, needed to be able to get into my apartment in case of an emergency. I would not have minded this arrangement had Ahmed not decided to visit me whenever he was bored or wanted to chat, even if that meant waking me up in the middle of the night. Nor did he believe in knocking.

He was frustrated, it seemed, because he had not the skills, education, or intelligence to advance in life. And there were problems in his marriage. He let it slip that Fatimah sometimes refused to sleep with him. Though handsome in an unshaven, thuggish way, he was an oaf, and I could imagine how his boudoir demeanor might have dampened her ardor. I had the temerity to ask whether he beat his wife. Puffing on his cigarette, he replied wryly that she would have left him long ago and gotten a divorce at the insistence of her own family had he laid a hand on her. But he did expect her to cook and to clean and to raise his children and to have sex with him when he wanted it—that was all—and she had the gall to throw back at him that she was not his "slave." I hinted that there was something beck-and-callish about his notion of marriage. One scene that could have come out of *A Streetcar Named Desire*, for example, was enacted almost daily. Ahmed would arrive at the house around noon, bellowing "Ahmo-o-o, ya Ahmo-o-o," at the top of his lungs while pounding on the front door. I did not understand at first why he called out his own name instead of his wife's until I learned that it was considered shameful to pronounce a woman's name in public, since it is deemed a metonym of her sex. I could hear Fatimah whispering fiercely to him that it was not necessary for him to shout clear across the village for her, as though he were summoning a dog, but he continued the practice. Whether to annoy her or because such delicacy was lost on him did not seem to matter.

I tried to imagine Fatimah's side of the story, though I may have been just projecting my own white, middle-class values on their marriage. "Perhaps she wants you to talk to her more and to help out with the housework once in a while."

"It's deeper than that, Seif. She wants me to buy her things when there's not enough money for basics." A husband is expected to give his wife gifts—jewelry, for example—as much for her own satisfaction and as a token of his affection as for the respect for her family's honor that this practice is supposed to show. Fatimah was clearly within her rights. The gifts could also serve a practical function, as a kind of insurance in her old age or to help support her parents, as Fatimah in fact was trying to do. Oh, yes, the in-laws were another source of irritation to Ahmed. "She spends more time with them than with me," he complained bitterly, "often sleeping overnight at their house." This, I now realized, might have explained his forlorn late-night appearances in my own quarters.

On those occasions, he sometimes brought along his livelier and wittier teenage brothers, Yahya and Abdullah. Because they were single, they did not have to be home after dark with wives and children, and so the four of us whiled away the evening hours playing cards and gossiping. Their horseplay and laughter cheered me up, and they were more than happy to pull me up from the floor and teach me some dance steps. *Sada* were not known for dancing, and indeed some of the more righteous ones frowned upon it, though the religious explanation for this, trotted out in one Qur'anic dogma and hadith (the Prophet's sayings and deeds) after another, always eluded me. Nonetheless, just in case a puritanical neighbor should come by and hear us, the shutters in my sitting room were tightly closed and the volume on the tape deck turned down low, imparting a deliciously clandestine air to our harmless sociality.

"Let's hear one of those tapes you made of the music at the tribal weddings," Yahya suggested.

"Left forward—together. Left forward—together. Keep the right arm up, Seif, and shake the dagger slightly. Now turn around on the right foot." I hadn't been instructed like this since Mrs. Wilson's dance class in junior high school. Yahya sprang up and stood beside me, unself-consciously grabbing me by the waist to demonstrate. I tried to tilt my body in the same direction as his, to bend slightly at the knees, and to sway as he did. Though Yahya and Abdullah had the agility of youth, even I could discern their lack of skill and precision compared with that of their tribal counterparts whose dancing they were emulating.

Ahmed, meanwhile, behaved like a wallflower. He dragged out a tome that had been lent to him, a sort of marriage manual produced by scholars of the Zaydi sect, a variant of Schiʿa Islam to which he belonged and which was predominant in North Yemen. He pronounced the words haltingly, not always sure of what they meant. After a while he gave up trying to understand the legalistic jargon and closed the book with a loud thud. "Maybe I'll just divorce her," he muttered petulantly. I could not help wondering whether that wasn't already his wife's wish.

Sometimes Fatimah would summon me to the door and talk through it, saying in her measured tones, like those of a trained singer, that she would leave me some freshly baked bread on the front steps. When I opened the house door to go on an errand, I'd find it there, on an old aluminum tray and covered with a cloth. The unleavened bread was the size and shape of a large pizza, delicate and spongy to the touch. It was delicious with a bean dip or *hilba*, a frothy sauce made from fenugreek. This too she would provide, in a blackened little tin pot. Aside from neighborliness, I cynically wondered what was behind this thoughtfulness. As she got to know me better, she would come to the front door and stand in the threshold with her little son on one hip. I knew better than to invite her into my apartment and she to accept, for then all the tongues in the neighborhood would wag.

One time she brought a friend, and holding their small children in their arms like passports into a foreign country, they pushed the door wide open and marched inside, brazenly inspecting the furnishings and informing me that they would like to have the first option of purchasing them when I left. I had hardly arrived and already they were anticipating my departure! I did not mean to sound condescending but asked as a matter of curiosity how they would pay for the furnishings. It was not that they were costly, but I needed every penny on my meager fellowship stipends and could not afford to give them away for a song. Oh, that would not be a problem, I was informed. The husband of Fatimah's friend worked in Saudi Arabia, and Fatimah had part ownership in a shop in the village souk. Women in Yemen could inherit money or own assets without their husbands having legal claim over them, and it was clear that these two intended to pay for my furnishings on their own. I was assured that they would make me a good offer. During these brief visits, I learned that Fatimah's parents were not in good health and that she spent as much time as possible in their house to help take care of them. Then, too, her brother's wedding was coming up, and there was anxiety over the expenses, so she had to make sure that her business was taking in enough money. She never spoke of the difficulties she was having with Ahmed, but I didn't expect her to, this being entirely inappropriate with a strange man. If truth be told, I liked her better than her husband.

Fatimah's friend invited me to visit her father, who was a caretaker of the Citadel, a house of imposing size located on the highest promontory in the sanctuary. He turned out to be the same Ali who had greeted me upon my entry into the village. Perhaps it was again cynical of me to think so, but I assumed she was banking on my becoming his friend in order to strengthen her claim on my household furnishings. He did not belong to the *sada* but was a tribesman, I learned, and she tried to intimate that he might have something specific to teach me about tribal poetry. It turned out he had very little to say on the subject, but his daughter was shrewd in suspecting that I would be won over by his charm anyway. He was indeed wonderful company and fun to talk to. It was precisely when I realized that I didn't want anything in particular from him that my visits to the Citadel became relaxing and refreshing. He would play with his little grandson until the boy fell asleep in his arms. I took a color slide of the two of them together and asked my father to have multiple copies printed so I could give some to the old man as a present. The daughter sent a copy to her husband in Saudi Arabia.

Ali the Bird began to attach himself to me for reasons that were not altogether clear. Perhaps he recognized a kindred spirit because of the books in my makeshift office. I in turn delighted in his subtle intelligence and gentleness. I nicknamed him the Bird because of his appearance. He had a beaklike nose and small, nervous eyes, and was always darting from one spot to the other as though in flight.

His ambition was to be a doctor. He had been fascinated by the American nurse "Jinni" and had often volunteered to be her escort on her daily rounds. Becoming a doctor would entail a long and arduous journey, however, leading farther and farther from the sanctuary he knew and loved: first a good secondary school in Sana'a; then the national university; then medical school in another Arab country or perhaps Europe or the United States. Besides the pang of separation, Ali's family worried that he might suffer a loss of faith in the lands of the infidel or succumb to alien ways. "It's what I want," he confessed to me, "to become a doctor. But it seems like such a far-off dream."

Afternoons were usually reserved for *qat* chews with friends. *Qat* is a mildly narcotic plant, the topmost leaves of which are chewed daily by

nearly every adult in Yemen. My jaw muscles weren't up to such a reg-
imen, so I would sometimes skip a session to take a walk with Ali the
Bird as my guide. We skirted the fields east of the village, which were
planted in barley, sorghum, wheat, and of course *qat*, the most lucrative
cash crop in Yemen. Or we strolled in the orchards, where the crab
apple, almond, and fig trees offered shade. Ali told me the names
of dozens of plants and other features, and I still am pleased when I
come across his beautiful handwriting in my notebooks, where he patiently corrected my spelling. The teenage boys we encountered on
our walks would ask me why I walked so much, and I told them it was
for exercise.

Once, I teasingly asked them whether they would like to join me in
a jog through the *seyla*, the watercourse outside the sanctuary that
flooded when the rains came in the winter and summer months but was
dry for the rest of the year. It extended for many kilometers through
rugged, dusty terrain.

"No thanks, we already know that Americans aren't quite right in
the head. We prefer soccer."

Turning to Ali the Bird, I asked, "Do you think I'm not right in the
head?"

"No," he responded shyly, "but I too prefer soccer," and he ran off
to play with his friends.

I continued on my own and scrambled to the top of an escarpment
where I could get a good view of the village. I gazed on a Cubist ab-
straction of planes: the tilting rectangles of fallow fields and the
smooth stone walls of houses, set at sharp angles to one another and
colored in delicate hues of brown, beige, yellow, and gray. The stillness that greeted me was like that of a wintry pond, with only the occasional gust of wind or throbbing of the water pump to break the
silence. No redolence of wildflowers penetrated the nostrils; no scent
of eucalyptus or pine such as one might smell in a California canyon,
nor, for that matter, the acrid stink of manure that almost makes one
faint as one bicycles past a freshly fertilized field in the Middle West. It
was long past the rainy season, but the land was even dryer than usual
because Yemen had been in the grips of a drought.

Running north-south was the road to Sana'a, about thirty kilometers away as the crow flies, but in 1980 it took at least two hours or more to reach it by car. I'd see the occasional "taxi" jeep dip and climb over the rugged terrain, looking like some ungainly, clambering beetle. Now and again the driver would stop to let off a passenger in the middle of nowhere. With his bag of belongings slung over his shoulder, he would trudge over neatly plowed fields toward some settlement perched on a rocky outcrop. Hajbah's store, no more than a wooden shed with a corrugated tin roof, was an important way station en route, where one could get soft drinks or fruit juice to slake one's thirst.

To the west was the tribal village of Sarkhan, nestled in a green valley. Above and quite far beyond it loomed a tabletop mountain, Kanin. Ali the Bird said that people bathed in hot and cold springs on the mountain. A treasure from the days of Yemen's ancient incense-and-spice kingdoms more than two and a half thousand years ago was said to be buried in its depths. No man has been able to find it because it's guarded by *jinn*. Did Ali, then, believe in *jinn*? I asked. Of course, he replied, they are mentioned in the Qur'an. But he sheepishly admitted that he'd never seen one.

The sanctuary had been nearly destroyed by Egyptian warplanes during the civil war, which had concluded only a few years before I arrived. Most people had rebuilt their houses using the rubble of the ruined old buildings, supplemented by stones from ancient sites. In effect, their homes became museums, the exterior walls studded with bas-relief snake sculptures and block writing, both being distinctive features of Himyaritic architecture. (The Himyarites were one of several powerful pre-Islamic kingdoms that flourished in Yemen about two thousand years ago.) Others who could afford it thought it more practical to start over, on the periphery of the settlement. Brand-new stone houses—the Citadel above where I lived being the most ostentatious among them—rose like phoenixes, built with money sent back by relatives working as migrant laborers in Saudi Arabia and the Gulf States during the 1960s and '70s. But this expansion sometimes occasioned disputes over land boundaries or fueled resentment among those who, like my upstairs neighbor Ahmed, could barely eke out a living. The man known as the Agent, who looked after my house and the other properties of several absentee landlords, had shots fired into his home one evening as a result of a feud he'd been having with a neighbor over land. Expansion even brought charges of encroachment from outside the sanctuary. A tribesman in an adjacent hamlet, Ali al-Mahjari, loudly proclaimed to anyone who would listen that the sada were stealing his ancestral lands. I began to realize that this was hardly the halcyon spot I had hoped to find.

I spent a lot of my mornings in the marketplace, the hub of the village's activities. There was no point in going before ten or ten-thirty, because store owners caught up on their sleep in the mornings after bouts of qat-induced insomnia, so I busied myself until then with household chores. I could see women making fuel for their ovens out of a mixture of cow dung and straw, which they shaped into pancake-sized patties and left to dry on the rooftops. I thanked God that I had puta gaz. The alternative would have been to gather firewood, of which there was very little on the hillsides, long since denuded by centuries of use and erosion. The main source of water was a well at the edge of town. Veiled, hip-swaying women walked to and fro with buckets carefully balanced on their heads. In the beginning, I paid a man with a truck to deliver water to me on a weekly basis, but he wasn't reliable, and since no sada woman was willing to hire herself out to me—not out of meanness or sloth but out of consideration of her social standing—I ended up hauling water myself. I tried to pick a time when the fewest women were at the well, to save all of us embarrassment, and then I lugged ten-liter plastic containers, one in each hand, up the three hundred yards to my house, swearing in English all the way. By midmorning, washing would appear all over the village, sometimes on clotheslines, sometimes spread out on rocks, and if it was the day on which I had scheduled a bath, I would do my laundry in my rinse water—a conservation idea I was quite proud of. Dan Varisco and Najwa Adra, friends of mine and fellow anthropologists who had been in Yemen, had sent me an audiotape of Casablanca, taken off television and complete with advertisements so that I could keep up with U.S.

consumerist tastes, and I liked to play it while doing my washing. As the Nazis invaded North Africa, I was stomping on my clothes like a winemaker on his grapes, and by the time Rick and Louis were swearing undying friendship, my shirts and pants were tugging on the line and snapping in the wind. When next I glanced out at the village, I might see women returning from the market with bags of groceries, a sign that I could begin my fieldwork in earnest. I would venture forth with a small spiral notebook and pencil wedged inside the waistband of my Yemeni skirt, or *futa*, my head covered in the cloth headdress called a *mushadda*. I knew better than to engage the women who crossed my path in conversation. Etiquette proscribed such familiarity.

My favorite shopkeeper, a man who was to become one of my dearest friends, was a dwarf nicknamed the Hunchback. He was respected not only for his keen intelligence but also for his shrewd and fair business practices as well as exemplary moral character. A man who seemed to know everyone, he might help me to make contact, or so I thought, with some of the best tribal poets in the region.

Muhammad the Hunchback would hail me with a broad smile, tell me to sit next to him, and ask what I had learned on the previous day. I would sit on his store counter or climb into the dark interior, perch on some sacks of grain, and talk to him about poetry, Islam, America, or anything else that came into my head. Grabbing my notebook, he would flip through the pages and read the words, phrases, and snatches of poetry I had recorded or a tribesman who was literate had written himself, then venture his own opinions as to whether the definitions and interpretations were correct or needed amplification. Why do you listen to so-and-so, he might mutter, seeing that I had jotted down information from someone he knew. He's not right in the head, he would say. Why don't you talk to X, who knows a tremendous amount about the subject? Why do you write down lies? When a tribesman came to his store who in the Hunchback's opinion might be interesting, he'd explain as best he could who I was and what I was looking for, and then ask the man to recite some poetry. I noted in my diary the Hunchback's efforts, and my own, to find poets:

Sunday, December 23, 1979

Late breakfast again and didn't arrive before 10:30. Sat mostly with the Hunchback and met Salih, the poet from the nearby village of Shadayg, whom I'd wanted to meet for some time. He seems to be a nice man—certainly had Muhammad the Hunchback's certificate of approval, which isn't given lightly—and he expressed interest in talking to me about poetry. I also met ʿUbad Ali, from Marhab, who said he'd come to see me tomorrow afternoon. It seems to have been the poets' bazaar day.

Friday, December 28, 1979

Got up late again. Did some household chores in the morning and went into the souk. Today being Friday, it was jammed with *qabilis* [tribesmen] who had come all the way from Marib [far to the east]. I also met some men from Bait al-Royshan, one of whom wrote down a *zamil* for me. He was enthusiastic about teaching me more poetry, so I hope we'll meet again sometime.

The Hunchback helped me with my project partly out of affection, partly out of intellectual curiosity, but also in an effort to control it. If I was a spy, he'd find out and alert the government. If I was not, he wanted to make sure I got "right" the information that I was planning to put in my book. But I suspected that after a while his sense of responsibility toward me became an unforeseen burden, and sensing that I was getting on his nerves, I'd change the topic to talk about more casual things or simply hang out without any agenda. When everything else failed, I often unwittingly provided comic relief.

December 22, 1979

One of the souk regulars offered me some *burtugan* [a kind of snuff], which I tried. You're supposed to take it under the tongue and then spit it out, but unfortunately I swallowed mine (after repeated and dire warnings from the Hunchback not to, and he scolded others for egging me on). The effect was instantaneous and as heavy as the blow from a sledgehammer. I almost passed out, broke into a cold sweat, felt very dizzy and slightly nauseous, as if I'd had too much to drink. My heart was pounding in my chest. I was a little giddy and laughed uproariously at everything people said, even if it wasn't very funny. The Hunchback was beside himself with alarm over my condition and amused by it.

At times the playfulness had sinister undertones.

December 9, 1979

In the souk today one of the boys called me a little devil for writing the words down that I hear in conversation. He later explicitly stated that I was a spy. I laughed. I can deny [the charge] until I'm blue in the face and they'll still suspect me. It astounds me that they think Khawlan is so important to America's security and interests that it would send an agent to spy on its people!

Reading this diary entry more than twenty years later, I am struck by its disingenuous näiveté. I knew perfectly well, and even admitted as much to myself at the time, that had I been in their shoes, I would not have trusted me either. What was a lone American, with such an awkward way of explaining himself to others, doing in this part of the world? Worse, I was ignorant of the political importance of Khawlan to Yemen. I had accepted the standard diplomatic line that regions like Khawlan were mere backwaters to the mainstream of national political events in Yemen or international ones in the Middle East. My defensive tone also belied anxiety about my safety. By November 1979, the Iranian Revolution was at its peak, and a group of student radicals, angered by the United States, whose government had granted asylum to the deposed Shah, had besieged the American Embassy in Tehran and held a large number of its personnel hostage. In the meantime, anti-American, pro-Iranian demonstrations were erupting throughout the Muslim world, and though Yemen was relatively quiet, U.S. citizens there were nonetheless anxious lest they be targets of assault or other aggression.

December 8, 1979

> Arrived [in the sanctuary] this afternoon . . . Paranoia is slowly
> spreading in the American community, especially among embassy
> personnel as the embassies in Islamabad and Tripoli were burned
> (also Iraq & Calcutta had anti-American incidents, as did Kuwait).
> The "voluntary" evacuees left Sana'a today for Rome, but they
> represent only a handful of the community. No emergency of any
> stage has yet been declared.
>
> HEW [Health, Education, and Welfare], which awards the
> Fulbright-Hays Grant by which I am financing the fieldwork, had
> the State Department send a secret cable to the ambassador in
> Sana'a requesting him to inform me of my options in case of an
> emergency: either fly to "safe haven" in Rome at my own expense,
> or remain in Sana'a at my own risk. What a thing to classify as
> secret, and everyone knew about it anyway. The State Department
> only sent the cable in order to cover its own ass in case something
> happened to me and it had failed to warn me of the danger.

One day the Hunchback sensed my concern and told me not to worry.
"If something happens in Sana'a, we'd protect you." It was not, however, the Iranian Revolution that he and others in the sanctuary were
excited about. During the Muslims' annual pilgrimage season, on November 20, a preacher by the name of Juhayman, who declared himself
mahdi (rightly guided one), laid siege to the Haram Mosque in Mecca
along with around two hundred of his followers (no one knew the exact number), protesting what they described as the moral degeneration
of the Saudi royal family and relations with "infidel" powers that their
policies led to. It took two weeks to crush the rebellion, and in the end
the *mahdi*, his general, and the theologian or theoretician of the movement, along with most of his followers and a number of innocent pil-
grims caught in the crossfire, were killed. This was the first time that
the Saudi royal family had been publicly attacked for misconduct and
misrule since King Abdul Aziz al-Saud, the founder of the modern nation, battled extreme Wahhabi elements over similar grievances in the
1920s—but it was not the last. In hindsight we can see that the rebel-

lion in Mecca was a harbinger of more ferocious and determined cam-
paigns against the Saudi state today, including those by Osama bin
Laden.

In a field note from November, I recorded the reaction of the people
in the sanctuary to the events of November 20: *For some of them it repre-*
sents the beginning of a revolution in Saudi Arabia against the King & the House of
*Sa*ᶜ*ud, just like the revolution that began a year ago against the former Shah of Iran.*
In the souk, I hear them say: huh huh, nafs ath-thowrah: iran wa saᶜudiyyah,
"It's the same thing, the same revolution: Iran & Saudi Arabia." And the fact that the
incident in the Haram Mosque co-occurred with the Iranian takeover of the U.S. Em-
bassy in Tehran, where over fifty hostages have been confined, may have added an-
other mental association between Saudi Arabia & the Revolution in Iran.

The curious and difficult question is: do [the people in the sanctuary] secretly hope
the same revolution will spread to Yemen and lead to what happened in Iran—that
is, the establishment of a theocracy with the clergy in control and an imam as absolute
ruler? This, after all, corresponds somewhat to the situation of the sada in Yemen dur-
ing the reign of the imams, and the [sanctuary] may be hoping secretly for the return
of its former power. This state of affairs could be brought about by a "religious" revo-
lution such as the one that is occurring in Iran.

The Hunchback's was one of nine stores in full, daily operation
when I was living in the sanctuary, with a new store being built by the
sons of a man called Hussein the Servant. Besides these stores, there
were some stalls whose owners eked out a living by serving Pepsi or tea
from beat-up, blackened aluminum kettles, while others belonged to
the better-off *qat* sellers. Shortly before noon each day, their motorcy-
cles or pickup trucks would roar into the souk laden with bundles
purchased from various growers in the region or from middlemen operating in Sana'a and Khawlan's administrative capital, Jihana. Shopkeep-
ers and customers would immediately stop what they were doing and
gather around the sellers, purchasing *qat* for themselves as well as for
their womenfolk. The Hunchback would often help me select succulent branches and, by the nod of his head and the lift of an eyebrow,
indicate whether the asking price was too steep.

Some of the tribesmen who showed up in the market to peddle their
dry goods came from as far away as Marib, on the fringes of the vast

central Arabian desert known as the Empty Quarter. This ancient town was once the capital of one of the great incense-and-spice kingdoms and thought by historians to have been ruled at one time by the Queen of Sheba. Though today a boomtown made prosperous by the discovery of oil in the 1980s, it was no more than a sleepy little place of a few hundred people when I was doing my fieldwork. The tribesmen from Marib were scragglier and tougher looking than even the men from these parts, and I learned that they were smugglers. The Hunchback would partly replenish his own stock from their supplies but would more often make trips with his sons to the spice souk in Sana'a for the rest of his purchases.

On Fridays I hoped to meet poets who would come to the market town, first to conduct their business, then to pray in the mosque and listen to the imam's sermon. One day the Hunchback gleefully waved to me from across the way to come and meet the man standing at his counter. He was Yahya al-Qiri, a son of Muhammad al-Qiri, a paramount sheikh in these parts and a poet in his own right. His shrewd eyes had a twinkle in them, and his face was as round and smooth as a cherub's.

"So you want to learn tribal poetry, eh?"

"Give him some poems, Yahya," the Hunchback urged him. "Give him some *zamils* from the civil war." A *zamil* poem is two lines in length with a strict meter and rhyme scheme (often with intricate internal rhymes) and is meant to be pithy or aphoristic. Most *zamil* poems are composed orally for certain ceremonial or political occasions and are remembered only if the poet or the event that occasioned the poem is famous. Because of their brevity, it was easy, or easier, for me at the beginning of my fieldwork to learn *zamils*.

Turning to me, Yahya asked, "Have you heard the famous *zamil* that al-Ghadir declaimed when he broke with the republic?" Naji al-Ghadir was one of the great Khawlani sheikhs of the previous half century. He had been an ardent supporter of the revolution until Egypt sent military forces to assist the republican forces, which in his mind was tantamount to occupation by a foreign power, and he had been assassinated by South Yemenis during the civil war.

Mount al-Tiyal, I summoned and cried out to every peak in Yemen:
"We shall never be a republic, not even if we were to be snuffed out
    forever from this world!
Even if yesterday were to return today and the sun were to rise in the
    south!
Even if the earth were to burn up in fire and the sky were to rain bul-
    lets!"

Though my literal translation captures the hyperbole of the original, it
cannot begin to render the beauty of its sound patterns. The most distinctive are internal rhymes: the Arabic for "he summoned" rhyming
with "Yemen" at the end of the first hemistich, for example.

    Yahya was taken aback but pleased that I knew the poem. He asked
me if I had collected the reply composed by the republican Sheikh al-
Royshan, another famous Khawlan leader of the civil-war era.

Pardon, if you please, someone who has wended a devious course.
The MIG, the Yushin with the helicopter, and the black fighter jet—
Neither cartridge belts nor M-1 rifles will stop the pilots.
Say to Hasan and Badr, O Naji, "Already silver has turned to
    brass!"

The two poems are coupled as "provocation" and "retort." Being a rejoinder, al-Royshan's poem must, according to the rules of the verbal
joust in Khawlan, replicate the meter and rhyme scheme of the challenge, but to be judged the superior poem, it must do more than this.
And indeed, al-Royshan's poem is a tour de force. For example, in Arabic the phrase "a devious course," whose final sound echoes the internal
rhyme in the first hemistich of al-Ghadir's poem, is also a chiasmus—
with the sequence of consonants in one word (t-l-w) being reversed in
the following one (w-l-t), conveying in sound the sense of someone
who has flip-flopped or reversed course. And the concluding line, because it alludes or indirectly refers to the monarchy (whose silver has
been debased and turned to brass), has the rhetorical force of a good
joke's punch line, the more so because it manages to include the names

of Naji al-Ghadir's allies—Imam Badr, whom the republicans had deposed, and Hasan al-ʿAmri, the imam's general.

A grin wrinkled Yahya's face. "And do you know what al-Ghadir said to that?" I shook my head. He began to recite:

> The Yushin will do you no good. We have something to combat it.
>   You are out of your mind!
> The land mine is certain to leave the tank in pieces.
> Of no use to you is Sallal the lunatic [the president of the republic] or
>   Hasan al-ʿAmri.
> O Satan, you are cursed, and the curse will be fulfilled in a narrow
>   grave.

A good poem, we agreed, but not up to the standard of al-Royshan's. It lacked the latter's imaginative flair. The Hunchback nonetheless exclaimed, "God be thanked, Seif, you've found the cycle of poems you've been searching for! Do you think you could invite Seif to come to your village, Yahya, to see your weddings and maybe to record some of your own poems?" Yahya said he would be honored to.

The Hunchback pressed him. "But when, Yahya, when?"

"Soon. We'll do it soon. Any time you want, Seif."

I could not resist reciting a proverb. "A promise is like thunder and fulfillment is the rain." He laughed, backing away from the store, waving and smiling, before he turned on his heel and was gone.

"Who taught you that proverb?" the Hunchback inquired admiringly.

"Hussein the Servant. Do you think he means it?" I asked doubtfully, thinking of all the other times a poet had promised to see me and then didn't.

"I think he does, Seif, but you'll have to be patient."

"I know, I know. 'Patience is beautiful,'" I said, quoting from the Qur'an and bringing a smile to the Hunchback's lips.

Meanwhile, I was diverted by the colorful scene before me. Vegetable sellers, usually women more thickly veiled than they would have been in their tribal villages, out of respect for the sanctuary, sat in shady lanes with their produce—onions, radishes, tomatoes, heads of lettuce—spread out on blankets while their menfolk hawked firewood. This happened to be one of the rare days when fresh vegetables were available, and I bought an armful. The women were joined by sellers of coffee, sheep's wool, carpets, used auto parts, motor oil, fencing wire, and spark plugs. I recognized some of these souk regulars from open-air markets in other Yemeni towns. A young man stood with his dagger aloft, slowly turning around and drawing people's attention to it by shouting loudly, "A thousand riyals! A thousand riyals!" An older man did the same thing with a rifle. A tribeswoman stepped up to the Hunchback's counter and thrust a clock at him; he was clever at fixing radios and other appliances, clothes irons, and small tools. Market-goers came to him for medicines, disinfectants, bandages, and palliative kinds of incense, which he dispensed with folk wisdom about bodily ailments and their reputed cures. Because his wife was a skilled seamstress and owned a sewing machine, he also received orders for women's and men's clothing. I had placed an order with her for several *zanna*, or male robes. And not least, since he knew how to read and write, the Hunchback was often called upon to decipher documents, for many of the older tribesmen had little if any formal schooling. Outside the main gate of the Old City of Sana'a, known as Bab al-Yemen, one would often see elderly men seated under umbrellas next to simple crates upon which they would write letters or documents dictated to them by tribesmen. To me, there is no more dramatic sign of the spread of education in Yemen than that these scribes have all but vanished today.

Most of the Hunchback's customers bought their goods on credit. He was a careful, even zealous bookkeeper, adding up accounts at the end of the month so that he would know exactly how much money his customers owed him. But unlike Shylock, he extended credit without interest, which is considered usurious according to Islam, and he allowed payment schedules to be flexible. "Running a store would be impossible without extending credit," he explained to me. "People don't always have the cash when they need to buy something." Only once did I see him lose his temper with a customer who he thought was taking advantage of him by letting the bill go unpaid too long. From below the counter, the Hunchback dragged out a large ledger in which he wrote down his accounts, which seemed even bigger next to his small, deformed body, like a holy tablet meant to last the ages, and opened it to the page where the young man's name was scrawled. He pointed out to him the date of sale, the amount of the purchase, and the cost. When the young man disputed the accuracy of the figures, the Hunchback swore up and down that there was no mistake and that the young man had to pay his debt or his name would be mud. This was a rather strong admonition, for it presumed dishonesty, so the young man took out his dagger to challenge the Hunchback's accounting, then handed it over to a bystander to act as mediator. Within half an hour the dispute was settled, the young man agreeing to pay the sum he owed at his next visit to the market. But the Hunchback was not sanguine about that prospect. "I'll probably never see him again," he muttered under his breath to me, "that son of a whore . . ." It is interesting that, for all his meticulous bookkeeping of sales made on credit, he did not keep a record of sales against his expenses and thus had no precise idea of his income. As far as I know, all the other souk merchants adopted the same methods: they were content to know that they were doing "well" or "poorly" or "average" in comparison to years past. It was difficult to estimate the Hunchback's net income in 1980, but I would surmise that it averaged between ten and twenty dollars per weekday and perhaps five times that amount on Friday, or souk day. This income was higher than that of the average merchant, primarily because his family owned the building where he kept his store and he had practically no overhead, but I also heard that he was a notorious skinflint.

In light of his altercation with the young man, I thought the Hunchback would appreciate the fact that I never asked for credit, but the contrary was true.

"Don't you trust each other in America?" he asked me one day, sarcastically.

"What do you mean?"

"You buy my stuff, but you always pay for it immediately. I thought we were friends, Seif."

"We *are* friends, Muhammad. I show my respect to you that way."

"No you don't. You show me that you don't trust me to be generous and understanding when you fall behind in your payment."

"I don't want to end up like that young man you had a fight with, Muhammad, and have our relationship spoiled."

"You're different, Seif, you wouldn't try to take advantage of me. I know that because I know you, and it's because I trust you that I don't ask you to pay for your purchases immediately. Otherwise I hurt your feelings, and you mine."

The Hunchback would invite me to spend an afternoon or two in his grape arbor, located in the western part of town, surrounded by walls or wire fences to keep out animals that might trample or eat the harvest. Being winter, it was time to prune back the vines, and I offered to help. Propped up on thin stone supports, they looked as unprepossessing as unraveled balls of yarn, madly twisted like the snakes in Medusa's hair, but in a month or two they would begin to sprout emerald green leaves. Then the Hunchback would cover the branches with thistles and thorns to ward off birds, and later, the most succulent or heavy clusters of grapes might be wrapped in canvas or paper for added protection. The vines produced mostly green grapes, wonderfully sweet, like the wine of the German Palatinate. I learned to identify the different types, with names like *razigi, atraf,* and *gawarir.* The Hunchback sold most of the grapes to middlemen in Sana'a, and the rest that were not immediately eaten were dried as raisins, which, along with locally grown almonds, made a delicious snack.

The arbor was a delightful spot for small gatherings. On matting and cushions we lay down and stretched ourselves and watched motes of dust gently swirl in the vine-filtered light. I tried to get the Hunchback to talk about the history of the village, but he deferred to Ibrahim, aka the Beltmaker. "Besides," he said, "Ibrahim travels to the tribes all over Khawlan, and you might go along with him and meet some of their poets." Though the Beltmaker did travel extensively, he had a reputation for being a recluse inside the sanctuary. He prayed in his house rather than in a mosque. Rarer still were his appearances in the market, for he preferred to send his youngest son, Ghazi, to run his errands for him while he sat at home studying his religious books or making the belts for which he was famous.

"Do you think he would talk to me?" I asked Muhammad the Hunchback.

"I don't see why not," he replied. "I'll speak to him about you."

It was Ghazi who came to my house one day with an invitation from his father. "Come on this day next week," the boy advised.

Ibrahim the Beltmaker lived in a modestly appointed, three-story house in the middle of town, one of those that had miraculously escaped destruction during the civil war. I pounded on its massive door with the brass knocker. This was always a suspenseful moment, exciting because of the new person I might meet but filled with dread lest I be turned away. No answer. A part of me was secretly relieved. It was always so much work getting to know someone here, and one never

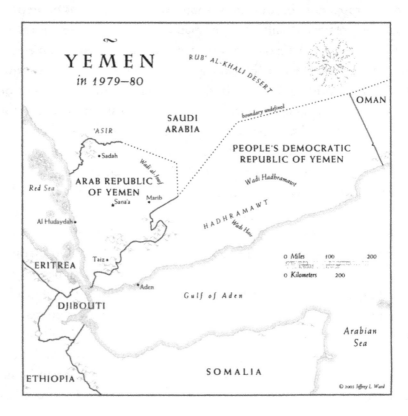

knew whether a person would be friendly or interesting. I moved away from the door to check the windows, but no face was pressed against the glass panes. For all its stillness, I nevertheless sensed that the house wasn't empty, that unseen eyes were watching me from behind the curtains. I knocked again, shouting, "It's Seif the American, come to visit Ibrahim." No answer.

When I told the Hunchback about what had happened, he seemed surprised and somewhat embarrassed. "Don't worry, Seif, I'll talk to Ibrahim about it."

In a few days I was summoned again to Ibrahim's house. When I knocked this time, a woman's voice came from the wooden-latticed peep box above me, uttering one loud and menacing staccato word. "*Man.*" "Who is it?" It sounded like the crack of a whip next to my ear.

"Seif the American."

The door opened from inside, pulled by a string that I imagined was operated by the invisible woman above my head.

"Proceed to the top floor," the same disembodied voice said, more gently. It was so dark I almost stumbled as I climbed the stairs. I uttered the formula "Allah, Allah, Allah," the customary warning to the women in the house that there was a man in their midst. Rather than causing them to scatter, it had the opposite effect, inviting them to draw near, checking me out through the cracks and keyholes in the doors while they remained hidden. I could hear a giggle as I passed, and an unintelligible exchange of whispers that made me feel self-conscious and foolish. As creatures of the forest, would they have been predator or prey?

As I entered a simple but cozy little room, Ibrahim rose from the floor with the suppleness of a dancer, though he was nearly twice my age. He was tall and erect in carriage, with a distinguished countenance. Only the gray stubble on his head betrayed his advancing years. I clasped his right hand, bringing the back of it to my lips as if to kiss it, and he did the same to mine. Thus did we ritually greet and gaze warmly into each other's eyes. I noticed flecks of green on his front teeth and a bulge in his cheek, telltale signs of *qat*. I was glad I had bought some sprigs in the marketplace that morning in preparation for my visit.

Ibrahim ushered me to my seat, propping up the back cushions, which had started to sag with age, straightening out the worn elbow rests, and in general trying to make me feel comfortable in spite of the threadbare furnishings. After a few minutes a discreet knock was heard at the door, and a woman's arm pushed a thermos across the threshold. He offered me a cup of scented water and, while we talked, picked up the strip of cotton cloth on which he had been working and spread it on his knee. He was making the decorative band sewn onto a leather backing that made up a belt. With a thick pencil, he carefully outlined the intertwined grape-and-almond design that his wife would later embroider in gold, silver, red, and green thread. I ordered two such lovely strips of cloth but never had the nerve to tell Ibrahim that I intended them as wall hangings instead of belts.

Belt-making was hardly more than a hobby for Ibrahim. His major source of income was from keeping the records of the religious endowments (*waqf*) scattered all over Khawlan. *Waqf* are properties (lands usually, but they can also be buildings, businesses, and so forth) donated by wealthier individuals to local mosques, the proceeds from which help to defray the cost of upkeep and repair of the mosques or to pay for new schools, clinics, and whatever else the congregation sees fit to support. As there are many mosques in Khawlan with *waqf* attached to them, Ibrahim was kept busy. Occasionally he might also be asked to adjudicate a divorce or settle an estate or perform graveside services. His religious knowledge and judicial skills were highly regarded, and because of his descent from the Prophet, he could move through tribal territories without the need for a person to guard him from potentially hostile tribesmen. However, there were times when it seemed wise to Ibrahim not to wander abroad, the tribes' obligation to protect *sada* not withstanding.

When hostilities broke out, the term *sanctuary* had real meaning, as Ibrahim's older brother, who now joined our conversation, could attest from his own experience. Hussein had been secretary to President al-Hamdi before the latter was assassinated in 1977. Fearing for his life because of his great admiration for the slain leader, Hussein took refuge in his ancestral home, where he had remained cooped up ever since. He was keen, alert, and suspicious, his personality alternately overbearing and immensely charming.

I noticed that Hussein did not chew *qat*. He was quite fastidious in his spotless white robe. "Do you not like it," I asked him, "or do you object to it on principle?"

"A filthy habit," he said with considerable disdain. "And far too expensive. I'd rather spend my money on other things. It's a scourge on our people as far as I'm concerned. Rather like your drugs." He did not look disapprovingly at his brother with his bulging cheek, nor did the latter seem to take offense.

"Certainly not that bad, I hope." I had to smile at the comparison. "It seems more benign. Like drinking a lot of coffee, though that isn't necessarily healthy either." The *Qat* Question, as I like to call it, is a topic of perennial debate in Yemen. *Qat*'s detractors are mainly foreigners or the Yemeni elite, who blame practically every social and economic ill of the country on *qat* consumption, but the general population refuses to give up its guilty pleasure. The government has enacted mild reforms, such as prohibiting the chewing of *qat* in the army or the state bureaucracy, but enforcement is lax. In general it is loath to interdict the cultivation and sale of a crop that has been so important to the livelihood of so many people in Yemen for such a long time.

"Here." Ibrahim passed the mouthpiece of the water pipe to his brother, who accepted it gratefully.

"You do not consider smoking a vice?" I asked him.

"Not when the smoke has to pass through all that water, filtering out the impurities. Anyway, it's not an addiction with me."

Sanctimonious sonovabitch, I thought to myself.

Hussein the Secretary asked the usual questions. Why was I in the village? What sort of study was I doing? How long did I plan to stay? When he learned how much money I "earned" from my research fellowships, he scoffed, saying that he spent that much in one month on the house he was building. He wasn't simply or only bragging, for through his probing and challenges he hoped to find out more about me. Ibrahim betrayed not a flicker of what he was thinking, but he must have sensed my growing discomfort under his brother's interrogation.

I congratulated Hussein on his good fortune, saying he was obviously beloved of God. I could see that he was not amused by this feeble attempt to fence with him, but I could not know until later how deeply ironical and even hurtful I had sounded. Grimly he got to the point.

"The president of Yemen has seen you on television and wanted to know whether you were a spy." Hussein smirked at the effect his words had on me. "Of course, I advised him that the American was a man of science and was in the sanctuary for the pursuit of knowledge."

"Very gratifying," I replied sarcastically. I proceeded to explain in detail all over again what I was doing in Khawlan, but he left the room before I could finish. As things turned out, it was the last I ever saw of him, but I had an intuition that he would somehow affect my life.

I tried to recover my composure. Ibrahim smiled and offered me the stem of the water pipe. I sucked at it gratefully, the deep drafts of the incense-flavored smoke acting like a sedative on my nerves.

After continuing to work on his belt in silence for a few minutes, Ibrahim tried to explain to me that his older brother was not a happy man. He had married many times but had not been able to father children. Now I could understand why Hussein might have been offended to be called "beloved of God." He had nurtured wealth and power but not offspring. In his old age, he was a lonely man. He had been like a father to Ibrahim's older sons, paying for their education and the bride wealth for their marriages to prominent *sada* families, neither of which Ibrahim could have afforded on his modest income.

"Your brother is going to tell you not to talk to me," I said.

"On the contrary." Ibrahim smiled. "It was my brother who asked me to invite you in the first place."

"He suspects I am a spy. That's what he wanted to confirm by my visit."

"Maybe so, maybe not. But he would not want me to keep talking to you now, would he, if he truly thought you were a spy? We all have to live under the uncertainties of what people think of us, Seif."

"Well, yes, that's true, but certain uncertainties put one at greater personal risk than others, no?"

"You mean that people might try to hurt you if they suspected you were a spy? That applies to me as well, for I or my family have enemies, and if they suspected you of being a spy, I might be accused of being a collaborator. I can only get to know you and judge for myself."

"But you can defend yourself. You have family and friends here. You're not alone."

"At the same time, Seif, because you have no family or friends, because you're alone, no one feels you're a threat to them."

"How can you say that I have no enemies, Ibrahim? There are people who hate America, and some of them are in this village." I was thinking of the Syrian teachers in the sanctuary school, who I had learned had been spreading rumors about me.

"Maybe they hate America, but as a rule they don't hate Americans. America is just an abstract concept to them. You're real, and people like you when they get to know you. Besides, the important thing to remember is that you're our guest. We have accepted you in our midst. We must protect and honor you."

Ibrahim continued to work on his belt. I had another, more desperate thought. "Does your brother think that he can win political favor by making others believe I'm a spy whom he can deliver into their hands?"

"What are you talking about, Seif? Which people? What political favor?"

I knew I had gone too far, but I could not stop myself. I had to bare my anxious suspicions to Ibrahim, even if their revelation made me seem ridiculous. "He did say, didn't he, that he had had a talk with the president about me? Doesn't that imply that he's working for him or at least trying to get back into his good graces? Handing me—or someone like me—over to the authorities would be the ticket back into government life and out of this sleepy little village."

"Maybe so, maybe not." Ibrahim laughed gently. "Are you then so valuable that you could become a pawn? Besides, that sounds like a dangerous game. If Hussein were wrong about you—which I would say to his face that he was—it would cost him dearly to accuse you falsely." He reached out to tap me on the shoulder. "You came to find out more about the history of the sanctuary, didn't you? What can I tell you about it?"

From my studies in Yemeni Islamic history, I had learned that the Arabic word for the sanctuary, *hijra*, has a precise reference to a historic event, the departure of the Prophet Muhammad from his hometown, Mecca, to Medina, where he was asked by its citizens to arbitrate a bitter dispute in exchange for accepting his religious message and leadership. The Zaydi *sada*, related to the Prophet through his son-in-law, Ali ibn Talib, and the Prophet's daughter, Fatimah, emigrated in the late ninth century A.D. from the Hijaz, in what is today western Saudi Arabia, and history says that they came to Yemen at the behest of the tribes there to help them settle internal disputes, thereby eventually becoming their rulers. Thus the story of Muhammad helped legitimate the *sada*, for by following its example they were constituting their own power.

But one ought to be skeptical of this history as a peculiarly *sada* invention, for it fits the classic rhetoric of colonial rule: that is, because the Other cannot rule themselves, they in turn need Others to bring governance and peace. Had I not been told by my friends in the sanctuary—and rather smugly, too—that "chaos" prevailed among the tribes? That if I ventured forth alone among them, they'd slit my throat?

Over time, the term *hijra* came to acquire other meanings. We know that it is used as the beginning date of the Muslim calendar, but it has a reference to a place as well. To continue the history, the Zaydi *sada* in Yemen became missionaries, instructing the tribes in Islamic credo and ritual and successfully converting many of them; in exchange for these services, they were given rights to land on which to build their settlements, from then on called *hijra*, and they were also granted protected status by the tribe or tribes in the area. It was in accordance with sacred covenants that a *hijra* could not be attacked by the tribes, nor could tribesmen who sought refuge in one. In Yemen, the term *hijra* thus has a more locally specific meaning than elsewhere in the Muslim world, as the name for a type of settlement in which *sada* have historically resided and in whose precincts certain protections are guaranteed. Yet not all such settlements in Yemen were established by the original emigrants from the Hijaz. In some cases, they were formed by someone who for one reason or another was moving from one region to a different one. This was apparently the case for the sanctuary where I was living, as Ibrahim explained. I did not tape his remarks, not having my tape recorder with me, but in the course of our talk I jotted down his comments in my small spiral notebook, which a later time I transcribed into a more complete field note.

Anthropologists like to distinguish between a diary and field notes, which are supposed to be the ethnographic reports they compile about the daily life of the people they are studying. In actual practice, it is hard to separate the two kinds of writing. Personal anecdotes constantly spill over into the supposedly objective field notes, and a diary contains much information of ethnographic import. When it comes to publishing, the habit has been to rework the information contained in both into a monograph or article, and to keep the diary and field notes invisible among one's private papers. Only rarely, as in the case of the great anthropologist Bronislaw Malinowski, one of the founders of anthropological fieldwork, has a field diary been published; in that particular case, the racist contents created such a scandal and an embarrassment for the profession that the experiment has not, to my knowledge, been repeated. At issue, however, is not merely the publication of diaries or field notes: it is the boundary between them and the ethnographic monograph. What I learned about Yemeni society, politics, and poetry in the sanctuary was facilitated as well as constrained by various circumstances—ranging from my psychological states, bordering at times on paranoia, through local conflicts, to world historical events like the Iranian hostage crisis. Here I want to show the complexities of these interconnected levels of life in Yemen, so I have interwoven diaries, field notes, post-fieldwork reflections, and my ethnographic reports.

Here's my field note containing the history of the sanctuary as told by Ibrahim the Beltmaker: *The founding ancestor of the sanctuary, a certain Mut'iq ibn Hayjan, came to Khawlan from Wadi al-Jowf [a large and important valley northeast of Khawlan], and this happened, oh, maybe three or four hundred years ago. As for why he left Wadi al-Jowf, it seems that Mut'iq got into a bad scrape with a tribesman whom he eventually killed. Did he kill the tribesman in self-defense? Did he strike the first blow? The details are obscure. What is certain is that he and his family were convinced they had to flee, either because he was guilty and would have been punished by death or because he was innocent and could not be assured of a fair hearing. The tribes of Khawlan al-Tiyal agreed to protect Mut'iq and to let him stay among them. [It is a common practice in Yemen for a fugitive, regardless of his guilt or innocence, to receive sanctuary from a politically powerful group or person. The protector is then honor-bound to keep his pledge of protection, even if in doing so he risks the enmity of the plaintiff and his tribe.] So Mut'iq moved his family to Khawlan and settled here, and that is how this place became a* hijra. *The remains of his home are still visible on the surface. In fact, they are not far from here, and Ibrahim said that he'd take me to see them someday.*

But why did he settle here? Khawlan is a big region, and there could have been other places to settle in. Ah, but the homestead is located on the border between two important sections of a very big tribe, probably the biggest at the time, Upper Yemeniya and Lower Yemeniya: These two sections were feuding over land boundaries, and Mut'iq offered to help settle their differences. Land boundaries are in general subject to dispute and therefore dangerous, and a sanctuary in this location, a "liminal" space as anthropologists since Arnold Van Gennep have been fond of calling it, has special symbolic significance. With no arms, just religious knowledge and legal reasoning, Mut'iq was able to persuade the sections of the tribe to remain at peace, and they gave him this land for his trouble.

Thinking about it now, I wonder whether Ibrahim was aware of the contradictions in his story or simply accepted them as a matter of course, but I never pressed him on this. It's one of those countless lapses—questions not asked, answers not pursued, invitations not followed up—that were due either to recalcitrant circumstances at the time, now no longer recoverable in memory, or to sloth and fatigue. The contradictions—as I see them, at least, though maybe not Ibrahim—suggest that the *sada* were harbingers of disorder as much as of peaceful harmony; indeed, the latter presupposes the former. It's not even as though Ibrahim tried to make excuses for Mut'iq's slaying a tribesman, unless he did this deliberately by obscuring the circumstances, which I doubt. Rather, he seemed to accept homicidal violence and peace as two sides of one coin. At the very time that he and I were talking about the history of the sanctuary, there were deep disputes among the villagers over land transactions, and they had led to shots being fired into a man's home, of all unpardonable things. And because of the building boom on the boundaries, a poor tribesman was being squeezed *out*, causing him to complain of the sanctuary's greed and heartlessness. Soon a bitter dispute between the sanctuary and a nearby village was to leave us all profoundly shaken, and this too seemed to confirm the dialectic between harmony and discord, peace and war.

The descendants of Mut'iq prospered, or so went the story Ibrahim told me, some of them becoming important as administrators in the imam's government, both in Sana'a and in other Yemeni cities, others as teachers and scribes. Their position did not change much until the overthrow of the last imam in 1962 and the ensuing civil war.

"What was it like," I asked Ibrahim, "to live here during the civil war?"

"On your way to the market from your house, Seif, do you notice the caves?" Ibrahim was referring to large underground passages whose openings were blocked by stones. "When the planes came, women, children, and old men took cover in them."

"How could all those people have found shelter in them? They don't seem big enough."

"They're bigger than you think. They extend very far and deep. That's why we've put stones in the entries to keep small children from playing in them and getting hurt. But the caves were not the only places where we found shelter. The tribes in the hills were our friends, and we would take cover with them. The people of Sarkhan often sheltered us against the bombs."

"Do you remember what the bombing was like?"

"Oh yes, the noise was terrifying, but few people died. Scouts would give us advance warnings when planes took off from Sana'a heading in our direction, so that we could take cover in plenty of time. Besides, the mountains are hard to get through, Seif. Easy to defend, hard to attack. The Ottomans had a tough time of it when they tried to occupy Yemen. In the end they could hold on only to Sana'a and a few other cities. And we fought back, too. You know what my younger son's name means? Ghazi? Raider. He was born at the height of the civil war. I wanted to honor the young men from the sanctuary who died attacking the Egyptian outposts."

"You fought back with what, Ibrahim? The Egyptians had planes with bombs."

"We had automatic weapons, even antiaircraft guns. We got pretty good at shooting down their planes, and after a while, they were afraid to fly over our village."

"So, the poet al-Royshan was wrong when he implied in his reply to al-Ghadir that the royalists had only small arms to combat the warplanes. Where did all this equipment come from?" Ibrahim was evasive, and I didn't press him for a straight answer. It was probably Saudi Arabia, which feared Egypt's backing of the Yemeni revolution, thinking it a ploy by President Gemal Abdul Nasser to gain a strategic foothold on the Arabian Peninsula, from which he could threaten their oil-rich and militarily vulnerable kingdom.

The people in the sanctuary had been royalist supporters for the most part, but this did not necessarily mean that their relatives elsewhere had been. In fact, among the earliest advocates of the new republic had been their own kinsmen, some of whom paid for it with their lives. As in the American Civil War, though perhaps not quite so bitterly, families were often divided, with brother pitted against brother. Ibrahim's family was a case in point. His brother had supported the republic and fought on its side, whereas Ibrahim had believed that the monarchy could have been reformed and salvaged.

"The monarchy had its faults, and the imam's government committed many abuses. Rule was supposed to pass down to the most qualified male among all the *sada* houses of Yemen, as determined by a special council, but in the end only one, his house, the Hamid ad-Din, and only Yahya's family within that house was permitted to rule. And then, Imam Yahya and Imam Ahmed were very closed-minded, refusing to allow things to come into Yemen from Egypt or the West, like up-to-date clinics and modern education. Before the revolution, we had fought the imams over these issues, demanding better care for the people, but they feared that the people would learn democracy, too, and crave it for our country. My family was involved in the coup that toppled Imam Yahya in 1948. And you know about al-Qardaʿi, the famous poet, whose *zamil* poems you've been collecting? We gave him sanctuary and then safe passage back to his tribe after he assassinated the imam."

"But why not have supported the republic, if it promised these things, too?"

"It had no legitimacy, Seif. Who was the first president? A half-literate butcher's son, Sallal, who rose through the ranks of the imam's army to become a colonel, a man who was part of the servant class of Yemen. A *muzeyyin!* What made him qualified to be president? He was only a puppet of the Egyptians."

"Would you want the monarchy back, then?"

He paused for a moment. "No, it's finished. But we don't have a strong republic, either. Al-Hamdi—now he was a president who could have unified us. He started to do good things for our people. That's why my brother believed in him and worked for him."

One day Ibrahim told me that his eldest son was home from school on a short visit, along with a nephew, the son of another brother, and I was invited to lunch (actually the equivalent of our dinner) with them. Yemen is outstanding in many arts—architecture, music, dance, handicrafts, jewelry, and poetry—but cooking is not one of them, and this in spite of Turkish occupation as well as centuries of contact with Indian and Southeast Asian traders. The one exception is bread—many unleavened breads made from wheat, millet, barley, or some combination of these baked in a special oven called the *tanour*. They may be oval—as large, say, as a dinner-table place mat and about a quarter inch thick—and either hard or spongy, or they may be small loaves, called *roti*. Chunks of bread are dipped in seasoned yoghurt or a sauce made from crushed tomatoes, onions, parsley, and hot peppers, but they are mainly used to scoop up mouthfuls of hot food in the absence of utensils. Overall, however, there is no style or art to Yemeni cooking that I could discern. Ibrahim's wife was thus all the more estimable a cook for doing so well with such conventional ingredients at that lunch: several varieties of unleavened bread; a scalding chicken soup surrounding like a moat a delicious dumpling called *asid*—this was a great delicacy; salads of mixed greens with fresh tomatoes, cucumbers, and hot radishes, which could be eaten with a kind of dressing called *zoam*; stuffed grape leaves; and for dessert, fresh fruit and a cake called *bint al-sahn* (literally, 'daughter of the plate'), topped with Yemeni honey, justly prized as among the finest in the world. The pièces de résistance were chunks of highly seasoned lamb served on a bed of saffroned rice. Meat is usually boiled rather than grilled in Yemen, which may kill bacteria but leaves the meat tough and stringy. Ibrahim's wife had avoided these shortcomings, perhaps by marinating the meat in advance or otherwise tenderizing it; whatever her secret, the tidbits were succulent. The dishes did not appear in sequence but all at once, spread out on the floor on top of a cloth. The rule was to sample a little of everything but to leave room for meat at the end. There was more food than we could possibly eat, which is a prerequisite of Arab hospitality but also because the leftovers were intended for the women and children of the house.

We men sat in a circle, one leg folded under the haunch, the other knee upright and touching the neighbor's. The local term for this position is *takhawlan-t*, literally meaning "I have khawlaned," or "I have assumed the position of a person from Khawlan." Uncomfortable for someone with long legs or arthritic joints, it takes getting used to. Ibrahim muttered the formula "In the name of God, the Merciful, the Compassionate," reaching out with his right hand for the food as he did so, and we followed suit. Except for Ibrahim's assiduous prompting to keep eating, which I found superfluous in light of the fact that I hadn't had such a delicious and filling meal in ages, we hardly spoke a word. Meals are for eating, not idle conversation. For that, there is the afternoon *qat* chew.

"Well, that was certainly a delicious meal," I said to Ibrahim. "Thank your wife for me." Later in my fieldwork, when I repeated this among the tribes, my faux pas was pointed out to me. It is the family and its generosity or nobility that should be thanked, not any individual or group within the household. Mindful that men were claiming this, I wondered whether the women, who did almost all the work, would have agreed. Probably. A feminist critique of women's labor in the patriarchal household had not yet made it to Yemen, let alone Khawlan. A scented towel was passed around on which we wiped our hands.

When I got up to stretch my legs, Rashid, Ibrahim's younger son, insisted that he pour rose water on my hands and then wanted to sprinkle a few drops on my jacket for good measure (a custom I rued because it spotted the material, which reeked of the sweet smell for weeks thereafter). I begged him not to, all the time thanking him profusely nonetheless, and he accepted my refusal of the honor graciously enough. Now his cousin Hamid appeared with some liquid refreshment. It was *gishr*, an infusion thought to be a digestive, made from the husk of the coffee bean and flavored with cardamom. Etiquette dictated that I slurp it loudly.

"What do you do for your meals, Seif?" asked Hamid.

I made them laugh when I described my kitchen, a counter and cabinet I had improvised from a shipping crate, which I had set on one side, the bottom toward the wall, the topside covered with vinyl, a curtain on a string to cover the opening, and the other sides painted a bright orange. Behind the curtain, hanging from nails or stacked on the bottom of the crate, were pots, pans, and various utensils. On the stone floor I had a little range with two burners hooked up by rubber hoses to a gas tank outside the house. Cupboards made from wooden fruit boxes, also painted orange—a little color coordination in the decor I was rather proud of—were nailed onto the wall, and in them I put my canned goods. This was where I prepared my food.

"And this arrangement is sufficient for you?" asked Hamid, incredulous.

"It's simple, but it works. I don't want to clutter up my life with things or chores that keep me away from my main task. The one thing I worry about, though, is rats. I can hear them scrambling about in the kitchen at night. Sometimes I wake up, terrified, thinking I felt one running over my bed. I've laid traps, but they don't seem to be effective."

"Ah, you need a cat," said Hamid.

"Indeed, and do you have one to lend me?"

"No"—he grinned—"but I'll keep my eyes open for one."

"And what about food?" asked Rashid. "Do you have enough to eat?"

"It's hard to get fresh food," I admitted. "Salads and vegetables I can get locally, but they don't come in many varieties, do they? And I can't afford meat. When you want a chicken"—I motioned to Ibrahim—"you go out to the barnyard and kill it for dinner. But I have to bring one frozen from Sana'a once every two or three weeks and then eat it the same day, because it's impossible to keep the meat refrigerated when the generator is turned on for only a few hours at night."

"Do you believe it, Seif, when it says on the wrapper for the frozen chicken 'slaughtered the Islamic way'?" This was Rashid's skeptical question.

"What do you eat, then, Seif?" asked Hamid. Almost none of what I consumed was food he had encountered, and it would have been difficult to describe to him. Omelets; bean salads and soups; pancakes and syrup; oatmeal with raisins; cheese melts; popcorn; pasta; peanut butter and jelly sandwiches; salads made from lettuce, horseradish leaves and leeks, canned mackerel and tuna. Especially tuna. By the time I was done with my fieldwork, I had figured out a thousand and one ways to prepare tuna: with mayonnaise and mustard in a spread, in casseroles, in salads, with rice and canned peas on the side, in stuffing. I'd never been fond of it; now, over twenty years later, I cannot stomach even the thought of it.

"A lot of vitamins," I answered, and he laughed at the jest. "If I'm lucky, eggplant or zucchini when they're in season, cooked with tomatoes, onions, garlic, and different spices. And one time my neighbor's wife gave me a yoghurt culture that I use in sauces and as a topping for mixed fruit. She also gives me fresh baked bread. I'll have you over for dinner at my place sometime and show you."

Hamid made a wry face.

Ibrahim was clearly happy to have his son around, but he excused himself after a little while to perform his prayers. "These two rascals have wanted to get to know you, Seif, so I leave you in their clutches. I'll be next door, should you need help." We broke out the *qat* and started our chew.

Rashid and Hamid were in their early twenties. Rashid was the more intense and scholarly of the two, no doubt taking after his father, and was attending the University of Sana'a. "I hope to become a professor of Arabic literature someday," he explained shyly. His cousin was the more attractive: handsome, lithe, affable, and fun-loving. He readily confessed to being a philistine, not liking school very much, and certainly not seeing much point in going on to university, since his ambition was to be a businessman, which he could learn by working in one of his uncle Hussein's establishments. I surmised that he had married recently, a Sana'ani woman of a powerful family evidently; from the way he talked about her, I thought his father-in-law might have been no less than Yemen's vice president, a member of a *sada* house different from that of the sanctuary but just as distinguished and even more powerful. "The dowry was a lot of money," he said in the first serious note he had struck, confirming that his uncle Hussein the Secretary had paid for it.

Hamid cuffed his cousin on the back of the head for making a fresh remark. The cousins were jolly and relaxed in each other's company. Their principal charm came from their having to remember they were no longer boys and to suppress the urge to tussle and tickle each other and break out in uncontrollable giggles. I was drawn into their affection and felt liked, really for the first time since I had arrived in the village. Whether this was intentional or not on their part, the effect was disarming. Rashid laughed and asked me innocently, "So you don't want your life to get too complicated and get in the way of your work. What is your work, anyway?"

They're checking me out after all, I thought. I suppose it was to be expected, but my heart sank a little. I explained, once again, the nature of my research, the fact that the authorities—like the Yemen Research Center, the governmental agency that oversaw all research being done in the country—had approved it, what I hoped to do with the material after I had collected it, and so on. Rashid understood most of what I said, since he was familiar with the idea of dissertations, but for Hamid it seemed to suffice that he liked me.

"How do you expect to meet the poets and tape them?" Rashid asked.

"I was hoping that the *sada* would take me to them."

"That's difficult, you know," he answered. "It's considered ᶜ*aib* [shameful] for us to visit the tribes uninvited. It's all right for the tribes to visit us, but not the other way around."

I was stunned by this revelation. "But what about your father? He visits the tribes, doesn't he?"

"Only on business and when they ask him to."

"I see."

I was barely able to conceal my disappointment, but Hamid offered some encouragement. "Of course, you could go with him. He's going to Harub next week, in fact. He wouldn't mind if you accompanied him." And he exchanged a sidelong glance with his cousin as if to say that he should play along.

When I left early that evening, I felt dejected. The point had finally been driven home: if I was to collect tribal poetry, I would have to do it on my own and in some place other than the sanctuary.

November 26, 1980

A little boy had been playing in the road when a car drove over the ditch in which he had been hiding and killed him. Though it was an accident, the driver was so grief-stricken that he threw himself at the bystanders and implored them to shoot him. The ᶜ*ugal [persons of reason, or headmen of the village] summoned to adjudicate happened to be Muhammad the Hunchback and Ibrahim the Beltmaker. Some of the people at the hearing were for punishing [the driver] with his life or at least levying a heavy fine. The judges, especially the Hunchback, strongly objected, saying they had no legal right to enforce such a penalty under Shariᶜa law. The boy's father accepted the judgment . . . Despite initial criticism, the people of the sanctuary were very proud of the way the case was handled. The Hunchback, in particular, was crowing to himself. "See how peacefully we managed to settle the matter. If this had happened among the tribes, or if the driver had killed a tribal boy, there would have been war." But the peo-*

ple of the sanctuary are sada, they are reasonable and peace-loving. A tribesman who was present at the discussions and final resolution was even supposed to have congratulated them on having been able to avoid bloodshed. The story, I suspect, is apocryphal.

The dead boy had lived in a house in back of mine, and outside it one morning I could see villagers gathering to perform the hajr, or ceremony of atonement. I decided to join them. The driver had come with a bull, which he presented to the boy's father. Some words were spoken, which I did not catch but assume came from the Qur'an, and then Nasir, a servant of the village, grasped the bull and with one swift stroke cut its throat. The beast collapsed onto its side, a dark stain like a gigantic pillow on the ground under his head. The legs kicked a bit, the shoulders shuddered, and then it lay still, its head thrown back and eyes wide open, looking as if it were more in delirium than in death.

This was not the first occasion on which I had seen an animal killed in the "Islamic way," but it was the first ritual sacrifice of its kind I had witnessed. I was squeamish at first but then surprised myself by getting caught up with the rest of the sanctuary in the majesty of the death. I remembered a much more mundane event, looking down from my window into a neighbor's courtyard at the precise instant when a woman cut a chicken's throat, holding its legs aloft and away from her body as it writhed and twisted in the air, spraying blood like a sprinkler. There was a gracefulness, even a gentleness, in her killing, that seemed not to have diminished in the countless times that she performed this act, at once everyday and religious. In the United States, massive deaths of a much cleaner—though perhaps not less cruel—kind are carried out by machines, and we eat the meat of the animals without the inconvenience of, perhaps the compunction about, first having to stare their death in the face.

Nasir now butchered the animal, hacking it into sections and cutting these into smaller pieces that he distributed, dripping with blood and slippery in his fingers, to the boy's father and relatives. His behavior was more than relaxed, it was positively irreverent. His was the laughter of the circus clown, the loudmouthed antics of a slapstick comic or alcoholic. He elicited guffaws by taking a sliver of meat and dangling it between his legs, a performance that was less coaxed than coerced by the people around him, which I supposed was intended to confirm his baseness and their superiority.

This was not the first time I had seen something like this charade. Waiting once for a taxi to take me back to Khawlan, I saw a very imposing man stride up to some sacks of grain, which he appraised with a calculating eye while their owner engaged him in some brisk bargaining. "He's a *doshan*, Seif," the owner whispered to me, meaning town crier, praise singer, and messenger, and then he asked the man to say a few conventional things in the way of his occupation. Mechanically, he complied with the request, as though commanded by royalty to the stage. He became boisterous to the point of seeming deranged, and then, as quickly as he had assumed the manner of a buffoon who delighted the onlookers, he dropped it and became again the shrewd, hard-driving bargainer.

Khaddam (servants) like Nasir could be found in villages all over Yemen. Unlike the darker-skinned ʿakhdam, who were said to have originated in Africa and who also performed menial tasks, the *khaddam* were virtually indistinguishable from tribesmen, except that they did not ordinarily carry guns. The old man Ali told me they were once tribesmen, even sons of Himyaritic kings, who lost their noble status because of cowardice or criminal offenses. Those who did not leave Yemen became servants known as "the people of the fifth," because they received one-fifth of the booty taken in warfare in return for performing menial services considered beneath the dignity of tribesmen. We already know what the *doshan* does. The one who butchers, barbers, and circumcises is called the *muzeyyin*. If a servant has a particularly beautiful voice, he may be given poetry to memorize and sing at weddings or make tapes for sale accompanying himself on a tambourine, in which case he is a *mulahhin*, literally composer of music, the most talented of whom can make a fairly good living in the cassette industry. This conceptualization of honor and categorization of work, ranking the tribesmen above the servants and regulating jobs as well as access to material resources, is central to the political economy of Yemen.

Of course, modern migrations to the oil-rich kingdoms of the Arabian Gulf complicated the economic picture, exerting pressure on the cultural boundary between tribesman and servant. At one time there had been several servant families in the sanctuary; now there were only two, and only Nasir, his wife, and youngest son actually remained in that line of work, his oldest boy having decided to strike out on his own as a *qat* seller. He had a shiny new Honda motorcycle, on which he scoured the countryside for good deals. In a picture I took of him, he grabs a goat and hoists it onto the seat, clowning in front of the camera, his pose at once deprecatory and defiant, like the *ᶜakhdam* that he is. Nasir always seemed congenial and friendly, ready with a smile. People said of him, "He's a nice, decent, hardworking fellow and deserves our respect." He had to be nice, for his support depended on how much people in the village liked him, and his demeanor sometimes bordered on obsequiousness. Because of his lowly status, he was not permitted to own land, so he rented his house, and this meant that in some deeper sense he never fully belonged to the community. If his landlord decided to develop the property and there was no other place for him in the village, he would have to pull up stakes and go elsewhere. And if he got into trouble, he had to throw himself on the mercy and justice of his patrons; the servant group had little, if any, power to defend themselves. Earnings may have been steady, if slight, but security was always precarious in Nasir's profession.

The other *khaddam* family in the sanctuary was headed by Hussein, but he no longer worked as a servant, having become rich—richer, in fact, than many of the *sada*. He had been blessed with several capable and hardworking sons, the oldest of whom made fair livings in Saudi Arabia as construction workers and regularly remitted money back to their father. Shrewdly foreseeing the boom that overtook Yemen in the 1970s, Hussein had invested in earth-hauling equipment, which he rented to home builders in the sanctuary and surrounding villages. As he was not permitted to own land himself, Hussein invested his and his sons' earnings in several businesses, one of which was a store that was going up in the souk at about the time I moved in. He turned its management over to his younger sons while he tended to other investments, the exact number and nature of which remained something of a mystery to me and others, not to speak of the profit they turned, though the Hunchback guessed that Hussein's net worth was well over a million riyals (about US $250,000 in 1980). I once saw a young man drop to his knees before him, kissing the hem of his skirt, a greeting usually reserved for either one of the *sada* or a venerable patriarch. Hussein turned red with embarrassment and nervously gestured for the young man to rise. It may have been an acknowledgment of some favor Hussein had done him, but whatever the reason, the gesture indicated Hussein's very real importance in the community, as well as the pressure that changing conditions were exerting on the cultural system of honor and status. Some *sada* spoke disapprovingly of him because he did not seem to know his place.

Before he had become well-to-do, Hussein had made his living as a *muzeyyin*. With his exuberant conviviality, he would have been an excellent one. He had great charm and an exceptional gift for telling jokes and stories—he could be the life of the party, as I knew from having observed him at several *qat* chews—which must have put him in great demand as a master of ceremonies at weddings and other public events. It was a talent appreciated also by the tribal sheikhs, whose acquaintance he cultivated assiduously. That was one reason that he could act so swiftly and efficiently as a mediator.

On the suggestion of the Hunchback, who claimed that Hussein knew everyone in the area with any influence, I hired him to take me to some of the leading regional poets. With his son at the wheel, we drove to the village of al-ʿAin, seat of the powerful al-Royshan house, where we were to meet Salih bin Gasim al-Sufi, one of Khawlan's renowned poets. But when we got there, we were told that neither the poet nor the sheikh was in town. Greatly flustered by this unexpected turn, Hussein hastily tried to arrange a meeting with some of the locals who had memorized verse, while the sheikh's family took me into their newly built home and gave me tea. But the session was not to be. Hussein had lost face, and not just with me but, more important, with the people in the sanctuary, some of whom gloated over this failure. In their perspective he was an upstart, a social climber, and now had his comeuppance. He was quite glum during our return journey and insisted that I should take back the money I had given him, which I refused to do. How could he make it up to me? he asked contritely. I suggested that I would like to chew *qat* with him and perhaps tape some of the stories he was known for.

A quite large but modest structure, Hussein's house was located on the outskirts of the sanctuary, which symbolized his marginal status. As usual, I was ushered into the sitting room on the top floor, where the males tended to congregate and where I found Hussein with his sons. I had not anticipated any resistance on his part to telling me his stories, which he said he considered to be no more than idle chatter, unworthy of being taped let alone transcribed, but when he finally did begin a story, he flubbed the ending and then excused himself. Pulling a book from a shelf and putting on his glasses, he began to read.

"You know how to read?" I blurted out and immediately regretted the remark.

"Yes, I taught myself."

"Why didn't you tell me a story that you tell in front of the assemblies, Hussein, instead of ones that you read?"

"Oh, they're no good. *These* are the real stories." He showed me a book of folktales that had been collected by a prominent Yemeni scholar. Not only had he learned to read but he had imbibed one of the prejudices of literacy: that only works of scholarship and writing are worthy of esteem. How thoughtless of me not to have realized that for Hussein storytelling was a performance of his own servility, and so it was painful to be pressed into it. Perhaps he had even flubbed on purpose. Reading the book with his eyeglasses was meant to signal his newly elevated status. That I did not appreciate this only compounded his consternation. I decided to drop my request and, as on other occasions, let the conversation drift where it might.

"There are blacks in the United States, are there not?" I was startled by the suddenness of the question. The anthropologist was being placed in the position of the informant. When people heard I was from Chicago, they thought of "al-Capone" and gunned me down with their index fingers. I found it harder to account for the images of women they saw in American movies. And they often wanted to know why the United States supported Israel. But Hussein's question I was not prepared for.

"There are problems between blacks and whites, or so I surmise from reading the newspapers and magazines. And yet it is true, is it not, that according to the law they are equal?" This was not the kind of question that was supposed to issue from the mouth of a servant, though at the same time it had an obvious bearing on his own experiences.

I tried as best I could to tell him about the civil-rights movement and the legislation that it helped to bring about. It turned out he was well aware of some of that history. Martin Luther King was a name that came to his lips in recognizable English, but his knowledge went deeper than that.

"Had you not fought your own civil war over the issue of black slavery?" he asked. Inequities still existed, I said.

"But the point is," he insisted, "that in the U.S. a black person is free, is he not, in the eyes of the law?" And as if in anticipation, he added, "Never mind that he might be poor. I know what poverty means. He has rights, doesn't he, that a court of law is obliged to defend?" He paused. "I don't own my home, Seif. I can afford to buy the land, I can afford to buy half this village, but I'm not permitted to own my own land. This house we're in is made from mud brick. I want to build in stone. But what's the point, if I can be cleared off whenever the *sada* say so? I have to move far away, to Sana'a, in order to own my own home."

I didn't know what to say, and didn't know enough about Yemeni law to help him. "You know I'm sorry, Hussein, that things are so difficult for you here."

"You're a nice guy, Seif. I want to make it up to you, by the way, for the mix-up in al-ʿAin. Do you trust me to go back with you one more time?"

"That would be splendid, Hussein."

"All right. Let me talk to the poet al-Sufi, and then I'll arrange a trip." He was true to his word.

———

One day I decided to pay a visit to the elementary school. I had been told by a Syrian school inspector who had passed through that conditions there were to be envied by comparison to other schools in Khawlan, some of which didn't even have roofs over the pupils' heads. For high school, boys—as far as I knew no girls from the sanctuary went beyond the elementary grades—went to school in Sana'a and lived with relatives there. The boys sat on one side of the classroom, the girls on the other—veiled if they had already passed puberty. Most of these pupils came from the sanctuary, but some were from nearby tribal settlements like Sarkhan.

I attended an English class first. An Egyptian schoolteacher by the name of Fathi spoke to his students in a soothing voice, explaining the grammar clearly, waiting for the answers patiently, and enforcing discipline with a gentle hand. Next came religious instruction by one of the village elders. He had a grandfatherly relationship with his charges, who obeyed him out of respect, not fear. The other teachers, all Syrian, were responsible for the rest of the curriculum: Arabic, history, and arithmetic. Unlike their colleagues, they were overbearing and harsh, striking students with rulers at the first sign of disobedience. I cringed at the sound of wood hitting their hands and could not bear to stay in their classrooms. They must have sensed the rebuke implicit in my retreat, and afterward their tepid demeanor toward me congealed into icy formality.

It had been not curiosity alone that inspired my ill-fated visit to the school but a belated gesture of tact or diplomacy. From the very beginning of my stay in the village, my relationship with the schoolteachers had been strained. When I first came looking for housing, I was told that I could stay in the school with the other "foreigners," a gracious offer I nevertheless politely and firmly declined, fearing that such a move would isolate me from the rest of the village even more than my presence as a stranger already had. I had wanted people to know that I was an anthropologist and to teach them what that meant. Though I may have been too earnest about it, I don't think that intention was misguided. It would have been dishonest to pass myself off as anything else, and at first I naïvely thought people would help me with my project, though they could only dimly understand it, and truth to tell, I wasn't certain myself what it was. I was experiencing the paradox of fieldwork—the invention and reinvention of one's study as one carries it out, sketching and drafting while also composing and performing. I couldn't do any of this if I was separated from the village with other "foreigners." Unfortunately, when word got back to the teachers that I didn't want to live with them, they took it as a snub, and they began to spread malicious rumors about me. So I had thought it wise to pay them a visit and do some fence-mending.

They were young men, in their late twenties and early thirties for the most part, therefore my contemporaries, and for that reason alone they had assumed I'd want to associate with them. I also think they presumed a certain fellowship, induced by their own loneliness and what they perceived to be the terrible hardship and isolation of living in the sanctuary. They left wives and families behind in some of the most exciting cities of the world—Cairo, Damascus, Aleppo—and were homesick and bored. I tried to befriend the Egyptian school-teacher, but it wasn't easy. I am sure he considered himself thoughtful and kind when he constantly shifted into English, even though I wanted the opportunity to speak Arabic. He condescendingly inti-mated that "as you know, life and these people are a little primitive here . . . We are alone in the middle of nowhere and need each other's company." My declining the honor of joining his outpost of civiliza-tion in the schoolhouse seemed to him either supremely arrogant or highly suspicious. What was I trying to hide?

His first target of criticism was the way I dressed, as I commented in my diary, but it was not the last:

November 27, 1979

In the late afternoon, dropped in to see I., who had just finished his lesson with the Egyptian schoolteacher. He [the schoolteacher, Fathi] was very gay and talkative. [He] remarked on the fact that I wear the *futa* and *sumata* [headdress], etc., as if to insinuate that it was a little silly . . . Fathi spoke to me mostly in English, of course, unless it was to tell me in Arabic how well I speak Arabic! I must remain on pleasant terms with him, however. He can be useful and at the same time could do me harm if we don't get along . . .

November 29, 1979

I met Fathi in the souk. He asked me why I chew *qat* since it tasted so awful—he would never indulge in the practice, and concluded that I would only stoop so low in order to ingratiate myself with the Yemenis. I asked him why he smoked the *madaᶜah* [water pipe], as I saw him do at I.'s house. I never would, I said, because I don't like it (a lie). "Well, of course, that's a different matter altogether . . . I guess we just have different attitudes about things," he concluded.

The question of dress was especially sensitive for me, and I bristled defensively at Fathi's innuendos. I brooded over what he had said for days. *Was* I wearing Yemeni clothes to ingratiate myself with the villagers? Obviously I didn't share his disdain for things Yemeni, but that didn't account for my unease. To imply, as he was, that I was trying to perpetrate a kind of scam on my Yemeni friends was not only to make them out as more gullible than they were but also to overlook that it was they who had suggested the fashion and encouraged me to adopt it. "You'd be a lot more comfortable, Seif, wearing the *futa* than your pants when you sit on the floor . . . You'll find our *mushadda* a lot more practical than a cap because you can pull it across your entire face for protection from the sun." Fear of my "going native" was a concern for Fathi and me but not for my Yemeni friends who never once mistook my appearance for that of a "native." To them I was just an American who dressed like a Yemeni. Fieldwork may have made me want to become the "Other," but the process seemed more like becoming an image of someone whom the "native" had invented—often enough with the anthropologist's collusion, I admit. I would have liked to have thought I was in control of the process, but in reality I was not. My Yemeni friends applauded my cultural impersonations rather as one would a child trying to dress up for a part, and the implicit infantilization unnerved me. Besides, I may have been repressing an anxiety over gender identity that wearing a "skirt" occasioned. But to Fathi my Yemeni clothing was a rejection of things western, and that made him even more insecure about his own ambivalent identification with the West.

December 26, 1979

Read the Qur'an in the morning & went into the souk. There I had a confrontation with [Ismael] about his insinuations that I am a spy. The whole incident was triggered by his having read in my notebook the names of the three ᶜagils [headmen of the sanctuary]. The fact that I had written this information down confirmed his worst suspicions of me, which had originally been aroused by the Syrian teachers. (They had told him not to talk to me because I was a spy!)

I asked him why this information was so sensitive. Others also seemed offended that I had noted it. But it was only the Hunchback who finally told me the reason: the ᶜagils didn't want to be known to the central government because they were afraid it would thrust responsibilities on them that they didn't want . . . I was fed up and, combined with irritation produced by bad health lately, lost my temper and more or less took it out on the boy . . .

I don't suppose I should ever expect to be trusted completely by anyone, and yet I am shocked at how deep the suspicions of me run . . .

In one sense, this has done me some good, for now I feel like breaking my ties a little with [the sanctuary] and going to the neighboring villages.

2

~

"ANGER BE NOW THY SONG"

January 19, 1980

There is a rumor making the rounds of the stores. Two young tribal
women from the neighboring hamlet, Sarkhan, were
supposed to have been abducted by a man from another tribe.

"See, Seif, how unruly and uncivilized the tribes are. Such a
dreadful thing could never happen here, a place of piety and
civilization. We are peace-loving and law-abiding."

My friends in the sanctuary never tire of telling me that tribal
Khawlan al-Tiyal is nothing but confusion and chaos, in which
their little village is a haven of tranquillity. *Fawdha*, a word akin to
anarchy, is how they describe the region.

Suddenly there is an uproar, every bit as shattering as an
explosion. The sheikh from the village of Sarkhan has stormed into
the marketplace, alone, unarmed, and furious. He announces that
two females, aged ten and fourteen, are missing from his village, and
accuses a nephew of one of the sanctuary *sada* of abducting them.

"It must be a terrible mistake or misunderstanding," one man
exclaims. His comrades concur, for it is unthinkable to them that
one of their own should have committed such a terrible deed.

"There's no mistake," the sheikh avers grimly. "Summon to me the man responsible for the boy."

When the latter—who happens to be the uncle, not the father—arrives, the sheikh from Sarkhan performs the ritual I have seen on other, less serious occasions of public disagreement or protest. He removes his dagger—the beautiful curved silver blade with the gazelle-horn handle known throughout Yemen as the *jambiyya*—from its sheath and, for an instant holding it aloft, where it catches the glint of the afternoon sun, pronounces the words "I challenge you!" He hands the dagger to a third party who happens to be standing nearby. He is Hussein the Servant. For the time being, this man is to be the mediator of the dispute, until the more important sheikhs can be summoned to resolve it. The uncle ruefully utters the conventional response, "And I am respectful," passing his thumb across his forehead, a gesture familiar to me from other occasions when I saw this ritual performed, and signaling the defendant's readiness to listen to the charges. He, too, then hands his dagger to the mediator.

In vain Hussein tries to soothe the sheikh's anger. Not only does he accuse the boy, and his uncle who is responsible for him, of the most heinous crime imaginable, but he holds the entire sanctuary accountable. He renews his challenge, only this time broadening its scope:

"If the girls and the boy are not found and returned to Sarkhan before sundown, the sanctuary will be plunged into war."

He then departs as quickly as he has come. Hussein the Servant scurries after him. The rest of the men in the marketplace close ranks around the uncle, reassuring him that there must be some grotesque misunderstanding, which will be cleared up momentarily—yet I can see that they are unnerved.

Giving a date to this incident suggests that it had a definite beginning, that one can say this event occurred at this-and-this time and at this-and-this place. Many of the most subtle and insightful analyses of events presume that we can reconstruct—not without difficulty, perhaps—what *actually* happened. It is tempting to think that, for an eye-witness like myself, it would be even easier to do this, since I was there in the sanctuary when the event occurred. And what could be more "immediate" than a diary entry written right after?

But this was not so easy as it sounds. How often do we say, "At first I thought . . . but later I realized . . ." The cliché has it that hindsight is twenty-twenty vision, but it is important to ask whether even hindsight might not be flawed. There are at least two conundrums. To arrive at a larger truth, for theoretical as much as political reasons, what do we have to simplify or flatten in our story? What do we have to leave out? And at what cost? Good field notes embody the tension and the strain between wanting to get at the truth and the inevitable messy confusion of the moment. There is also the reverse problem: not of leaving out things but of unavoidable gaps in the record that are not likely to be filled. These are perhaps more common than we like to admit, and the interesting question, it seems to me, is what to do with them.

An event is saturated with ambiguity as to its meaning or explana-tion, and this is not only because, as another cliché would have it, there are always two sides to a story. I have in mind several things here. One is what the literary critic Mikhail Bakhtin called multivocality: stories about an event multiply and contest each other, leaving one un-certain as to the event's origin, course, or even outcome, let alone the moral culpability of the actors, and no clear basis on which to sort through and decide upon competing versions. In Baktrin's view, this multivocality is an inevitable condition of ordinary human existence, not to be dispelled even if one does think life would be more bearable without it. This is certainly what I experienced on January 19, 1980. My companions in the sanctuary thought the rumor that a tribesman was responsible for the kidnapping showed once again how unruly or immoral the tribes were. In other words, to them the event was time-less because it was emblematic of essentialized identities and therefore had no real beginning and no real end; surely something like it would happen again, given the tribes' supposedly incorrigible warlike nature. Almost immediately this complacency gave way to chagrin, when the sanctuary realized it was being accused of exactly the sort of crime for which only moments earlier it had condemned the "Other." Later, some of the tribes impugned the piety of the sanctuary's people. Whose story was to be believed? Both? Neither?

Another difficulty is that, though an event appears to be singular or unique, it isn't; or rather it is *and* it isn't. What made the abduction an event for the *sada* was that none of their own, so far as they knew, had ever done anything like it, and yet that opinion would become complicated in the following weeks. Had the culprit acted alone? Was it, after all, unimaginable for one of their own to have committed this crime? Might the event be emblematic or symptomatic of some deeper moral rot in the sanctuary? Was it therefore less exceptional than the people of the sanctuary insisted? The impression of an event's uniqueness is attenuated when it is seen to be linked to other events, as it almost always is, not in causal chains so much as in complex webs. The event in Khawlan brought to the surface of collective memory events of the past that were associated with it, such as the civil war, and this convinced me all the more that I should not think of it as having started on January 19, 1980. Furthermore, whatever did happen on that day spawned other local events that became entangled in it, producing a web from which neither the sanctuary nor I could extricate ourselves.

Related to the multivocality and ramification of an event is what I call, borrowing from the great American literary critic Kenneth Burke, its interpretive "recalcitrance" and simultaneous ineluctability. In the former, the issue is not so much that there are contested stories about an event, in any one of which a partisan may firmly believe, but that the stories fail to make sense. There is a terrifying breakdown in meaning, a yawning gap between our naming of the event and its being or existence (what the psychiatrist Jacques Lacan calls "the Real"). Concomitantly, we have a helpless sense that things will happen that are unforeseeable and therefore uncontrollable. In the months to come, my friends in the *hijra* struggled to make sense of what had happened and were occasionally shocked, not to say frightened, that nothing made sense. They tried to control or manage the event so as to minimize the damage to themselves and their sanctuary, even when they harbored the apprehension that it was out of their hands and they might be overcome and undone by it in the end—if there ever was an end. I shared their fear and foreboding, not least because the fieldwork I had only just begun might be doomed.

To be sure, certain facts were knowable. For example, it is true that on January 19, 1980, the sheikh of the neighboring village entered the sanctuary and, in a ritualized action of challenge-and-response, accused one of its members of having abducted his daughter and niece; he alleged that this heinous deed had occurred sometime that same morning. But on what exactly were his truth claims based? Rumor, allegation, innuendo. In the ensuing weeks the parties summoned to mediate this conflict strained to determine the truth of the sheikh's claims, and after hearing testimonies based on sworn oaths (or, in one instance, extracted through torture), weighed the evidence again and again, and came to only limited conclusions. One was that the two girls from Sarkhan, one aged fourteen, the other ten, had indeed disappeared. The other was that the accused young man from the sanctuary had indeed taken them out of their village, and this was illegal. Little else could be agreed upon with certainty. People kept wondering, How culpable were the girls themselves in the crime for which the boy was held responsible? What had happened to them? And yet, what was talked about *during* the event and was said *about* the event far exceeded the certainties. It had to, or there would have been little to speak of. What was this excess of discussion all about? How do we understand it anthropologically? In the end, what people said about the event and why were more important than what actually happened, which I submit, is probably knowable only to a limited extent.

To indicate here how my presumed friends, their presumed enemies, and the presumed mediators tried to make sense of the event, I have tried, wherever possible, to re-present their discourse, whether it was in the form of a full-blown poetic ode or on the wings of a conversation. To preserve a sense of my own presence in the event, and the consequent confusions or uncertainties in my understanding of it, I continue to cite my field notes (in italics), and diary entries separately. However, a goodly part of this text is based not on either of these but on my memory, which represents an obvious problem for the credibility of my account about an event that occurred more than twenty-five years ago. Why should the reader trust my memory? Then again, why believe an account based on private field notes and sources kept anonymous for ethical reasons that cannot, because of their anonymity, be questioned?

The philosopher Paul Ricoeur, in his magisterial three-volume work *Time and Narrative*, posed for historical texts a similar set of questions, and his answer is the one adopted here. Like the historian, the anthropologist enters into an implicit "contract" with the reader averring that his ethnographic representation of the world is as factually true as he can make it. Unlike the historian or anthropologist (or for that matter, journalist), a writer of fiction is bound by no such contract. This is not to say, of course, that the historian and anthropologist are free from fictional or narrative devices in the construction of their truths—far from it—a point made by Hayden White, Paul Ricoeur, and James Clifford, among others. Nor does it mean that the historian and anthropologist may not include speculative or fantastic passages in their texts, so long as it is clear to the reader that that is what they are.

These matters have been discussed at length in scholarly literature on ethnographic writing and "hybrid" genres, but a reliance on one's memory to write about an event—far more an issue for the anthropologist than for the historian—goes virtually unremarked. Not only is it the case that far more material based on memory enters into an ethnographic account than has been acknowledged but it is also the case that there's little to be done about it. For one thing, there are not enough hours to record everything learned about a culture in a given day of fieldwork; experiences, judgments, and facts retained in memory may never be inscribed in notes. For another, information may be forgotten or repressed and not be recorded even if one has the time, then resurface years later only because of an association that has triggered one's memory. Would not the ethnographic account be greatly impoverished without this information? Why not, then, combine diary, field note, and memory fragment? We could call this book, perhaps, an "ethno-memoir."

Of course, there was one way to check the accuracy of my memory, or so I thought: I went back to Yemen in the summer of 2001 to see what other people remembered of the event, if they remembered it at all, and to see whether their memories jibed with mine. I was not a little surprised by what I found. But I would not want the reader to think that because I wrote this book after that, that it represents my final word on the subject, that it somehow gives me the closure I sorely wanted and came back to Yemen for. But I am getting ahead of my story.

By late afternoon of January 19, marksmen from Sarkhan had taken positions on the mountaintops facing the sanctuary and were waiting. I was told that Hussein the Servant was busy talking to the sheikh and his followers, trying hard to persuade them to agree to a truce. I enjoyed not a little the irony that the inhabitants of the sanctuary would entrust such an important task to a virtual outcast. There had been no choice in the matter, the Hunchback later told me, for he was the only person present at the time of the sheikh's challenge who did not belong to the descent group of either the sanctuary or Sarkhan and could therefore be expected to be neutral.

I refused to be alarmist and persuaded myself that the incident would be resolved peacefully and quickly. I returned to my house to relax. But toward nightfall, just after the call to prayer, shots rang out and a cry went up from one of the mosques. An older man had been hit in the leg.

I heard shouts of "A cowardly deed! To wound a man while he is at his prayers!"

The shots were answered by a barrage of gunfire from the sanctuary. It was not a heavy exchange, but it continued desultorily throughout the night. I learned that nighttime fighting was not only common among the tribes but preferred. Naturally, I became more apprehensive.

And more self-pitying, as I am now embarrassed to admit. I was affronted that no one—not the Hunchback or the Beltmaker or Ali the Bird—was concerned with my safety. They had to worry about the well-being of their own families, of course. I felt so forlorn that I almost knocked on Ahmed's door to see if he and Fatimah wanted company, but I knew they were away, probably at Fatimah's parents' home, where she and her young son would be safer than on the second story of our house.

I sat on the outside steps to catch the last glimmer of the sun, as I often did at twilight when it was too dark to read but the village electric generator had not yet been turned on. The black bulk of the house was behind me and served as a shield from the gunfire that might come from the direction of Sarkhan. I never thought of the possibility of bullets ricocheting off neighboring house walls. I was hoping that someone might come along with whom I could talk about the situation. But though an occasional beam of a flashlight raked the village path and shadows of passersby loomed and then faded on the walls, they only added to the impression of a village abandoned rather than, as was assuredly the case, holding its breath.

Then a couple of local boys came along, and I had to laugh when I saw them carrying slingshots. One of them was Abdullah, the same teenager who sometimes came to my apartment clandestinely at night to listen to music and dance with me, and his brother Yahya.

"That's not going to do you much good against the 'enemy,'" I joked.

"We're hunting pigeons," he explained. I plied them with questions, but they didn't seem to know much. If these lads were not afraid to venture forth, I figured the situation could not be too dire, and I tried to relieve the uncertainty by gathering news in the souk.

By now, there was hardly any daylight left to illuminate the way. Just as well, I thought, for I would be invisible to sharpshooters above the village. I was like a blind man without a cane, my feet in their plastic sandals serving to tap a large stone I remembered being in front of me *here*, my hand stretching out to confirm a jutting house wall just around the corner *there*. When I finally got to the market, I found that the metal barriers had been pulled down over the storefronts and locked. No one was in the street. I turned back, disappointment mingling with dread.

That night I decided to sleep in my bedroom, a stupid thing to do as I admitted to myself at the time, since its shuttered windows faced Sarkhan and presumably the enemy line of fire. But I decided to take the risk because I was too tired to move my bedding into the window-less hallway or the kitchen, which faced the courtyard in back.

In the morning I was awakened by gunfire. The truce must have been broken, I thought to myself with a sinking feeling. I was torn about what to do. Then I heard some voices from above calling, "Seif, can you brew us some tea?" They belonged to *sada* marksmen on the roof.

"Tea?" I laughed incredulously. One should never underestimate the fine Yemeni sense of the absurd.

"If it's no bother. We've been here all night and haven't had any breakfast."

Minutes later, fumbling up the dark stairwell to the roof and crouch-ing as low as possible, I made my way forward with teapot and porce-lain cups rattling on a tin tray.

Now it was their turn to sound incredulous. "Why are you so fright-ened? They're not trying to kill us—not yet anyway."

They might have had a point. Hadn't the man in the mosque been shot in the leg, not to kill or even maim him but as a warning? Had not the two boys gone hunting birds without much concern? My new friends on the roof explained that this fighting was more like a game through which the tribe hoped to make its rhetorical point—namely, that such a disgrace as had been perpetrated on them by a *sada* boy would not go unpunished. As I had learned from an anthropological literature that analyzed Arab tribal violence, through such a show of force they could construct themselves as honorable men and demand honorable actions in return; only on this basis of mutual honor could any negotiation start, let alone proceed. Still, it was a fine line between a show of violence and the real thing, an ambiguity that continued to the point when events tipped the violence into something altogether more dangerous, like the switch on a railroad track redirecting a speed-ing train to a disastrous end.

Suddenly, it was announced that a cease-fire had been declared for three days. Hussein the Servant had accomplished a truce after all. Men began to emerge from their cover and congratulate themselves that the worst-case scenario had been avoided. This was the beginning of a long process in which spurts of staged violence that became increasingly dangerous punctuated the ongoing negotiations, which involved more and more powerful men at higher and higher structural levels of the tribal system and national government.

Crowding the hillside below my house later that morning, I and dozens of other people clutched our shawls tightly in the crisp early morning air as we watched the proceedings in the wadi below. Ibrahim the Beltmaker represented the sanctuary. He was resplendent in a traditional outfit of the sada: *the round, white turban in the shape of a large pillbox; the elegant, snow-white robes cleaned and ironed; and the silver dagger affixed to one of his own magnificent belts. I could faintly see his lips pronouncing the sacred words of forgiveness and atonement to the sheikh of Sarkhan, who all the while was gazing at him sternly. A large bull and calf were handed over to [the sheikh], which would be eaten at lunch that day by the aggrieved family of the girls and the delegation of sheikhs from the region that had come to mediate the dispute.*

With Ibrahim were two members of the sanctuary. They were hostages, in accordance with the rules of conflict resolution, and they would be kept until the criminal was found and delivered into the hands of the mediators for trial and punishment. One of them was the grim-looking uncle of the alleged culprit, Abdullah. I was a bit surprised to see that the other was my upstairs neighbor Ahmed. I wondered what he was doing there, as he bore no relationship to Abdullah's family. He had volunteered, I learned subsequently, because he would get paid a minimal sum of money from the sanctuary to serve as a hostage. He would be fed regularly, allowed to listen to a radio and chat with his fellow hostage, and allowed fresh air and exercise whenever he wanted it. That was probably the best salaried work he would find, I said to myself unkindly. He would be relieved in a few days by another man from the sanctuary, or just as soon as Abdullah's father arrived from the capital to take his place. Besides hostages, the sanctuary handed over a large cache of weapons (old flintlock rifles for symbolic purposes, automatic weapons otherwise) as an initial payment of damages, the exact sum of which would be determined in the course of the negotiations.

Salah al-Qiri and his father, a powerful sheikh of the region, were standing behind Ibrahim. They had arrived with an entourage of some half dozen men, chanting a zamil *poem that Salah had composed for the occasion.*

This is the bull and calf, these the hostages and guns.
We shall add our dagger, with its polished gazelle-horn handle.
Until the accused is among us, we shall wage hot pursuit,
Even if we have to drag him from Lahaj or Taiz.

They had walked down the wadi floodplain in rows, their guns slung over their shoulders, clasping each other's hands. One half carried the first line, the other the second, and thus they alternated in their high-pitched, nasal cries, which echoed off the mountainsides. It was difficult for me to make out the words at first, having always had trouble with sung lyrics even in American pop tunes, and I asked a neighbor to repeat them to me in a plain speaking voice so that I could write them down in my little spiral notebook. When they got to the spot where the sheikh of Sarkhan was standing, a ritual greeting was performed, which was very different from the one I had encountered in the sanctuary. I had heard it before at tribal gatherings, but this spectacle was rendered more sublime by the beauty of the outdoor setting and the seriousness of the occasion. The sheikh of Sarkhan exhorted his men to greet the arrivals, and his companions responded in unison with a hearty kef al-Hal, ya rijal. "How is it going, men?" a greeting made more musical by its internal rhyme (-al). The father of Salah now took out his dagger and solemnly handed it over to the sheikh of Sarkhan, who accepted it as a sign of his willingness to negotiate.

The Qiri clan had not been the first to attempt mediation, though I did not learn this until later, and not from my friends in the sanctuary but from the great poet of al-ᶜAin, whom I had missed on my trip with Hussein the Servant but would visit a few weeks later. He explained to me that his own kinsman and benefactor, a member of the house of Royshan, had offered to mediate for the descendants of the Prophet, claiming that he could resolve the conflict quickly. But this man had a reputation for being ambitious and ruthless, and some said that he was vying to become paramount sheikh of Khawlan. If he succeeded in resolving the differences between the sanctuary and Sarkhan, his prestige would be enhanced immeasurably, and so would his grasp on political power. The sheikh was a man in his fifties, imposing in stature but with a face gnarled by a perpetual scowl. His son, who went everywhere with him (and presumably was in training to become his father's successor), was by contrast exceptionally handsome, gracious, and modest. One had the sense that he might be exuberantly outgoing were he not kept in check by his stern father. The poet Salih of al-ᶜAin later informed me that this son had considerable poetic talent, but on the couple of occasions *when the latter tried to speak to me, he seemed to rue his father's displeasure and thought better of it. I felt a slight pang of regret, for the opportunity lost not only of working with a tribal poet on tribal poetry—at long last—but also of experiencing a friendship.*

Seeking later to confirm what the poet from al-ᶜAin had told me about the sheikh of Royshan's intervention, I asked the Hunchback about it. "It's true," he said, "they did offer to negotiate for us, but we turned them down because we didn't trust Royshan. We suspected that he was behind an attempt to assassinate one of our headmen, perhaps at the behest of the president. That's one reason why we decided that the conflict had to be mediated by all of Khawlan, not just a section of it, so that the peace would be lasting."

That afternoon deliberations began in earnest, overseen by the Qiri clan but joined by one sheikh after another from the immediate vicinity, in compliance with the wishes of the sanctuary. As for the leadership of the sanctuary, which remained obscure to me, a crisis had now brought it to the fore, though it still attempted to operate discreetly. I would be surprised in the coming months by its depth, flexibility, and resilience. I would learn, for example, that men like Ibrahim the Beltmaker or Muhammad the Hunchback, though quite visible in the early stages of the conflict, turned out to be secondary players.

During these discussions another of the sada, whom I had been friends with in the market, a man with a painful limp and a face that was often haggard and drawn but that would always light up with a smile for me, distinguished himself. I will call him Muhammad the Lame. He seemed the most knowledgeable in the sanctuary about tribal poetry, and I sought him out for help on my project. Perhaps because he had a more profound understanding of tribal ways than any of his colleagues in the sanctuary, he had been put forward as their spokesman.

I didn't know at the time that more than seven hundred carloads of tribesmen from all over Khawlan had descended on the sanctuary, waiting on the outskirts and along the roads. They came as soon as Sarkhan announced that it had asked the tribe of which it was a part, called al-Dhubayyinah, to support it in its conflict with the sanctuary and its allies. It was within its rights to do so, kinsmen being expected to help out kinsmen, but as a consequence of the forces now allied with Sarkhan, the sanctuary was outnumbered. The mobilization by the carloads to aid the sanctuary was based on the rhetoric not of blood descent but of religious devotion. "It is our sanctuary," it was explained to me by some of the tribesmen who crowded the souk in those dramatic days, "and we must help to defend it." In addition to tribesmen, sada from Sana'a and other parts of Yemen—related to the sanctuary by blood as well as many who were not—came straggling in. Handsome young Hamid, the nephew of Ibrahim, stopped me in the street to say hello and ask how I was doing. "Well, Seif, I'll see you on the battlements!" The conflict was still at that stage when violence seemed to be a matter more of theater than of aggression, and the younger men were acting their parts with relish.

The dispute was not merely a local affair for other reasons as well. The Yemeni state sent a representative, one rumor claiming that he was the uncle of the president and one of his most trusted henchmen. To what ends he had been sent remained, however, a question altogether complex and shifting. The president may have had a grudge against one or two sada whom he had wanted to get rid of or at least neutralize through exile or confinement, but that was altogether different from wanting to see the whole sanctuary endangered; after all, the daily running of the Yemeni state bureaucracy was made possible largely by educated men such as the descendants of the Prophet, among whom quite a number hailed from the sanctuary. On the other hand, being dependent on both the political and military backing of the tribes in times of international conflict, such as in the quite recent war with South Yemen, the president would also want to make sure not to antagonize Sarkhan and its tribal allies. It was important that both sides could count on his blessing or, at the very least, his neutrality.

What the state could do more concretely in the meantime was to alert its checkpoints on the Sana'a–Taiz highway to be on the lookout for a white Toyota passenger car with a certain license plate number. Seeing that they would probably be secondary in the dispute mediation, the powerful but out-of-favor Royshans volunteered to head up a search party for the boy and the two missing girls. The sheikhs of Sarkhan and the Dhubayyinah were adamant that the disgrace perpetrated on their tribe would never be cleansed unless they were found, and if the Royshans succeeded in apprehending the fugitives, they could claim credit for having provided the crucial piece in the resolution of the dispute and thereby enhance their political standing. But the inhabitants of the sanctuary were not going to let the Royshans co-opt the manhunt, so they sent out their own party.

In the afternoon, discussions were held concurrently in both the sanctuary and Sarkhan. Testimony was heard and evidence weighed. I debated with myself whether I should crash one of them and decided I had to try. Wearing my headdress and futa, *with a dagger around my waist, and carrying a bundle of qat leaves wrapped in red cellophane, I resolutely marched off to the chew where Salah al-Qiri was holding forth. He was quite charming to me when I entered the sitting room, but I could sense that others were surprised and far less inclined to be welcoming. One man could not hold back his sarcasm. "Does he think he's going to collect some interesting poetry here?" Perhaps he thought I was attempting to divert attention from the more serious matter at hand. In spite of how uncomfortable the stares made me, I resolved to stay, as was my right according to the dictates of hospitality, hoping to make myself inconspicuous by sitting near the door.*

One tribesman next to me, a strapping young man with hair made unruly by the headdress he had pulled off and draped around his shoulders, smiled and gave me a sprig of qat. I asked him, "Why keep on fighting?"

"In order 'to cleanse the shame ['ar],' " he answered proverbially.

The rest stared at me coldly and said nothing. After a few moments, I decided to gather together my qat and leave.

The next day I spoke to the Hunchback, the Beltmaker, and the Lame about what had happened. It turned out that there had been a witness to the disappearance of the girls, a shepherd boy from Sarkhan who had seen them gathering firewood on the hillside. He had noticed them put down their baskets, descend to the wadi floor, and walk up to an idling white Toyota. The sheikhs questioned him closely. He admitted that he had not actually seen them get into the car, nor did he clearly see its driver. Many questions remained, not the least of which was whether in fact the Toyota, a common enough vehicle in Yemen, belonged to the boy Abdullah who was alleged to have abducted them. But another witness gave potentially more conclusive and damning testimony. This was Hajbah, the owner of the tiny convenience store on the road to Sana'a, who claimed that Abdullah stopped to buy petrol and soft drinks while two women remained in the backseat of his car, a white Toyota. They were veiled, of course, so it was impossible to identify them positively as the sheikh's daughter and niece. But the most urgent question was why the women hadn't spoken up, if indeed they had been forced into the car against their will. Could they have been drugged? Hajbah, had not gotten a clear enough view of them to hazard a guess as to that possibility. Others speculated that they might have been too frightened to speak up. But frightened of whom and of what? Of Abdullah and a possible threat of harm, even of death, if they should give him away? Or of their father and a terrible punishment that might include death if he were persuaded that they had cooperated with Abdullah in their disappearance? After all, it was his word against theirs, and no guarantee that their word would be believed. What was clear, however, was the astonishing self-possession of this young man who calmly spoke to the store owner, made his purchases, filled his gas tank, and then slowly drove off. In fact, Hajbah's suspicions had not even been aroused at the time, for it was a relatively common occurrence, after all, for a man to drive his female relatives to and fro on family business.

What Abdullah had done was unspeakably shocking, and it took time for the sanctuary to absorb the magnitude of it. Even then, his viciousness beggared the imagination. What could possibly have motivated him? He was either completely out of his mind or totally depraved, or both.

Leaders of the sanctuary such as Muhammad the Lame not surprisingly tried to distance themselves from Abdullah and the consequences of his crime. *Abdullah had not grown up in their midst, having been taken by his father to live in the capital after his parents had been divorced. They hardly knew him. It is true that he had visited his mother in the sanctuary from time to time, but his trips had been more infrequent in later years. They insisted that he was a stranger in their midst, a pariah, over whose upbringing they had had no control. It was the father who bore that responsibility, a father who had remained in the capital, which everyone knew to be filled with temptation and sin. Therefore, the punishment of the crime should fall on the culprit Abdullah and the people most responsible for him, not on the entire sanctuary.*

The descendants of the Prophet were not simply trying to get themselves off the hook. A theological principle was at stake. Muhammad the Lame—he among the *sada* who ultimately taught me the most about tribal poetry and tribal ways—understood better than anyone the clash or discrepancy between the two legal systems. *In arguing for individual culpability, [the sanctuary leaders] were invoking religious doctrine and law (Shariʿa). The sheikh of Sarkhan and his people, on the other hand, insisted that the sanctuary could not so easily be absolved of guilt, invoking tribal customary law (ʿurf or taghut as it is sometimes also known) and its principle of collective responsibility.*

In Yemen, the two legal systems, the one Islamic, the other tribal, have coexisted for centuries but not always harmoniously, and here was a case in which they were in conflict. Each side was invoking law for its own tactical advantage, but one could not reduce their claims to political machinations. At stake were fundamental issues of identity and, even more profoundly, conflicts in those identities, which existed not only between but also within groups and individuals. Muhammad the Lame, who seemed to be able to place himself in the other's position better than most of the *sada* while remaining clearheaded about his own, understood this profoundly.

*Not being themselves tribal, the descendants of the Prophet felt their primary allegiance to be to Shari*ᶜ*a, yet they realized only too well that the sanctuary owed its survival to the sufferance of the tribes, whose customs, including tribal law, they had to respect. At the same time, the people of Sarkhan were deeply committed to worship in the Islamic way and deferred to the descendants of the Prophet in matters of religion. Had they not for generations come to the sanctuary to pray in its mosque and to be inspired by the imam's sermons? Had they not sent their children to the sanctuary school to be "rightly guided"? Which, now, would take precedence for them: Shari*ᶜ*ya or* ᶜ*urf?*

The negotiation continued the next day but remained inconclusive. My neighbor at the chew had warned me that fighting would resume, and it threatened to do so with every passing hour that the boy and the girls were not found. The sanctuary once again closed ranks and prepared for a fight. That night I wrote in my diary:

> Talks have been going on between the sanctuary and the tribes (see my notes). The mood of the townsmen is grim. They don't want war, but the tribes are not going to be satisfied until they've spilled blood [in the sanctuary] in revenge for the disgrace caused by the boy. I debated with myself whether to stay . . . or whether to leave. Unfortunately, there is never enough time to prepare for leaving if hostilities are resumed, and I learned at sundown tonight that fighting would begin in the morning. No car leaves for Sana'a tonight, and so I am stuck.
>
> Except for stray bullets, I really don't think there is any danger for me as long as I seek adequate shelter during the fighting. I've moved my desk and some study materials into my *mafraj* [sitting room], where I also plan to sleep tonight. I understand they're

going to install a machine gun on the roof of my house. There's a
cannon above us in the Citadel. It looks as though my house will
be a central target, so maybe I should think about moving out to be
with someone else.

Such an irony that I chose the sanctuary because I thought I'd
be safer here than elsewhere in Khawlan. Nerves are frayed.
Muhammad the Lame, who seems to be one of the main leaders of
the sanctuary, looks exhausted. I see him everywhere, tirelessly
tending to a thousand details.

Cars are coming in and out, constantly bringing in *sada* from
Sana'a, perhaps to help in the fighting. Everyone is carrying a
weapon, and the men are now preparing their positions.

I once had a dream in Hyde Park . . . that I would land in the
center of something—I didn't know what it would be, except that
it involved a lot of fighting in the Middle East. I wonder if my
dream has now become reality. I stop worrying about myself and
think about what might happen to the *sada*—some of them may die
in this war, and the men who are now bearing arms must be
wondering whether they will be the ones to die. Or perhaps one of
their women or children? And what of the tribesmen? One of them
might be killed as well! And for what reason? In order to avenge a
shame. I feel that I'm in the middle of a Greek tragedy.

A dark night. Only a silver cuticle of a moon in the sky. There is
none of the strange, unearthly pallor, the platinum sheen of light
that the earth reflects when the moon is full. At those times there
would be enough light to see the enemy, but now I doubt that a
marksman could distinguish anything that is more than a hundred
yards away.

In the distance one can hear the tribes singing their *zamils*—
otherwise the night is still. The eerie chant, loud and shrill, is
repeated over and over again. It's like a war cry, a rallying call, and
a summons to defend the tribe's honor. One wonders whether
they're working themselves up into launching a major attack on the
village. And then again, it seems only that they want to make a
moral, symbolic point rather than exact any horrible revenge.

What I am struck by most now, in rereading this passage, is the ambiguity of the violence. Thanks to the marksmen on my roof, I had understood that it was a kind of theater, necessary to reconstitute the honor of Sarkhan and its tribal allies so that serious negotiations could get under way, as indeed they did. Yet if the aggrieved party wasn't satisfied, negotiations could be broken off and a state of war resumed. Was the threat of attack, then, an admonition to the sanctuary to negotiate in all seriousness, with the intent of continuing the next day? Or did it signal something more ominous, that the Sarkhan were giving up on negotiations altogether and would settle their score through blood? There was no way to decide between these alternative interpretations. The meaning of violence, as also the intent of the perpetrators, had to remain ambiguous, paradoxically enough, if the negotiations were to continue.

As it turned out, a truce (*sulh*) was declared the next day, and negotiations began again in earnest.

One day soon thereafter, as I came through the market as usual and headed toward my house, a young man hailed me from the back of a Toyota pickup. This was Muhammad the Maswari. I base the following description of our first meeting on recollection and not on the record of either my field notes or my diary, in neither of which this first meeting is mentioned. It is one of those ironies of fieldwork, as of life, that a person or incident that will be so important appears coincidentally and unheralded at the time. But not unnoticed. Muhammad made a tremendous first impression, which is why I have such a vivid recollection of that first encounter.

"You're the guy who was on TV, aren't you? You said you wanted to study tribal poetry. Did you finally find a house?" he asked, grinning. Muhammad was around twenty years old, medium height, wiry, with quick, agile movements. Except for his nose, which was slightly crooked and short, making his open face appear slightly squashed, he had fine features, with straight, white teeth and intelligent eyes that would fix one with a disarmingly level gaze.

He grabbed my hand and shook it heartily. "I've wanted to meet you, Seif. I've wanted to talk to you about your project. You've come to the right place. Khawlan has the best poets in all of Yemen."

"So I've been told. I've met some of them. Not as many as I'd like, though."

"I can fix that. Where do you live?"

I pointed to the Citadel. "Just below that big house over there."

"I'll visit you this afternoon and we can chew *qat* together. Some of our people visiting the sanctuary are poets and I'll ask them to come along. If, that is, we don't have a big meeting. My uncle is one of the sheikhs of Wadi Maswar who is trying to mediate the dispute."

"You will come, then?"

"Yes, God willing."

"You swear?"

"I swear," he replied.

"You swear 'by God and all that is holy'?"

"I swear 'by God and all that is holy,'" he repeated, amused that I was getting him to commit to a promise in accordance with the rather pushy local norms of speaking.

Muhammad was true to his word. That afternoon he appeared at my doorstep with two companions from his wadi. I could tell they meant to stay when I saw the bundles of *qat* under their arms.

I joyfully ushered them into my sitting room. Had I been able to afford one, I would have spread out a carpet, but it was just as well that I had settled for pale blue plastic mats instead. They were easier to keep clean after a chew. Curtains of white, translucent gauze hung from the bottom windows and diffused the glare, while a soft light—colored red, amber, and green—angled down from the half-moon windows and spilled like wine at our feet. I preferred to keep the whitewashed walls with their texture of cake icing bare, except for a peg or two on which jackets, walking sticks, or the occasional gun could hang, and perhaps some books on the ledge that ran around the room just above the head.

While my guests helped themselves to tea, I filled some thermoses with water, which kept surprisingly cool in the moistened clay pots that I had in my kitchen, and, as is customary, added a pinch of incense to help disguise the brackish taste. After we felt comfortable, *qat* bundles were unfolded from their banana-leaf casings and spread out on our laps.

Before the conversation got rolling, I busied myself with the preparation of the water pipe. I went out on my front steps to light some charcoal in a small brazier. In one hand I held a funnel-shaped clay container with tobacco leaves, crumpled and lightly pressed on the bottom, in the other a metal clamp, with which I stirred the charcoal, occasionally fanning the flames with my breath. When the lumps were furry with ash, I carefully placed them on top of the tobacco until they rose over the rim of the container in the shape of a small mound or pyramid. In the middle of its glowing heart I inserted a sliver of aromatic incense. Muhammad had already set up the water pipe in the *mafraj*, to whose stem I now carefully affixed the clay container. This was often tricky, for the opening at its base was not necessarily of the same size as the top of the stem and one had to wedge in bits of a rag or newspaper to secure a tight fit. In addition, the base of the stem, with its brass water bowl, had to be stable, and the thick snake coil of the leather tube through which the smoke was pulled had to be extended carefully from the bowl, otherwise the top-heavy contraption might tip over and spill cinders on the floor or, worse, burn the visitors. Another reason why plastic mats rather than wool carpets were practical, I thought. Once Muhammad had gotten the smoke to draw easily through the water in a low gurgle, the mouthpiece was passed around the room. It mattered little that it might be smeared with bits of *qat* from the last user; one simply cleaned it off with one's hand or sleeve before sucking gently on the stem, perhaps letting it rest momentarily on the lower lip as one savored the scented smoke curling upward into the nostrils.

I had always been the guest, especially in this village, where only Ahmed and his younger brothers might visit me. I was excited to be a host for a change and gratified to be able to extend my modest hospitality to some newfound friends who, moreover, seemed like "the real thing." It was as if someone were finally taking me and my presence seriously.

I hauled out notebooks of poetry, proverbs, jokes, and other sayings. One of the young men who was quite literate served as our scribe, writing down in my small spiral notebook a number of *zamil* poems remembered by him or dictated to him by his comrades. His name was Yahya, and he was a son of the sheikh from Wadi Maswar. Definitions of words, many of them part of the local dialect, were appended and explanations provided of historic events unknown to me. Now I had collaborators instead of debunkers, I thought. I pinched myself to see whether I was dreaming. I asked if they would mind my taping some of their melodic chants. Whereas he had been rather subdued until then, Muhammad became quite animated at the start of the taping. I discovered later that he had learned to read in school but could not write proficiently. In fact, he could barely scribble his name. His inability to write was such a source of consternation, even mild embarrassment, to him that I had it in the back of my mind to try to teach him someday. Regrettably, I never had the chance.

Attitudes toward literacy and its practice were important topics I would have explored more systematically if the outlines of the tribe's primarily oral poetic system hadn't consumed all my time and attention. For tribesmen, mastery of the written word was more tenuous, and their attitude toward it ambivalent. Many of them, like Muhammad's friends, were functionally literate, and all of them could see the need for writing in their rapidly modernizing lives, which were spent in the army, in some sort of commerce, or in the state bureaucracy. Yet the traditional system of tribal leadership was and to a large extent continued to be face-to-face, depending more upon the charisma of speech than upon print. The *sada*, like all other literate classes with an ideological allegiance to written, standard language, denigrated colloquial speech and its verse forms, including tribal Arabic and poetry, which they saw as simply another dialect. But the tribes took considerable pride in their spoken language, claiming it to be a survival of a great oral tradition that extended back to the glorious days of ancient Yemen—even to the kingdoms of Himyar and Saba, which existed before the advent of Islam. And some tribesmen had a tacit and not altogether unjustified fear that if they embraced literacy wholeheartedly, they would lose their linguistic identity and come under the rhetorical sway of the forces that controlled printing and writing. I can still hear Muhammad's eloquence, to which his companions inevitably deferred. In spite of the fact that he had a large pouch in one cheek filled with *qat*, he managed to preserve the crisp diction that made him the easiest to comprehend of all my Yemeni consultants. As I continue today to listen to his voice, captured by the miracle of sound recording over two decades ago, I notice the concision, clarity, and vividness of his answers, which reveal his trenchant intelligence and commanding personality.

The room would have gotten quite warm after a while, a chew having to become like a sweat bath to be considered truly climactic, and Muhammad unwound his headdress and let it fall over his shoulders as he reached for a thermos to sip some water. His words tumbled out of him as his mind raced under the influence of the *qat*. I'm sure I tossed him a particularly succulent branch in appreciation for his lively company, a gesture often extended to an honored guest at a chew. I remember that, if his hands were not busily plucking the leaves off the stem, which he waved like a conductor's baton, their strong, tapered fingers would be bunched in a characteristic jabbing gesture, with which he emphasized his points. The strain of following his subtle, rapid explanations, particularly toward the end of the afternoon, sometimes proved too much for me, and I would lean back on my pillow, all the while keeping eye contact, nodding my head in agreement as though I were following every word, and occasionally digging or prodding or questioning to demonstrate my interest.

When we had arrived at that time—it's about three hours into every chew—when the slightly madcap pace of conversation slowed and people held a silent colloquy with their thoughts, I was secretly relieved. I may have tried to revive the dying embers in the clay container of the water pipe or add more water to the thermoses, though I do not now recall the particulars. Then, it would have been time for Muhammad and his friends to rejoin their companions, who would have been heading for their homes in another wadi, while I, exhausted by the session but at the same time exhilarated by the *qat*, would pick up and throw away the refuse of branches, extinguish and dismantle the water pipe, and sweep the floors. Thank God *qat* kills the appetite, for I would not have had the strength to prepare dinner after such an intense session.

"I'll be back," Muhammad assured me as he walked away with his companions into the night.

It was around this time that Abdullah the Culprit, who was responsible for the disappearance of the girls, was apprehended and brought back to the sanctuary.

Quite by chance one day, I happened to come across him. I was hailed by a group of men bearing arms and recognized one of them as my upstairs neighbor's brother, Mohammed, the successful mason and carpenter whom I had always liked far more than Ahmed. I came over to say hello. As I approached, I saw that they were standing around someone who was sitting on his haunches. When I saw that his legs were in iron shackles, I suddenly understood. So this was Abdullah, the young man who had caused the "troubles." He was smoking a cigarette—evidently, he was being let out of his prison for his daily breath of fresh air—and when he turned to me, I saw purple bruises on his face. The sight was chilling. Something else about his looks unnerved me, though I could not quite put my finger on it.

I was told that the young man had been made to undergo an ordeal (he was tortured with electricity) to determine whether he was telling the truth. He confessed that the girls had paid him to take them out of the village, and so he had driven them to Taiz, checked into a room, and had sex with the older of them. (Did he rape her, or was it consensual? No one except the parties involved know the answer, and only one of them ever had the chance to tell the story.) He insisted that he did not know what had happened to them after he left the girls in the room together.

We were introduced.

"Don't you want to talk to him?" Ahmed's brother Mohammed asked.

"Why should I?"

I was being coy. A sense of perhaps excessive discretion overwhelmed me. To be honest, this sense was newly acquired. I hadn't felt it necessary in my relations with people until I started fieldwork, but it was a lesson well learned, and I haven't forgotten it. The "troubles" were generally thought to be none of my business, though such opinions were not uniform or uniformly hostile; my business, some people thought, was to collect and study tribal poetry. At the time I took consolation in the thought—erroneous as it turned out—that that task was remote from the sanctuary and its dispute with Sarkhan. I didn't want to rock the boat by poking my nose into what was deemed not my business. But in retrospect, I suspect I also must have had a psychological reason for my readiness to shun this young man, apart from the abhorrent nature of his crime. I had been in the village only two months—after more than nine months of trying to locate myself in a field site—and the prospect of moving and starting over again because of the calamity that was bearing down on it was unnerving to contemplate. This young man became the scapegoat for my "troubles," too, and I resented him.

"He's ordinary," said Ahmed's brother, trying to coax me into a conversation. "He won't bite. He's just like me—or you, for that matter."

I was secretly horrified and bewildered. I could not tell whether Ahmed's brother was joking or, worse, slyly insinuating that, for all he knew, I was as bad as the Culprit.

"What do you mean, 'just like me or you'?" I asked defensively.

"Well, his story is not so different from anyone else's."

This was not the way others in the village had spoken about the fellow. "A dog," they had said, "a crazy maniac," and of course, in their arguments with Sarkhan and its supporters, they had painted him as someone whom they did not know and absolutely disavowed. Now Ahmed's brother was claiming a certain kinship, a shared identity. "I still don't understand. Why is he so ordinary?"

Abdullah remained silent, watching me intently while he listened to the story about himself, a smirk playing on his lips. Ahmed's brother explained that Abdullah had grown up in Sana'a, where he had gone to school and found a clerical job in the government administration. He had wanted to get married, but like so many other young men, he could not afford the marriage payments on his salary. He'd come to the sanctuary to see whether he could marry a local girl, expecting the price to be lower, but found the prospects here no better. Of course what he did was horrible, taking those two girls out of Khawlan, and inexcusable, but you can understand maybe why he was angry at the old men for this arrangement and crazy enough to make trouble for them.

This was an extraordinary "explanation," but at least it provided some context for what the Culprit had done. Until now all I had heard was that the youth of Yemen were being corrupted by foreign ways and unduly influenced by godless beliefs. Abdullah's story, as I heard it from the man guarding him, offered another version: the younger generation was chafing against the older one's demands for exorbitantly high marriage payments, which stood in the way of its happiness.

Abdullah's appearance was as unexpected as Muhammad the Maswari's, if far more uncanny. Again I did not refer to my meeting with him in either my diary or my field notes, but as with Muhammad I retain a vivid memory of the encounter. It was the first and the last time I saw him, in fact. This cannot be a simple lapse, the sort of thing one doesn't mention because it is trivial or because one has other, more pressing details to write down. There was nothing *more* important that I could have recorded at that time. I ought to have written something about it. Thinking back on it now, the omission was, more probably, due to repression. Abdullah the Culprit and Seif the Anthropologist were merging into one phantasmagorical figure in my mind.

I looked forward to the next time Muhammad the Maswari would return to the sanctuary and visit me. When that moment came, I was still shy about talking about the "troubles," but I had resolved to get to the bottom of at least one subject, namely the different tribes of Khawlan, the approximate sizes of their territory, their political significance, and their locations relative to one another. Nothing much had been written about this question in the western or Yemeni literature, and the picture that Ibrahim the Beltmaker had drawn for me, though helpful, was sketchy. In the process of clarifying these points, I hoped to make better sense of the people involved in this dispute.

"Poetry is always referring to the seven tribes of Khawlan. Who are they, Muhammad?"

"They are the Bani Jabr, Bani Siham, Bani Dhubyan, Bani Shadad, Bani Bahlul, al-Garwa, and al-Yamaniyaten."

"I thought that the Bani Suhman were a separate tribe."

"No, they belong to the Bani Siham."

"This is the first time I've heard al-Garwa mentioned as one of the seven tribes."

"It used to be a part of the Bani Jabr. Now it's its own tribe. You know the poem of Sheikh al-Ghadir, composed during the civil war, which starts out 'Mount al-Tiyal, I summoned'?" I certainly remembered it well, and I remembered how I had recited it to Yahya al-Qiri, early on in my days at the sanctuary. "Well, he was sheikh of al-Garwa before he became head sheikh of the region and one of the most powerful men in Yemen. Because of his stature, and the commanding presence of his son in today's assemblies, al-Garwa has become a tribe." This possibly apocryphal history would be fascinating to trace, and I made a mental note to do so. It could be an example of the process of tribal formation and the factors behind it. As in so many other instances, however, I never had the opportunity to follow up.

"Where are all these tribes located, Muhammad? Maybe you can draw them for me on a map."

I knew that he understood the term *kharitah*, "map," but I did not realize that he meant something quite different from what I or Arab cartographers meant by it. I left him in my sitting room, comfortably ensconced with a water pipe and some *qat*. When I returned an hour later, I was astonished at what he had drawn.

Muhammad had visualized the region not from a bird's-eye perspective—from a fixed point above the space being surveyed—but from the point of view of a traveler passing through on the ground along a particular route. This is sometimes called an experiential map. The routes he might have taken from his home in Wadi Maswar to one end of Khawlan or the other were his axes of orientation, and he duly noted the main features to be seen along the way. It was more a visual record or memory of a journey than a map of a space, as I had learned to think of it from my schooling. There was not even a starting or end point, with arrows telling the direction of travel. He had drawn page after page of zigzags and curves, straight lines and wavy lines, going in one direction and then veering off in the opposite; if they had been tacked on to one another, they would have spread from my house to the other end of the village. It has been said that Queen Victoria was entertained by travelogues that consisted of a giant canvas scroll slowly unfurled in front of her court to reveal everything seen along a particular route or journey, say, along one bank of the Nile River. Muhammad's map was based on a similar principle: he simply recorded what was in front of him at various points of a journey. Consider written directions that you might give someone trying to find your home: drive two miles on Tower Road and turn right at the stoplight; continue for three blocks until you get to a railroad intersection, et cetera. These are more abbreviated and anemic than Muhammad's drawings were but comparable in their logic. I had in mind to study Muhammad's sense of spatial orientation and try to understand it in its own terms, a culturally specific cartography, but it seemed at the time to be taking me away from the information I wanted. Now, I don't even know what happened to all those sheets of paper Muhammad had filled out so laboriously.

I tried a different tack. "What are the boundaries of Khawlan, Muhammad?"

He rattled off ancient and reliable markers, the most important of which were mountains that I could locate on a conventional cartographic map. I pulled out a detailed map of Yemen and pointed out the features he had listed. "See, Muhammad, here's Mount al-Tiyal and if you drew a line between it and Mount Nugum in Sana'a on one side to the west and Mount Sirwah to the east, you'd almost have the northern boundary of Khawlan. Then you have Mount Sahal over here, forming the eastern boundary with Sirwah."

He caught on quickly and began to trace the rest of the boundary himself. "And here's the village of Dhuraᶜ al-Kalb, Mount Kanin to the north of it, and here is Sana'a."

Any indication of the sizes of the tribal territories should be taken with a grain of salt, and to draw the boundaries in anything like a straight line would be pure fiction. Undoubtedly, there are other

TERRITORIES of the SEVEN TRIBES of KHAWLAN

The seven tribes of Khawlan al-Tiyal: Bani Jabr, Bani Siham, Bani Dhubyan, Bani Shadad, Bani Bahlul, Bani Garwa, and al-Yamaniyaten. The Bani Suhman are a subsection of the Bani Siham, al-Dhubayina a subsection of the Bani Dhubyan. Al-Yamaniyaten (literally, "two Yemenis") has two sections, one at the higher elevation and one at the lower. The tribes' noncontiguous territorial organization complicates their alliances. The territory of the Sinhan, the President's tribe, is technically not part of Khawlan.

Marib

Sabal

Haylam

Sirwah

BANI JABR

BANI DHUBYAN

BANI SUHMAN

Naqil al-'Urqub

al-Tiyal

BANI SHADAD

Wadi Maswar

BANI GARWA

AL-YAMANIYATEN (upper and lower)

BANI SIHAM

Jihana

sanctuary

Sarkhan

AL-DHUBAYINA

BANI BAHLUL

Kanin

Nugum

SINHAN

Sana'a

Dhura' al-Kalb

0 Miles 10 20

0 Kilometers 20

© 2005 Jeffrey L. Ward

anomalies. I was puzzled, for example, by the fact that al-Garwa, which Muhammad had just told me had been part of the Bani Jabr at one time, was not even adjacent to it. So sections of tribal territories need not be contiguous? Muhammad insisted the location of al-Garwa was correct. As he reminded me, people at first found it puzzling that Sarkhan and the villages under its sheikh should claim affiliation with the Bani Dhubyan, a tribe whose main territory was even more distant from them than al-Garwa was from the Bani Jabr, but they had nonetheless accepted it as plausible.

"Could al-Garwa," I asked, "claim descent from the Bani Jabr and seek its help if it needed it, just as Sarkhan has done from its distant cousins?"

"I suppose so," he answered. "But other factors come into play as well. It doesn't really help if the section you call on is weak, even though you share a blood connection. The Bani Dhubyan are not weak. And you know, sometimes your neighbor means a lot to you and you feel closer to him, even if you don't share descent."

I began to understand more clearly what marked the boundaries between political entities. The mountain gap of Nagil al-ʿUrgub, for instance, was the point of convergence of no fewer than five tribal entities: the Bani Jabr, Shadad, Dhubyan, and Suhman, and al-Yamaniyaten. Muhammad referred to this point again and again, in part because it marked the easternmost extent of Wadi Maswar, his home. Mount Haylan was another marker of this kind, located at the boundary between the Bani Jabr and the Bani Dhubyan, and the town of Jihana, which was the administrative hub of Khawlan from the Yemeni state's point of view, also lay at the intersection of the Bani Shadad, al-Garwa, Bani Bahlul, and al-Yamaniyaten. It, like the sanctuary where I lived, had a small contingent of *sada* who performed various functions for the tribes.

"You say, Muhammad, that the Bani Dhubyan are not weak. What makes them strong? Do they have great wealth?"

"Not really. Their lands are not nearly so fertile as ours in Wadi Maswar, for example. On the western edge of Khawlan, where they live, near the great desert, cultivation is sparse, and many of them are

Bedouin. There might be a little bit of smuggling across the border with Saudi Arabia, but it doesn't amount to much. No, they're a military power. Just last year, for example, they helped stop the advance of enemy troops from South Yemen and secured the eastern border for the president. The state gave them weaponry for that purpose, although they have always been heavily armed."

"That makes them a formidable opponent, no? I mean, it seems that the sanctuary might easily get beaten."

"True, but that's why we're here. If the Bani Dhubyan attack, they will be opposed by not only the inhabitants of the sanctuary but nearly the rest of Khawlan too. 'It's our sanctuary and we shall defend it.' " (I knew this sentence had become something of a rallying cry.)

"What about the state? Why doesn't it keep the Bani Dhubyan in check?"

"As I told you, the president can't afford to anger the Bani Dhubyan because his defense of the east depends on them. Besides, even if he did try to prevent an attack, we wouldn't let him. Let the army in, and you compromise your autonomy."

Muhammad wasn't telling me everything I needed to know to understand the relationship of the Khawlan tribes to the Yemeni state. I surmised this much later when he revealed to me that Khawlan had been perturbed at the agreement the president had been "forced" to sign with South Yemen in 1979 to the effect that North and South Yemen would work toward national unity. "Never shall we allow unification. We haven't forgiven South Yemen for its treachery in the civil war," said Muhammad. He was remembering the assassination of several royalist sheikhs, many from Khawlan, at a luncheon to which they had been invited by southerners who said they wanted reconciliation with North Yemen. "Not only was Sheikh al-Ghadir of al-Garwa killed," he reminded me, "but practically the whole tribal leadership of Khawlan was wiped out!" It would make sense that Khawlan was alienated from the president's policy of working toward unification with South Yemen. The question was how far its tribesmen would go to oppose it, and whether they would seize on the current situation to do so.

"What do you think will happen?"

"Hard to say. Right now the sheikh of Sarkhan says he won't stop fighting until the two girls show up. Some of the sheikhs from Khawlan are questioning the hotel owner in Taiz to see whether he knows anything about their disappearance."

"It's his honor, isn't it?"

"Of course, but you know he really does want to get his women back, and not just because he wants to 'cleanse the disgrace.' Suppose it had been your sisters, Seif. Wouldn't you want them back? Unless he holds out to the very last minute, he can't be sure that every effort hasn't really been made to retrieve them."

"But what will happen to them if they are found?"

"Well, it depends on their guilt. If the girls paid Abdullah to take them away because one of them was pregnant, as the boy insists, then the punishment will be severe. Probably death. But if it turns out that she wasn't pregnant and probably had no reason to leave the village secretly, no one will believe the boy's story, and their lives will be spared. However, no man will want to marry either of them."

"Why is that?"

"Damaged goods."

"How are you going to know what they did independently of the boy, if you can't find them?"

"Ah, that's why the sheikhs are questioning the hotel owner in Taiz." It was clear that these people weren't going to permit an investigation by mere policemen or governmental functionaries. They were taking matters in their own hands.

January 29, 1980

The Prophet's Birthday. It was a brisk morning, and the schoolboys were huddled against the wind that whipped around the corners of the houses. Some of them smiled and waved when they saw me coming.

The schoolmasters prodded us to form a procession, and soon we were wending our way slowly through the streets to the house of Muhammad the Hunchback, the proud host of this year's celebration. He had told me about it the day before and had encouraged me to attend. "It will be very moving, Seif." "And what will I hear?" "Hymns, speeches, stories—all things you'd be interested in."

I made a tape recording of this celebration, and listening to it now, I'm not only amazed that the tape has held up but struck by how many different sounds it captured: the crunching of our footsteps on the gravelly paths; the mumblings of the younger boys, who were only half paying attention to a hymn an old man (Fatimah's elderly father?); was plaintively singing; the impatient honking of a car in another part of the village; the mad barking of dogs. I didn't bring my camera along this time, out of discretion (misguided, as it turned out—they all wanted me to take their picture), for I didn't want to piss anyone off, least of all the old-timers, and especially on such a sacred occasion.

It was an unusually bright morning, and the whole village gleamed like a polished kettle. Veiled faces peered down silently from the rooftops, and I could not but wonder whether the peripheral presence of the women was a sign of their inclusion or exclusion.

As I strain to make out Fatimah's father's singing on the tape, I remember that at the time I caught only half his words and understood even fewer of them. Being able to stop and replay the tape (or, to be precise, a copy of the tape, for I worry that the original might break under this kind of wear) doesn't help much, for his voice was broken with age and many of his teeth were missing. The assembly, by contrast, had no trouble following him. They had heard the same hymn countless times and after each of his offerings would catch the line and repeat it.

> Peace be upon you, O Messenger [*rasul*] of ours, Peace be upon you.
> Peace be upon you, O Prophet [*nabi*], Peace be upon you.
> O Loved one, Peace be upon you, God's prayer be upon you.

The first half of the line was delivered on a languid musical beat, with the concluding portion on a melodic line soaring heavenward. Approaching the Hunchback's house, we abruptly changed rhythms. The tune became jaunty and staccato, like feet stomping in a vigorous dance.

WELCOME, Light of Hussein, WELCOME.
WELCOME, O house of Hussein, WELCOME.
WELCOME, O light of my eyes, WELCOME.

From deep inside the house could be faintly heard high, paper-thin voices echoing us in song, and suddenly I realized that the youngest boys had already congregated there to meet us. The antiphony of voices symbolized a generational difference between older and younger, leaders and followers; and given that the little boys occupied the interior space of the house—the protected sphere of women and children—another difference became apparent, that between guardian and ward. As we made our way up the dimly lit interior stairs, the boys' voices grew louder and more boisterous. When we finally entered the sitting room, little bodies swaying and rocking in the brilliant white light joyfully greeted us in deafening song. There we all were, crammed into one room: boys, young men, village elders, schoolteachers, and one anthropologist. Ali the Bird's brother, a nice young man who had a little shop I used to frequent in the market, smiled radiantly and beckoned me to his side. We all sat down.

Now the headmaster of the school, one of the most learned men in the sanctuary, delivered a homily in flawless classical Arabic. Everyone knew this to be the Prophet's language, the language in which the Qur'an is revealed. By enunciating distinctly, as well as observing the written or standardized grammatical rules, he was showing himself to be a worthy representative of the religious elite. In the context of the ongoing dispute with Sarkhan, in which the very legitimacy of the sanctuary to lead religiously was called into question, this performance was not a little poignant. This is not to say that everyone listened with rapt attention: little kids were chattering to themselves and had to be hushed occasionally; thermoses were lifted and poured, teacups clinked, and people would get up or stretch their legs, occasionally disturbing the speaker's concentration.

The Mighty One [the Prophet Muhammad] was chosen by God over
all creatures,

The prayers of God and peace be upon him and his people.

He indeed loved them all, but His Blessing fell upon the loins of
Adam, peace be upon him.

And this is how we arrive at The Chosen One: He divided [the progeny of Adam] into two parts;

One part was derived from Abdullah, the other part from the progeny
of Abu Talib.

"For he made me rich in prophecy and produced Ali as my
successor."

And God chose Ibrahim from among the sons of Adam, and He chose
Isma^cil

From among the sons of Ibrahim. He chose Kananah from among the
sons of Isma^cil

And from among the Kananah, he chose the Qur'esh. From the
Qur'esh, He chose

The Bani Hashim. "And He chose me from among the Bani Qur'esh.
For I am the Chosen One from

Among the chosen ones." And now, we are happy and honored on this
blessed day

To commemorate the birthday of the Messenger of God, Muhammad
ibn Abdullah ibn Abi Talib

Ibn Hashim. God's prayer be upon him and his people.

This was a genealogy of the *sada* that went back to the Prophet
Muhammad and beyond, all the way to Adam. It legitimated their
religious status. To perform this ritual speech act in the context of
the recent events that had so shaken the sanctuary gave it added
significance.

Now one of the older boys in the audience, a prize pupil in the
sanctuary school, recited a portion of the Qur'an. As it is thought that
the Qur'an was transmitted in similar fashion to Muhammad and from
him to his faithful followers, this *tartil*, as it is called, is symbolic of an
unbroken chain going back many generations to the founder of Islam.

Mastery of this chanting is no mean achievement. It requires memory of the correct voweling of the script and a slow, deliberate chanting of the text. A hush came over the room as the audience prepared to hear the sacred words of God Himself. The boy raised his voice confidently and began "Victory," the verse that commemorates the taking of Mecca in A.D. 630 by the Prophet and his followers:

> *We have given you a glorious victory,*
> *So that God may forgive your past and future sins.*
> *He completes His goodness to you,*
> *So that He may guide you to a straight path.*
> *God helped you mightily.*
> *It was He who made tranquil*
> *The hearts of the faithful*
> *So that their faith might grow stronger.*
> *To God belong the armies of the sky*
> *And the earth God is all knowing and wise,*
> *God-on-high has spoken truthfully.*

He had hardly finished when an elder came crashing in like a wave over a beach, raucously singing a familiar devotional hymn. He was quickly joined by Fatimah's father in a loud, scratchy voice, and together they led us in song, older teaching younger. As the little boys began to catch on, their voices drowned out our own. Each line began and ended with the formula "Peace be upon you," but in the middle was inserted fresh poetry.

> *Peace be upon you,* Ahmed Muhammad, *Peace be upon you.*
> *Peace be upon you,* O highest on high, *Peace be upon you.*
> *Peace be upon you,* O deepest of the deep, *Peace be upon you.*
> *Peace be upon you,* O lord of irrigation, *Peace be upon you.*
> *Peace be upon you,* O lord of the skies, *Peace be upon you.*

Chanting epithets of the Prophet is a common devotional practice, often performed with a rosary. This time they were sung, and the fact

that they appeared in no particular order—at least that I could discern—lent a certain surprise and spontaneity to the act and the qualities of a game.

> *Peace be upon you,* Ahmed, O Beloved, *Peace be upon you.*
> *Peace be upon you,* Chosen One, my doctor, *Peace be upon you.*
> *Peace be upon you,* O love of my heart, *Peace be upon you.*
> *Peace be upon you,* O light of my darkness, *Peace be upon you.*
> *Peace be upon you,* O first of the imams, *Peace be upon you.*

The hymn continued for several minutes in this fashion, the droning
gently lulling us, or at least me, into a trancelike stupor. The Hunchback noticed my state and called me to account for it later. "We're not
mystics, like the Sufis," he declared, with a disapproving sniff. I tried to
explain that the heat and stuffiness in the room had made me drowsy.

Our master of ceremonies now introduced a teacher in the school, a
member of the sanctuary. He was an older man whom I knew only
slightly.

"Peace be upon you," he began in a thick voice. It sounded as if he
had a potato in his throat. "And the compassion of God and His blessings." We murmured the expected response. "And upon you peace."
What he lacked in diction he made up for in volume, bellowing at the
top of his lungs. He may have been suffering from a bad case of nerves.
In the middle of his speech, no doubt realizing that he did not have
the strength to sustain this volume, he suddenly dropped to a fierce
whisper. Intentional or not, it had a dramatic effect, for everyone suddenly got very quiet and listened.

Much of what the teacher had to say only repeated the common
pieties heard about the Prophet: that he had brought the Qur'an to
Muslims; that he was an example, through word and deed, to his followers and to all other Muslims, past and future; that he fought to
preserve the religion against infidels; and so forth. The teacher's
presentation was immediately followed by that of a younger student in
the local school, and here what mattered was not the content (for he
repeated many of the sentiments of his predecessor) but that he suc-

cessfully mimicked the oratorical style of an elder, with its religious and intellectual overtones.

More singing of hymns.

The master of ceremonies said there were many youngsters and adults who would like to speak on this occasion (rather overstating the case, I thought) but not enough time to listen to them all. (I heaved a secret sigh of relief.) But he did want to make sure to call on some other persons. (Please not me, I thought.) He turned now to the foreign schoolteachers. They were dressed in neat western clothes—pants, white shirts, jackets, and ties—and had been sitting quietly and rather stiffly throughout the ceremony.

Fathi, the Egyptian, was the first to address us, his voice low. I couldn't tell whether he was shy or embarrassed or simply modest. Almost as if on cue, unfortunately, a car started spinning its wheels in the muddy street outside and racing its engine. The noise made Fathi pause, and he became slightly flustered when it persisted in spite of efforts from the celebrants to get it to stop. He continued above the din with a pleasant, resonant voice that was easy to listen to. But unlike that of the Yemeni schoolmaster, his oral command of the classical tongue was insecure, and he slid into Egyptian colloquial Arabic, with its hard *g*'s, which may have been one reason, besides the noise of the vehicle outside, that he was hard for me to understand. (The difference between the colloquial spoken Arabic language and classical Arabic tends to be greater in some linguistic communities than in others.) Children began to squirm. Adults leaned toward one another to chat in hushed tones. But Fathi was able to make his points in a gentle, unstilted way, giving the impression that his speech was "natural" and did not merely follow rhetorical models, as in the case of the previous speakers. I began to warm to him. He took as his theme the *muᶜgizat* (miracles) purported to have occurred on the Prophet's Birthday, which heralded his coming greatness. A great blinding light was supposed to have been visible on that day. And why? Because the Prophet—"the prayers of God be upon him and his family"—was a "light" and a "fire." (Every time the Prophet's name is mentioned, a Muslim is expected to utter the ritual response "the prayers of God be upon him and his family.") He was a light by which the whole world was guided. He was a fire in that all who doubted his message and worshiped idols would be punished in everlasting Hell. Then, without transition or warning, Fathi suddenly brought us into the present. "And what about today? We regret that we have not all been good Muslims." His speech went on in this vein.

Once again, hymn singing rolled over us like a wave.

> *Welcome, welcome, to our Prophet,*
> *God's Mercy upon him and his family.*
> *Welcome, welcome, we celebrate*
> *His birthday, our Prophet.*

Some of the tunes were better known than others, and the boys would sing them lustily. Others required a bit of backstage coaching by the schoolmaster.

Now it was the turn of one of the Syrians, the Arabic instructor, soft-spoken like his Egyptian compatriot, and with a voice that was if anything even sweeter. Dialect sounds, in his case the sibilants *z* and *j*, also crept into his pronunciation, and this sent his command of the classical Arabic into a nosedive. A kid with a persistent dry, hacking cough distracted him. Other children seemed to be losing their ability to pay attention and startled babbling. Hisses from adults failed to quiet them. The Syrian got rattled. He paused and started again, paused and started again. This was not like a classroom, in which iron discipline could be enforced. All of a sudden he was shouting at the top of his voice, whether out of anger or dramatic effect, I wasn't sure.

> Who is it who conquered the earth? WHO IS IT WHO CONQUERED THE EARTH? WHO IS IT? WHO IS IT WHO BROUGHT OUR EXISTENCE INTO BEING?

The room was suddenly still. "This is an amazing creation that warrants our thanks and remembrance," he continued. He may have lowered his voice, but the tone had the clarion quality of struck steel. "But there were some who had strayed, who did not know the right way, the path of goodness, who exchanged it for the path of sin." His tone was now full of pathos.

> Until, that is, our Prophet—the prayers of God be upon him and his family—our Prophet came as a light that flooded the Arabian Peninsula. "I am the seer of the age. The pathfinder." He taught them the right path. They came from all corners to hear the word of God.

He paused and became hushed.

> There is no God but God. And you are the Prophet of God. You are our guide, our teacher, our leader, the beating of our heart, everything good that has come into our lives. For there is only one God. And Muhammad is the Prophet of God. He came and saved us from blasphemy and sin. So to you go our prayers and our thanks.

A slight pause and a change in voice marked a transition to a new idea.

> O fellow Muslims, they were brothers and united. They put an end to idolatry. They cut off dissension at the head. They tried to do the same for the rest of the world, to save the world from darkness. And now we live uncleanly and we'll burn.

He raised his finger in the air and shouted.

> WE SHALL BURN! WE SHALL BURN! We shall go to Hell! [Dramatic pause] But we are Muslims and united, and I have no doubt that we shall still follow the right path.

Was he alluding to the troubles in the sanctuary, or was this just another pious reference to sin and redemption? I got the feeling that he was accusing us of sliding into sin because of Abdullah's crime. And of course, given that he was the one spreading rumors that I was a spy, I couldn't help suspecting that he meant I was the cause of "dissension" that had to be cut off at the head. But now he was going on too long and losing his audience. To his credit, he sensed their mood and abruptly ended. "And prayers be upon the Prophet and his family."

The speech left a lasting impression on the youngsters, though not perhaps as the Syrian teacher had intended. With no small pleasure, I heard them running through the streets of the village for weeks after, yelling at the top of their voices, "WHO IS IT WHO CONQUERED THE EARTH? WHO IS IT?"

Hymns again.

The master of ceremonies now spoke. "Peace be upon you." The place grew quiet. He continued in a rapid-fire, monotone voice.

> And the Compassion of God and His Blessings. O noble ones in at-
> tendance in this lofty place belonging to a wise man [the Hunchback
> beamed] for the *sada's* annual celebration of the Prophet's birthday,
> Muhammad ibn Abdullah, God's prayers be upon him, his compan-
> ions and his family. And now . . .

He gestured to one of the older boys to recite a speech in classical Arabic. My heart went out to him, for it wasn't easy to remember the proper case endings. He had trouble getting started and then became flustered as the language teacher kept correcting his mistakes. But he composed himself, and his memory came rushing back.

> You who are here, greetings to you,
> And the students who have gathered to celebrate
> The Prophet's great birthday.
> The Prophet who is noble,
> To whom we owe our lands and buildings,
> He who began Islam,
> Rescuing the Ignorant from the Devil,
> Establishing Mecca as the holy city
> In whose direction we pray . . .

Already the smaller boys were poking one another in the ribs. This was a poem of praise in a mold they had heard many times before. The grammar teacher continued to follow the speech but, sensing that people were losing interest, wisely let the student rattle on without correcting him too much and slowing down his progress.

> Blessing of God be upon him
> And his companions and his family . . .

Another hymn. One of the elders would sing the line and the boys repeat it in unison—more or less.

> Peace be upon you, O Prophet,
> Our prayers to you, O happy one,
> Peace be upon you.
> Ahmed the Chosen One,
> Light of the creation of the world,
> Creator of the folk's religion,
> God's prayers upon him and his family.

It often happened that someone sitting next to me would tell me what to record and what not. At this point as I relisten to the old tape, an admonitory voice is audible: "Be sure that it's recording now. This is a nice one . . . Turn it off, turn it off! They're not in unison, they're losing it!"

As the ceremony drew to a close and the singing became more intense, even impassioned and beautiful, my neighbor stopped finding fault. He raised his voice with everyone else, and we became, in that unity of song and spirit, the boisterous embodiment of the Durkheimian conscience collective.

3

~

"WE ARE ALL ONE"

Meetings took place in several locales between the intermediaries and the two sides in the conflict throughout February and March, but I was again discouraged from attending and had to get my information secondhand. It was Muhammad the Hunchback and Ibrahim the Belt-maker who mostly supplied it from the side of the sanctuary and my newfound friend Muhammad the Maswari from the side of the mediators. I had no access to the story from the Sarkhan side except through its poetry. Had I attempted to go to Sarkhan and ask questions, I would have jeopardized my relations with the sanctuary. That is a limitation of the "eyewitness" account, positioned on one side or another of an event because of the politics of fieldwork itself.

It was clear that condemnation had now spread from Abdullah the Culprit to the sanctuary as a whole. Indeed, the descendants of the Prophet were being vilified, and it seemed as though there was one person who was leading the charge, the poet from al-Mahjari who had been in a land dispute with them some months before.

The poet harangued the assemblies about the "moral problem" of the *sada*. The descendants of the Prophet sent their sons to cities like Sana'a, supposedly to get an education, he began sarcastically, and then they left them unsupervised, so that they turned to evil ways:

drinking, drugs, whoring, gambling, pornography. All sorts of godless people—Somali, Chinese, Russian, American—taught them. They were so intent on aping foreign ways that they tended to forget their own: decency, respect for women, the honor of their kinfolk. Then these sons of pollution, like Abdullah, came back to Khawlan thinking they could behave in the same way that they had in the cesspools of the cities. But did Abdullah, this whoremonger, pick on one of the beautiful *sada* women to have his way with? Oh, no. He chose tribal girls, and for good reason: because he had been taught by his kinfolk, as much by their tongue as by their example, that they were beneath him, no better than clods of earth. And that was why the sanctuary was to blame, because deep down it had no respect for us and instilled none in its children. It was haughty, arrogant, and condescending. It thought it could do what it wanted with us and get away with it.

The poet's people were just a few against the sanctuary's hundreds. The poet's people's houses were simple mud dwellings compared with the sanctuary's stone fortresses. While the poet's people scratched a living from the soil with their bare hands, the *sada* hired others to do their work. Now they wanted to take the land away from his people because one of their own had grown rich and meant to build a lordly manor for himself. It's cheaper to do that on the outskirts than to buy someone else's decrepit house in town, and it's only the poor, defenseless poet who stood in the way. But they hadn't reckoned with his sharp words and stout heart.

The sanctuary erupted in protest. The poet was being slanderous, and his attack was clearly motivated by his feud with them. As for his allegations that they had cheated him of his land, the case was now being adjudicated and the documents would show that the boundaries were as they had claimed all along. But they were not here to settle the dispute between themselves and the poet from al-Mahjari. They were here to talk about the "problem," the tragic affair, between the sanctuary and Sarkhan. They had been friends. Their histories had been intertwined like tendrils of a vine. When Sarkhan was attacked by enemies ten years earlier, did the sanctuary not come to its defense with men and weapons? And the sanctuary men remembered with gratitude how the people of Sarkhan took their wives and daughters into their homes when the village was bombed by the Egyptians during the civil war. Was it not unthinkable that the sanctuary would repay this kindness with such a horrendous deed? No, the culprit Abdullah, that mad one, that dog, had acted alone. Maybe he was corrupted by sinners in Sana'a, but other descendants of the Prophet living in the sanctuary were good men and women. They are among us now and have come to reason with us and find an end to this problem. If you, friends of Sarkhan, truly believed that the people of the sanctuary were no good, you wouldn't have sent your own sons and daughters to be schooled here, you wouldn't come to hear the imam deliver the sermon in the mosque on Fridays. It was as if the boy Abdullah had been made by *jinn* or the Devil himself to commit this sin, for men to talk about long after he is dead. He may have been born in the sanctuary, but he no longer is one of us. From now on, he is stripped of his name.

Perhaps it was wishful thinking on their part, but the *sada* reported to me that the sheikh of Sarkhan had been moved by their plea for understanding and forgiveness. But he was still overcome by sadness over the loss of his daughter and anger at the dishonor the abduction had caused him and his tribe. Or so it was said, for he remained strangely silent. No speeches of his were ever reported, only poetry; he had something of a reputation in that regard. How could we have heard what the poet from al-Mahjari had said, and the various intermediaries, but nothing from the sheikh of Sarkhan, the man most fundamentally wronged in this affair? Did he mean his silence to be a rebuke? Had the tragedy made him mute with despair? Was he choking on his own anger? Was it linked to his unutterable shame? If the people of the sanctuary were being made to take the heat for Abdullah the Culprit's crime, one could not help wondering whether the sheikh and his kinsmen blamed themselves for not having been able to prevent it in the first place. After all, the abduction had happened on their own doorstep and in plain daylight, which made the violation even more treacherous, like that of a stranger who has dared to step into the harem. True, the boy was from the sanctuary, and therefore his presence would not ordinarily have aroused suspicion, but an honorable man never lets down his guard. It was almost as if the sheikh was impotent, as weak as the poor, helpless creatures who were stolen from under his nose.

Because of his eloquence and passion, the voice of the poet from al-Mahjari was listened to in the assembly, but a purely partisan attack, as his was accused of being, would not have been persuasive had it not also struck a chord. One day early on in the conflict, I took a taxi to the capital with the Hunchback and a tribesman from the region, the latter affiliated with neither Sarkhan nor the intermediaries. Inevitably, the two of them got into a heated discussion about the dispute. The Hunchback expressed his dismay at the outpouring of ill feeling toward the sanctuary. Indeed, he really could not explain its provocation or understand its ferocity.

"Well, I'll tell you," his interlocutor said, exasperated. "I fought for you and your people all through the civil war because you had been the rightful rulers of the country for a thousand years—rightful, perhaps, but not righteous."

"But we didn't do anything!" my friend protested. "It was all that crazy boy's fault, the one they call Abdullah."

"You know," the tribesman went on, glaring at the Hunchback, "I lost everything in that war, everything, and what do I have to show for it? What I carry around with me in this sack on my lap. I now work land that no longer belongs to me but to a descendant of the Prophet. When I come to the sanctuary and look around, I see prosperity, but in my own village only hardship. I have helped you, but I can't see the benefit of it to me."

"I understand that you feel bitter about the war. And I am deeply grateful that you fought on our side, doing as God willed. But do you think that we haven't had to struggle also?" asked the Hunchback. "It wasn't your village that was bombed nearly out of existence but ours. It wasn't your sons and relatives who were hunted down and executed by the Egyptians but mine. Those of us who could flee had to spend long, hard years abroad in Saudi Arabia, Kuwait, Abu Dhabi, Bahrain—cut off from our relatives, living in difficult conditions, working as servants for people who despised us because we didn't grow rich on oil as they did. If we have money now, it's because we had to work like slaves to earn it."

When I related this conversation to my friend Muhammad the Maswari, I asked him whether he agreed with the tribesman. All he would say was, "They were dogs, Seif, they were dogs, before the revolution kicked them out of power. Now the *sada* have to be nice because they're living in a republic."

Sometime in late January, I learned that a poem had been composed about the dispute. The author, Abu Talib, was a distinguished religious scholar and a *sada* from another part of Yemen who had come to the sanctuary to help mediate. The text was in classical Arabic—the written, standard language of Arabic-speaking countries. This literate register befitted Abu Talib's reputation and status. Though the text of his poem was written, a great singer, al-Badda, a servant from Khawlan, composed a melody for it. His performance of the song was captured on tape and sold in stereo stores all over Yemen. People from other parts of the country learned of the dispute between the sanctuary and the Sarkhan by hearing the tape, and some of them were moved to respond with verses of their own, which, too, were committed to tape and circulated. In time, a rich trove of poetry was built up on the "event," or *al-hadith*.

Whenever I hear these tapes today, sung by the great al-Badda, I seem to feel the wheel-rutted road in my legs, to see a landscape of browns and grays passing before my window in wintry, metallic light. Most of all, I sense the solitude of the land. Al-Badda's voice was a high, perfectly pitched baritone, and he was admired not so much for the sweetness of his timbre as for the clarity of his diction. He could be highly expressive, sometimes purring or raspy—even sexy—at other times hollow and sad or brooding. His voice was inimitable and immediately recognizable. No wonder that he was the most popular singer in Khawlan. He accompanied himself on a musical instrument called the *tasa*, which looks like a tambourine except without the jingling disks.

> Heroes of Khawlan, heroes of the great mountain al-Tiyal,
> A brother greets you, O dearest of brothers,

A descendant of the Chosen One,
Himself a descendant of that legendary Arab Adnan.
Of the eminence of such descent, the Qur'an is an agreement,
And no one dares contradict the sacred text.

Why this anger, these insults against the sanctuary?
My beloved people of Sarkhan: by the All Merciful, I swear
That your estrangement has gone on long enough.
It has distressed me greatly.

The sanctuary has handed over the crazy boy,
Handed him over for torture by fire
So that he will tell the truth. Nothing remains for which
The sanctuary can stand condemned
In any code of law, be it far or near.
The sanctuary is a piece of Khawlan, like the tendril to the grape.
It is its hijra, its sacred place, and must be protected,
Like a brother of the mother, a loved one by marriage.
All are brothers, and I appeal to you, O intermediaries,
To solve the problem.

There is no one but you who can judge,
Who can rip out the weed of discord that grows rank.
The two parties in the dispute will thank you. A whole
    community will thank you,
And I pray to Muhammad, the Chosen One, for your success.

This type of poem is called a *qasida*, regarded as the greatest genre of Arabic literature. It is also very ancient. The most highly esteemed odes were composed (whether orally or in writing remains a point of controversy) by tribal poets in pre-Islamic times; seven of them hang inside the Ka'ba in Mecca. Thus, Abu Talib's selection of this genre was not arbitrary. As with genealogy, so with literature: when you go back far enough in time, traditions of tribesmen and *sada* merge— precisely the rhetorical point Abu Talib was making.

One morning I was distracted from my note-scribbling by the sound of vigorous drumming, the signal that a wedding was to take place. The village servant Nasir and his son were standing on the knoll just above my house, announcing in stentorian tones the wedding celebration of the brother of my upstairs neighbor Fatimah and the daughter of Muhammad Muhammad Abu-Dim. The wedding, which had been continuously postponed when it seemed that hostilities might break out into open fighting at any moment, could now take place. (Though there were still tensions, the truce appeared to be holding.) People in the sanctuary hoped that the gaiety of the wedding would temporarily loosen the fear and anguish that had gripped their hearts in the last couple of weeks. While I shared in this respite, however temporary, I got something else out of the celebration. The wedding drove home the realization that there was a difference between an event and a ritual, formal similarities notwithstanding. And features were added to this wedding, or given special emphasis, because of the recent hostilities with Sarkhan.

It was still winter, but a golden sunlight made the village seem dipped in honey. Looking out my window, I could see people bestirring themselves in preparation for the festivities. Fine clothes, washed and pressed, would be retrieved from wooden chests. Gifts and other goods to be distributed to the houses of the groom and bride would be made ready. (My gift, a robe for her brother, which I had ordered from the Hunchback's seamstress wife was already in Fatimah's hands.) Firecrackers to be set off at the groom's procession that afternoon and fine *qat* for the chew following it had to be purchased in the souk.

I stepped out of my house just before the noonday prayer, my *mushadda* wrapped around my head, my camera and tape recorder slung over my shoulder, and my spiral notebook tucked inside the elastic waistband of my *futa*. This is how I would appear "armed," I thought to myself, in these days of conflict. I headed toward the groom's house.

When Fatimah's brother came out the door and into the street, he was smiling happily though also a little shyly and nervously. He had not expected so many people. His family's social standing, not to mention his own modest employment as a car mechanic, hardly warranted such a turnout. Of course, many in attendance came not because of the wedding but to defend the sanctuary in the event of fighting. In a salute to the groom, the air exploded with loud bursts of gunfire.

A stately procession of men now made its way slowly to the mosque, headed by the drummers, then the rest of us, with Fatimah's brother and his family and friends in the rear, carrying a large wedding bouquet. It was laden with non-too-subtle fertility symbols, such as big white eggs dangling from strong acacia branches, on which were impaled pieces of red paper as well. In the middle of the bouquet was tucked a picture of the Haram Mosque in Mecca, a symbol of blessing.

Occasionally the younger men would go off to the side and start to dance. Some of the older, more fanatical *sada* frowned, exclaiming that dancing was forbidden by prophetic hadith (though this opinion was contested). Only tribes, and by implication they meant only the "pagan" ones, would indulge in such a suspect pastime! I thought silently of the shenanigans that went on some nights in my house with Fatimah's husband and his brothers. The loud, boisterous, and colorful celebrations continued in the streets, but what I did not hear was the chanting of poetry, a custom I was told more common of tribal than of *sada* weddings. Meanwhile, I thought I saw curtains shivering in the windows as the women watched the dancing, though they might have been too busy with their own dancing to take notice of the men for long. The bride had her separate celebrations with the women of the sanctuary, which regrettably, I couldn't see.

Young men, still boys really, would hold on to a string of firecrackers until the very last one sizzled between thumb and index finger and then toss it into the air with a flick of the wrist. Pale smoke wafted in the air behind them like wraiths. Timing was everything, for they had to wait until the very last possible moment to let go, and nothing less than looks of utter nonchalance on their faces would do. During these displays of macho daring, little regard was shown for the safety of the rest of us, who more than once had to sidestep an exploding firecracker or quickly brush off one that landed on the shoulder. But this was not the least of our perils. I had heard stories of men being wounded or killed by stray or ricocheting bullets during the deafening rounds of periodic gun salutes. The wedding seemed more dangerous than the war.

Fortunately, we arrived at the mosque without mishap. Fatimah's brother ducked inside to pray and hear some final words of blessing from the imam. He then changed into his wedding finery, symbolically marking the end of his bachelor status, though legally the couple had been married several days before, when the contract was signed and the imam blessed them as they clasped hands with their respective parents over a copy of the Qur'an. It was not as if the bride and groom had been strangers or had not seen each other before the wedding, for they had grown up in the sanctuary and had played together as children. But the familiarity they had known ceased at puberty, when she took up the veil and they both began to move in their separate worlds. They would not meet publicly again until marriage, though they continued to keep track of each other by word of mouth and through intermediary relatives and friends.

Either in the evening of the same day or the next, the bride would be brought to the groom's house in her own procession, accompanied by her male kinsmen. When husband and wife had had intercourse for the first time, their marriage was proclaimed consummated. This was not done by some bloodied sheet waved from the bedroom window, as in other places. It was enough for the in-laws to be satisfied that the act had taken place. This might not happen right away, however; it depended on the age and "readiness" of the bride (even of the groom, if he was very young). If they were deemed "unready" for conjugal relations, the couple would live under the same roof and the supervision of the groom's family but without sleeping together. This situation was not uncommon and in a way reduced the sexual pressure on the couple while they were trying to get used to each other. At that afternoon's chew, I asked why couples got married if it was clear they weren't ready sexually. Is marriage about sex or about responsibility to spouse and child? I was asked in turn. Exactly. So first they learn this lesson, as well as how to get along with each other, and the sex comes later.

Another gun salute deafened our ears, the signal that the bridegroom had reemerged in his wedding finery. I turned to encounter a wholly transformed person. The difference in his demeanor made me smile broadly. In contrast to the playful, boyish awkwardness of a few moments ago, we were now confronted by dignified reserve; his body was stiff, his posture ramrod straight, his glance downcast. A young man at my side joked that the imam must have scared him with the litany of responsibilities he faced as a husband and father. But then, in a more serious tone, he told me the significance of the pose. "The groom should act like a *samad*, a statue." To test the groom's resolve, he was sometimes poked in the ribs or even pricked with needles secretly hidden for that purpose, though neither at this wedding nor at any other did I actually see this happen. I suppose it was better than having one's front teeth knocked out or one's face scarred, as in some rituals of manhood.

The second thing that struck me was the finery. Fatimah's brother was resplendent. A minor potentate. Every item of clothing signaled that its wearer was of *sada* descent. If anything, that message was over the top. He wore a gleaming white turban, a white robe with wide, long sleeves pulled back over the shoulders (and probably a piece of fragrant incense tucked in its pocket to ward off *jinn*), a belt beautifully stitched in gold, silver, green, and red thread—precisely of the sort for which Ibrahim the Beltmaker was renowned—and a silver-plaited dagger hilt at the waist. In his right hand he dangled a rosary while uttering some of the hundred and one names of God. "God is Great, God is Merciful, God is Compassionate." No doubt they had been invoked more than once by the worried inhabitants of the sanctuary during the current crisis. A magnificent full-length black wool coat lined in soft white silk completed the outfit, and on his left shoulder, instead of a rifle, as would be customary for tribesmen, he bore an exquisite silver sword. It was a sign of calm and courage, and on another level it also stood for the authority of the former Islamic state. (I had been named Seif, "sword," in part because the name reminded the old man who first met me of the former prince regent.)

It was rumored that Fatimah's brother had not wanted to wear this outfit, and indeed the clothing looked awkward and even pretentious on him. After all, he was a manual laborer, not an aspiring scholar or judge, and he did not hail from a prominent family. But he was apparently pressured by the sanctuary to conform to this older, traditional style of dress. His wedding was a pretext for turning him into a symbol. For what the crisis had cast in doubt, even perhaps in the minds of some of the inhabitants of the *hijra*, was the legitimacy of the *sada* as standard-bearers of Islam in Khawlan. The fact that one of their own could be shown to incarnate those values gave them the opportunity to affirm their faith in themselves and to convey it to others as well. Yet it could not have escaped the more thoughtful in the assembly that the pageant might have been more persuasive had a more believable actor been cast in the lead role.

The procession continued to make its grand and noisy progress. Now we entered the house at which the *qat* chew was to take place. Because of the unusually large numbers, it could not be held in the sitting room of the father's house, a modest structure that could accommodate only a handful of people. Adequate space was found instead in an assembly room in a more majestic house. As always upon entering such rooms, what impressed me most was the magic and beauty of the light. Along the street side of the room and at both ends were clear glass windows framed in simple wood, recessed half a foot or more and covered by plain curtains that cut the glare of the Arabian sun. Above them were smaller circular or semicircular windows, made from colored glass arranged either in an abstract pattern or as symbols like the Eagle of the Republic or the Star of David. This particular room also had round windows, the size and shape of ship portholes, made of translucent alabaster, which at once softened and enriched the light. This window is sometimes known as *gamariyya*, "moon," which, indeed, it resembles. Propped on the ledge atop the stained-glass windows was the groom's wedding bouquet. To the left of it was hung his silver sword, to the right the long black overcoat with its creamy silk lining exposed like the delicious flesh inside a coconut. And below these ancient symbols of *sada* authority sat the groom like a sultan in some minor court, chewing *qat* with his father and other close relatives.

The rest of the assembled guests sat facing the windows. In the middle of the room lay a forest of *qat* branches, entangled with the long hoses of the water pipes that gurgled over the conversation, a sound as contented as the purring of cats. A young man perched in the middle of the room was ready at a signal to change the tobacco, refill the thermoses, or help a guest straighten out a back cushion or an elbow rest. Patterns of colored light like tilted constellations in the sky crisscrossed the wall in back of us.

This chew, like others held during weddings, was noteworthy for its singing of *anashid* "hymns." They are not oral poems of the kind heard at many tribal weddings, composed especially for the occasion, but texts taken from a religious book and chanted by an expert singer. The father of the groom, as we already knew from the Prophet's Birthday celebration, was well-practiced in this art form, and though long past his prime, he took up the task with a zeal that was both admirable and infectious. Droning a few lines in a nasal voice, he would stop for the assembly to repeat a refrain, the deep voices resounding like an echo in a cave. After the completion of the hymn, the groom's father softly intoned the *du^ca*, or invocation of God, with hands outstretched before his face. The assembly followed suit. Feeling uncomfortable repeating these religiously charged words, I would listen appreciatively but silently.

During a lull in the singing, Nasir the Servant entered the room. In stentorian tones he uttered the proverbial saying "There has come to you from the groom a gift." In unison we gave the ritual response, "Verily, O God, honor him." He was bearing in his hands an incense burner, which he gave us to pass around. When it came to me, I imitated what I had seen others doing, placed it on the floor before me and, with my *mushadda* drawn over my head, leaned over to inhale the sweet-smelling smoke. A memory of childhood unexpectedly surfaced. When sick with bronchitis, I was made to inhale steam infused with medicinal jellies on the theory prevalent in those days that it would loosen my cough. As far as I could determine, however, it only burned my cheeks. The same thing seemed to happen to me now. As the temperature in the room climbed and the air became stuffier, I seemed like that sick child swathed in blankets, trying to break the fever. For the Yemenis in the room, however, the atmosphere was as comfortable as it gets: *qat* really doesn't "take" unless one works up a good sweat.

Conversation alternated with hymn singing until the call to prayer at sunset. The whole assembly including the groom then departed for their various mosques. Since I could not join them, I as usual felt a pang of regret. One moment, as at this chew, I was plunged into the midst of the community, and the next I felt washed up on the beach like a piece of driftwood. My neighbors deserting me was perfectly understandable, but it was hard to accept. I was very lonely at the time.

As I went off to my house, a boy stopped me to ask whether I had heard the news. Two tribesmen, hailing from a subsection of the Dhubayyinah, which had surrounded and fired upon the sanctuary only a month ago, were in the village. Why had they come, when relations were still strained? They happened to be passing through the village, the boy explained to me, and were on their way to the capital when some of the *sada* insisted they stay for dinner. Though they had at first demurred, the tribesmen were finally persuaded to stay for the wedding festivities. The significance of such an invitation could not have been lost on them. The moral bonds of ʿesh wa milh "bread and salt," or what we call "breaking bread," ran deep. Nevertheless, I noticed a certain hesitancy on their part to lay down their rifles before joining the meal. Sacred trusts were known, after all, to have been broken.

Fortified by the excellent dinner and humored by their hosts' charming conversation, the tribesmen were persuaded to remain overnight. The evening continued, first of all with a tremendous procession that wended its way from the house where all the men had eaten dinner to the assembly hall, where they kept the groom company until the arrival of his bride, passing the time in storytelling, pleasant conversation, and joking—the occasion known as the *samra*.

As the procession started to form itself in an open area outside the groom's house, a dance began. I was startled to see with what gusto it was performed. More astounding still was that even the older men joined in. One instigator of the dance was a charismatic young man who had sought refuge in the sanctuary for political reasons and was thought to be a protégé of Hussein, brother of Ibrahim the Beltmaker. He was exhorting everyone to participate—pulling on this man's sleeve, murmuring something in that man's ear. By the light of kerosene lanterns, the dancers were stepping vigorously and whirling their daggers in the air. Ironically, the only ones who could not be persuaded to join in were the tribal guests, who politely but resolutely remained as spectators on the sidelines—an interesting decision, since dancing was prescribed etiquette for guests at their weddings.

When we all retired to the assembly hall for the *samra*, the tribesmen were seated in the place next to the groom, as befitted their status as honored guests, and were catered to hand and foot. Then the younger men proceeded to do something unheard of at *sada* weddings: they performed, or rather attempted to perform, a genre of poetry-and-dance commonly seen at tribal wedding *samra*s and known as the *razfa*. The poem is short, only two lines long, and is either spontaneously composed or recited from memory. A *razfa* was what the men at the wedding *tried* to compose, but I could hardly make out the words. However, the text was the least of their problems, for they also had to sing it while vigorously stepping and whirling, their daggers aloft in the air. Words, music, and dance never quite meshed, and one tribal guest leaned over to his companion and asked, "Do you understand what they're doing?" Perhaps he thought he was witnessing a parody of his own traditions and was offended. The young man who had earlier engineered the dance and was behind this performance sheepishly apologized to them. With a disarming smile he confessed, "You'll have to excuse us, but we're still learning."

The intention was clear: a diplomatic effort to show that the sanctuary was respectful of tribal traditions despite what the poet al-Mahjari and others had claimed. But I do not mean to cast the performance in a solely utilitarian, ultimately even cynical, light. It was not simply that the sanctuary wanted the tribesmen to believe that it esteemed their customs, a kind of Goffmanesque impression management, but also that the *sada* wanted to believe it themselves. Indeed, I would propose that a concept of the self ("like the tendril to the grape," as Abu Talib said in his poem) was being constructed of inextricably entwined tribal and *sada* traditions, as indeed they had been at earlier times in Yemen's troubled history. The sanctuary leaders knew they had to restore this belief in themselves and instill it in the tribes if the two groups were to survive the crisis as friends.

The tribal guests, however, seemed to want to resist the implied rhetoric of the *samra*, and they found a way to do so without offending their hosts. They waited until the final event of the evening, the climax of the wedding, to make their point. This was the groom's procession to his house, where he would greet his bride. One tribesman had apparently excused himself on the grounds of fatigue and illness. No one believed him, of course. In a society where almost every act is a public statement and every statement is read between the lines, his absence was construed as criticism. As for his younger companion, he may have been genuinely moved by the attempt at fence mending or at least may not have wished unduly to offend his generous hosts; he stayed to the end.

During the procession I was amazed to hear *zamil* poetry, ordinarily a tribal genre, not a *sada* one, and quite good poetry at that, but I noticed that the poems were first written down "backstage" and then chanted in the manner of tribal performances. The act of composition, in other words, was still grounded in literacy and not a spontaneously produced oral performance. Though by rights the visiting tribesman could have composed a response as a return gift, he did not.

Then word came that the bride was ready to be brought to her husband. The final procession of the evening would begin.

It was near midnight, and there was no moon. Had our way not been lit by candle lanterns and kerosene lamps held high by the older boys, we would certainly have stumbled on the uneven pathways of the village. Another memory of my own childhood sprang up, that of going with paper lanterns from house to house asking for treats during the German Oktoberfest. Smiling faces, winking eyes were caught in the soft amber glow. The stillness of the mountain air, which usually nothing disturbed after the electric generators had been turned off, was shattered once again by firecrackers and rifle fire as the groom emerged from the *samra*. Gradually a procession formed in front of him, the pace slow and solemn on the way to his house.

Now resumed what to me was the most beautiful and moving part of the wedding ritual, the hymn singing. Since I had heard it before, I concentrated on watching the tribesman's face to see what responses he might have. He seemed to be shivering. This being February, the nights were still cold, and someone had given him a blanket to wrap around his shoulders. Or perhaps it was fear that he was in the enemy's midst, where after all, an "accidental" shot might claim his life. He looked around self-consciously, observing what others were doing and imitating them, momentarily an ethnographer like myself. But gradually his self-consciousness vanished as he became as much enthralled with the spectacle as the rest of us. The joy that the ordinarily reserved *sada* allowed themselves to express burst forth like an explosion and rocked the company. The tribesman and I joined them in song. Hand in hand we all took a few strides and, after a brief pause, struck up a hymn in a voice pure and strong. It was one of those rare moments when I felt part of this community.

A mule carrying the bride came into view. More startling than the suddenness of her appearance was the swiftness with which she was conveyed into the house. Covered in a tie-dyed sheet, she was impossible to see, and I wondered what her wedding finery looked like underneath. Her brother lifted her off the mount, and her delicate hennaed hand clasped his neck while he held her in his arms. A poignant moment for brother and sister, for this would be the last time they would be physically close. The brother gently placed her in the arms of the groom, who then carried her through the doorway of the house. An outburst of women's joyful ululation greeted the couple inside.

In the souk next day I discussed the wedding with the Hunchback. I remarked on the tribal elements in the ceremony. I had not noticed them in any previous weddings of the descendants of the Prophet and wanted to know what they were doing there. He denied that they were "tribal," however.

"You mean to say they're sada*?"*

"They're neither sada *nor* qabili *[tribal]," he said, beaming. "They're one and the same, Seif. We're all one." He gave me one of his sweet looks that I took to mean he was not interested in pursuing the matter. He nonetheless believed what he was claiming, which was that tribesmen and* sada *shared a common identity—in spite of the talk in the meetings of late—a claim that was essential to be believed for the future*

well-being of the sanctuary. Who was the real groom that night, Fatimah's brother or the tribesmen who had come to watch? Rhetorically, the tribes were being married to the sanctuary: that was the deeper meaning of the wedding, just as surely as in reality Fatimah's brother was married to his intended bride. It was important that the tribesmen were there to witness it, not only because they were the figurative grooms but because they could report back on what they saw to their own people, and offset their negative opinions of the sada. *It was also important that the Hunchback (and he was not alone in this) believed in this consubstantiality—again, it was not a cynical act of impression management—for, in order for the dispute to have a positive outcome, Sarkhan and the Dhubayyinah had to trust the people of the sanctuary again. And that is one reason that the ritual was so seductively beautiful: both sides wanted to believe in that possibility and hope, complicated as their feelings might have been toward each other.*

In the afternoon of the next day, I was mulling over these thoughts when I heard the distant ring of gunshots again. What was it this time, I wondered, a wedding or a war? I'd had my fill of both. Opening the door to my house just wide enough to look out, I saw Sayyid Ali—the same man who had greeted me upon my arrival in the sanctuary—making his way down the street. Well, it couldn't be a war if he was walking in plain sight, but I was mystified concerning what the shooting was about, since I had heard nothing about another wedding celebration. I supposed I'd better check. I put on my headdress, slung the camera from my shoulder, made sure the batteries were still operating in the tape recorder, stuck a spiral notebook inside the waistband of my Yemeni dress in place of the *jambiyya* that might have been there, and gingerly ventured forth.

"How are you, Sayyid Ali?"

"Very well, praise be to God. And you?"

"Praise be to God. I was wondering what was happening. Is it a wedding or a war?"

"Neither one. It's a circumcision."

"Here in the sanctuary?"

"No, among the tribes. But some of our *sada,* like Ibrahim the Beltmaker, are officiating."

"Do you celebrate everything in Yemen with gunfire?"

"Well, Seif, in some parts of Yemen they cut it off [and he made a small sawing motion with his two fingers], but here in Khawlan the men are true heroes, and so [his fingers now forming the barrel of a gun] they shoot it off."

As if to confirm what he was saying, we heard a loud volley of gunshots. I stared at him in horror. With a twinkle in his eye and pointing to my waist, he said, "And don't forget to write that down in your little notebook, Seif."

A parable for anthropology if there ever was one, I thought.

4

∾

INTERLUDE

June 13, 2001

Onboard Yemen Airlines Flight 605 to Sana'a . . . I am arriving in the late afternoon but can see the city plainly. And as I look out my window I think for a moment that the pilot has made a mistake. This is not the Sana'a I knew. The airplane circles once before making its landing to the north, and I have a chance to see the full sweep of the city. I remember two halves like the division of a cell, one being the Old City, the other the New, which had grown on the other side of the wall. The Old City is still intact, but the New must be three times its former size. It looks more like a cancer ready to attack the ovum. Thankfully, the United Nations has declared the Old City a World Heritage City, which might make it safe from developers.

In February 1980 I made one of my monthly trips to Sana'a to replenish my household supplies and check my mail. I missed my friends, too, and wanted to see them again. The community I had formed there, among both Americans and Yemenis, sustained me professionally, intellectually, and emotionally. I cannot imagine having continued my research in Khawlan without it. Still, it was in fact politically vulnerable and culturally isolated and after a while I was thankful to escape its self-absorption and anxieties and return to the field. Nor was it anymore a safe haven, as I once naïvely thought the sanctuary would be. I don't think foreigners in Sana'a, particularly Americans, ever fully unpacked their belongings, since they imagined that at any time they might have to leave Yemen because of political turmoil. But stories about fieldwork tend to overlook the backstage arena to which anthropologists retreat to get away from the tensions they experience in the field or sometimes to continue fieldwork from other angles. (In Sana'a, the first chance I had I went straight to The World of Happiness, which may sound like a house of prostitution but was in fact a stereo store, and asked for the tape about the two girls abducted from Khawlan.) But above all it is a place to relax and be rejuvenated. And let us not forget the creature comforts of modern life. Ice-cold beer. A steak. *Washing machines.*

I had reserved a seat on the van belonging to the son of my next-door neighbor, the fellow who operated a daily taxi service to the capital that left early in the morning. When I asked Ismail about the departure time, he shrugged his shoulders and said only "I leave when the van is full."

To make sure I wouldn't miss it, I got up before dawn. In the moonlight I could barely see the shadowy hulk of the vehicle, its roof rack already laden with baggage. It tilted slightly toward the wall of my neighbor's house, like a weary beast of burden dreaming over its front paws.

I reached out for the jeans that I knew to be on the chair at my desk and pulled them on, tucking in the tails of a white cotton shirt. The chill mountain air felt like a bee sting on my ankles. The flimsy plastic sandals of Chinese manufacture that were the footwear of choice in Yemen, had thongs between the big and second toes, which made wearing socks impossible, so I opted for sneakers. I didn't need a mirror to make sure my headdress was wound correctly around my head, this action having become as familiar as tugging a belt through the loops of a pair of trousers. Then it came to checking I had everything packed for my stay in Sana'a. I propped a flashlight on top of the folding table that served as my desk, its orb of light expanded by the eggshell white-ness of the walls, and found the items I was looking for in my back-pack: tapes that I wanted to transcribe into written Arabic with the help of a tutor; canisters of film I planned to send to the United States for development; and two copies of field notes, which I had finished transcribing the night before, one of which I would send (along with the film) via diplomatic pouch to the United States, and the other I would ship by regular mail to my parents. The originals I had put away in three-ring, loose-leaf notebooks that I kept in a box under my desk. These maniacal little routines, these magical rituals of forethought that I followed in Yemen, at first drove me nuts, since I am not a particularly well-organized person at home. But the effort to correct a mistake or find a lost article or retrace steps was too costly in the field, so I be-came a happy obsessive-compulsive. Then, too, it was comforting to think several steps ahead—not to make a plan but to run through alter-natives in the face of contingencies—because doing so gave me a sense of security and control. An entirely false sense, to be sure, but that is not the point.

I made some instant coffee to be jolted awake but swilled only a mouthful of the putrid stuff.

When I stepped out of the house, it was as though someone had switched on a light, dawn had come so suddenly. While the driver was busy with some last-minute check under the hood, I took a seat in the back and waited for us to push off. It was bit uncomfortable to have el-bows poking into ribs when the van jostled on the uneven road, but at least we were all kept warm with our bodies pressed tightly together. As gloves were unheard of, my companions kept their hands covered in the folds of their robes while I stuffed mine in the sleeves of my sweatshirt. Drowsiness overcame us, and heads gently bobbed with the motion of the vehicle. The stillness was broken only by the chanting of the Qur'an played from a tape deck.

Two hours later we arrived in Sana'a, disembarking at a "station" for travelers from Khawlan al-Tiyal called the Sha'ub Gate. Each region of the country had its own depot of sorts, usually no more than a place with grease-smeared pits slashed in the earth, over which cars were parked and mechanics worked from below. The street looked like a crude archaeological dig. Urchins circulated among the passersby, shrilly selling tea, army bread, and canned fruit juices. " 'Allo, 'allo," they shouted, running up to me with mischievous grins. And then in Arabic, "Picture! Picture!" "Scoot," I said, and to a particularly insistent urchin hissed, "Get away from me, you little *jinn*." Obviously I was not a tourist, he concluded, and quickly lost interest.

A stone bridge took me over the dry riverbed that skirted the northern part of the Old City, and I entered the labyrinth of streets and alleys that soon led me to the bustling heart of modern Sana'a. Street sweepers and garbage collectors, many of them South Asian, were completing their early morning work. Storekeepers were flinging open clanging shutters and placing merchandise for display on the sidewalks, like riches spilling from a cornucopia. Specialty shops were clustered together on a street rather than scattered, so all the jewelry stores were next to one another on one corner, spice emporiums alongside, textile shops on another block, and so forth. This arrangement not only was more convenient for the comparative shopper but also worked to the advantage of the retailer, who if he ran out of some item, might be able to procure it from an obliging neighbor. The appliance stores, stationery shops, and bookstores were clustered nearer the center of the capital, Liberation Square, in squat cinder-block buildings from the 1970s. Since I was out of my small spiral notebooks, I stopped in at one of the office supply stores to buy a few. I also checked to see whether any new collections of written colloquial poetry had been published or older ones reprinted. Both tended to sell out quickly. I was unlucky this time, though I did manage to find a book of religious hymns to give as a present to Ali the Bird. The lines would not be very long in the post office in the midmorning, so I dropped in to get some stamps and mail letters.

Only one more alley and I was at the hostel, a three-story house built in the traditional Yemeni style. That is, the first story was built of large stone blocks, with several floors above made of dried adobe bricks, the topmost having slightly tapered walls with intricate decorations that incorporated religious inscriptions such as "Allah, Allah."

The cornices of Yemeni buildings show elaborate decorative brick-work, like a crown.

"Welcome back!" yelled Janet, the wife of the Institute director.

In the United States, Janet had worked for a government agency concerned with urban affairs in which she had risen to a position of some importance. She had forfeited that job when she came to Yemen to begin the Institute with her husband, Jon Mandaville. They had had a wonderful time in Turkey some years before, and she had been look-ing forward to Yemen even though she knew it to be a very different place. For one thing, it was less accessible to an independent woman. For another, there was less to do for an energetic, hardworking, and ef-ficient person who spoke no Arabic. Her three children were not much trouble, and she found it difficult to fill up the hours of the day as part concierge for the hostel, part confidante to the researchers. It was like hooking up a jet-propulsion engine to an egg beater, which is why per-haps her head was always in a book. She raised it from one now to come over and greet me with a hug.

"Jon, Steve's here." Janet's voice was as big as her personality, and it boomed throughout the house, but this time it was for the benefit of her husband, who was a little hard of hearing. "He just got in from Khawlan." She tripped over the pronunciation of the initial consonant. I teasingly reminded her that it sounded like the German -*ch*, as in *Bach*. "Well, that doesn't help. I don't know German either." She re-peated the word, but now it sounded as if she was clearing her throat. She giggled self-consciously and gave up. "Well, how've you been? You look healthy enough, if a little thinner." I loved the big-sister routine she adopted with me. It reminded me of my own sisters back home.

Janet poured some real coffee and offered me a seat at the table while she retrieved the mail that had piled up since my last visit. Her two girls had gone off to the international school, while her eight-year old son, Heath, was just getting up. Researchers became part of the Mandaville family if they chose to, and in many ways I felt like an honorary uncle to the Mandaville children. I wasn't living in a family household or having much contact with families in the sanctuary, so I cherished these interactions.

I asked about some of our mutual friends, many of them working in the U.S. Embassy, USAID, or the World Bank. The scare that had swept through the community when American government organizations were attacked in other countries of the Middle East after the Iranian hostage crisis and the anti-American demonstrations in Tunis, Cairo, and Bahrain had apparently died down.

"And how is Taha?" He was a young Yemeni, a recent graduate from the university who had gotten to know the Mandavilles. When the Institute had to relocate to less expensive quarters in Sana'a, he helped them find their new house. I knew that Janet and Jon were quite fond of him. In time I got to know him too and to appreciate his deep intelligence and warm personality. Moreover, he was what one affectionately calls a "character."

October 13, 1979

Taha . . . came to dinner. I felt sorry for him when I learned that he'd been out of work for over four months and amused to discover how he works off his frustrations. The following events all happened today. Taha was sipping tea in his favorite restaurant on Abdul-Mughni Street and was charged 1 riyal instead of 0.5 for his drink. The price is apparently regulated by law, so Taha argued about it with the restaurant owner, who threatened Taha or, more exactly, challenged him to do something about it. So Taha went to the Office of Supplies and got an injunction out against him, returning with the police to the restaurant. The owner by this time had fled, leaving his son in charge of the matter, so the boy went to jail from 9 to 12 the next morning, the owner paid a fine of 200 riyals, and to make the punishment even more galling, Taha insisted that the man reimburse him 20 riyals to cover the transportation costs incurred when traveling back and forth between offices and the restaurant.

But this was not to be the only social injustice Taha was to right that day. Heading to the back of one of the public buses, he was charged 1 riyal instead of 0.5, and he was quite sure that this was in excess of the limit set by law. He wasn't able to persuade the driver to see the correctness of his views and so took up the matter with a nearby policeman, who happened to be one of his friends. The policeman ruled in Taha's favor, and so the driver was dispossessed of his license and his keys and was made to pay a 500-riyal fine. And again, Taha claimed & won his 20 riyals transportation costs!

A busy day, but it wasn't over yet. Recently having bought a pair of pants which ripped on first washing, Taha tried to have them exchanged in the store he bought them from. The owner, however, wouldn't agree to exchange them because he claimed they were not new. Taha gave in but only if the owner gave him 20 riyals transportation costs!

This tenacious young man picked up badly needed money by doing, among other things (I never knew the full extent of his entrepreneurial activities), little odd jobs such as translations for the Institute. Eventually we became close friends, and I hired him to help me with translations of poetry, but that wasn't until much later in my fieldwork. I liked him, but to be honest, I was also a little wary. Was I being paranoid in thinking that he might be paid by Internal Security to check up on us from time to time and report on what we were doing? Was I projecting onto him suspicions that were laid on me when I was in the sanctuary?

Jon looked like the fit version of Kris Kringle, with an iron gray beard, twinkling blue eyes, and an "aw shucks" demeanor. An Aramco "brat" with many years' experience living in Saudi Arabia, he had become one of the world's leading authorities on the history of the Arabian Peninsula, specializing in the Ottoman period. "How's the research going on the poetry?" he asked.

I explained that I had been making contacts with some poets when trouble broke out. He asked me what I would do if I couldn't stay in the sanctuary. "I'm not sure. Relocate to Sana'a, I suppose, and work with tribal poets who are here. It certainly would be safer."

"I'm not so sure about that," said Jon.

"That's true," I conceded. "You know, when the mess with the hostages was happening in Tehran, the people of the sanctuary were telling me, 'Don't worry, Seif. If the government makes trouble for Americans, we'll protect you. We'll hide you or move you, but we won't let them get their hands on you.' Of course, when push comes to shove . . ."

Everyone had assumed that North Yemen would receive several hundred million dollars' worth of U.S. military equipment to combat the communist South, and it was rumored that the new equipment went instead to Saudi Arabia, which in turn gave the equivalent value of used equipment to North Yemen. Naturally, the regime in Sana'a was said to be furious. Worse, the Saudis were said to be doling it out in dribs and drabs and keeping North Yemen dependent on its archrival for spare parts. The arrangement seemed to make it painfully obvious which of the two countries the United States favored.

"There were some tense moments," Jon explained, "when it seemed that the military aid wasn't going to pan out."

"Is there talk now that Sana'a might lean more toward the Soviets if they promise to come through with the equipment?" I asked.

"There is."

I shook my head at how convoluted cold war politics was. Here the Soviet Union was militarily supplying North Yemen, a country that was defending itself against the incursions of the USSR's own satellite, the Cuba of the Middle East. But then again, who was to say that the influence the Soviet Union might thereby exert over North Yemen might not work toward the unification of the two countries? That accomplishment would pose a greater threat to Saudi Arabia than either half of Yemen could on its own. The Soviets, it seemed, were developing a more subtle and flexible policy than the United States at the moment.

"What do you think this means for the future of the Institute?" I asked. I knew how vulnerable to international politics our research was.

"Our relations with the government seem pretty good at the moment. They're not as bloody minded as you might think, shutting us down, say, in retaliation for the way they've been treated by our government. Poor Yemen has to walk a tightrope between the two superpowers. If anything causes us to shut down, it's lack of money. We need to increase our membership if we're going to pay our bills. Which reminds me, have you sent in your annual dues?"

I helped myself to a second cup of Janet's coffee and climbed to the aerie that was to be my room for the next few days. Traditional Yemeni houses often have such a room on the roof, to which the men of the household retreat from time to time to chew *qat*. It was small—one had to remember to crouch in order not to bump one's head—and there were no amenities such as cupboards or closets. I stacked my few clothes in one corner, my books and notes in another, and used a clipboard instead of a desk to write on. The room's discomfort was more than amply compensated for by its seclusion from the rest of the hostel and, best of all, its expansive views of the city from windows on all four sides.

I relaxed by reading my mail, letters from my parents first.

Dad's, written in minuscule but extraordinarily legible script, were as methodical as his business letters, informing me of the status of various items I had asked him to look into, but they were also chatty. He was glad to report that the color film I had sent to be developed had turned out well. They had purchased a slide projector and screen so that he and my mother could check out the pictures. (They thought I wouldn't mind.) They were pretty sure they had figured out which ones were of my village. Very beautiful, but a little desolate, no? There was one of me among the lot that they liked and decided to have printed and blown up. I'm wearing a Yemeni headdress, sweatshirt, and jeans. They got a kick out of the fact that I seem confident, even serene, although I'm standing under a large, dangerous-looking ledge. Second, the Fulbright-Hays officer in charge of processing my field grant had received my report and found it in order. (I must not have told the officer anything about the dispute with Sarkhan, I thought to myself.) Third, my last check was in the mail and I should receive it at the bank shortly. (This reminded me that I would have to be extra frugal until I could figure out a way to earn money to tide me over while I finished my fieldwork.) I was to let Dad know if it hadn't arrived by the time of my next visit to Sana'a so that he could alert Fulbright-Hays to put a trace on it. (Ah, these were the times when I appreciated my father's managerial background. I hadn't always.) And then family matters. They'd had to take the dog to the vet because of some infection, but he now seemed fine. It being so bitterly cold in Chicago, Dad wasn't sure whether Hoover would want to go on his regular walks, and he did require a little coaxing, especially at five in the morning, when Dad usually got up. But once out the door he would amble down the snow-plowed street, his Nietzschean eyebrows fluttering in the wind. It must be that Airedale coat that keeps him warm. Take care of yourself. Love, Dad.

A letter from my mother next. A clipping fell out from the *Chicago Tribune*, a review of a symphony concert she had attended with a friend. (She knew how much I missed hearing classical music.) She had scribbled across it a caustic remark about Georg Solti's conducting. Was she the only one in Chicago who found him cold and unfeeling? The words, typed with a slightly faded ribbon on plain white stationery, have ink marks sprinkled on them—corrections, accents on foreign words, last-minute second thoughts. A brief opening, telling me how much she misses me and how difficult it is to keep in touch across such vast distances of time and space, is neither maudlin nor self-pitying but stoical. Well, I was away and the circumstances were hard but one had to get on with life, didn't one?

There was usually a pastoral first movement, sometimes in French, which she liked to practice, perhaps a description of her lovely suburb, knowing as she did that I missed the changing seasons, and knowing as I did that her moods were highly sensitive to the weather. Then a sharp-edged, witty scherzo about neighbors, including their children's foibles, and amusing snippets of conversations with her friends (mainly widows and divorcées), who were entertainingly eccentric (she had a knack for finding what my father derisively called "screwball friends"). There was usually less news about my sisters, for she figured that I should and would be writing to them separately. An avid reader with philosophical tastes, she knew I would be interested in what she had been studying. "I have been digging up Schopenhauer these days, because someone asked me questions about him. I certainly do not like him. In this day and age he probably would have fallen victim to some feminist like Friedan who would have had a field day with him. An arch–male chauvinist, a cynic, a pessimist, a nihilist: I'm surprised he lived to the age of 72. We don't need him to point out the ills and sufferings of life. He says that knowledge increases sorrow, but he forgets that knowledge also may increase joy and health. He only sees one side of the coin on almost all of his statements. Woman is to blame for the misery in the world because her whole goal in life is to seduce man with her dubious charm; men are too generous to turn them down. (*Dass ich nicht lache!*) In that statement he admits that (according to his opinion) men are the weaker sex (if they can't resist the temptation of women). Well, from what I read, he had hard luck with women who found it easy to resist his charms; he also hated his mother, who was more prominent than he, and probably smarter."

The final movement usually consisted of a loving yet ambivalent reference to my father. It had been six years since his retirement, and he still hadn't any friends except for the mailman or the garbage people and didn't want to see too many of his old cronies from the office and could think of no better project to occupy himself with than reorganizing her kitchen, and it was always worse in the winter, when he couldn't go outdoors on his bike or putter around in the garden. *Nevertheless*, he was still affectionate and quite helpful to her when she had colitis; she was depending on him more and more, in fact, which was both a blessing and a curse. The lingering coda was an apology for not having anything really "interesting" to talk about, followed by a swift admonition to eat properly (have I been taking my vitamins?) and to look after my health (there's nothing more important), and a quiet expression of hope that I would return soon in one piece. With all her love, "Hanni." I cherish a crude, sappy drawing of the dog wagging its tail next to her signature.

I folded the letters and carefully put them back in their envelopes. There was no rush in replying to them. I had already sent some off this morning; they would arrive in a week, and I would probably be back in Sana'a in a month with another batch. I wanted the pleasure of rereading them back in the sanctuary, where they would mean more to me because I would be alone again, and lonely. I wondered how much I should tell my parents about the recent upheavals. In some respects, I could be more frank with my father than with my mother, who would worry too much; if I asked my father to keep what I told him under his hat, he would.

The homesickness these letters provoked made me wonder all over again why I was in Yemen and doing whatever it was that I was supposed to be doing. How could I justify my Olympian perch, high above this city that Noah and his sons had built? I could argue that my graduate work required my living overseas for a while. Was a dissertation worth this separation from family and friends? Five years for a work that would be read by a committee of four, if I was lucky, and then gather dust on a shelf at the university library? And on poetry? If it had been a comparative study of the military forces of Saudi Arabia and Yemen maybe, or better yet, the oil industries on the Peninsula, fine, but poetry? Who on earth could benefit from this? The absurdity was almost unbearable to think about, and I laughed at myself. And then I began to succumb to the utilitarian view of knowledge that I always criticized in others. Perhaps if things didn't work out, I might be able to use my language skills and travel experience to get a job in the private sector, following in my father's footsteps. Had I not been virtually offered a job once by an executive of a big American-owned oil company whom I met in Riyadh? I had told him over lunch that I wanted to finish my degree and then think about it. He did not scoff at my answer. Surprisingly, he seemed to understand it better than I. I was only twenty-five and wanted to see more of this fascinating world. That would make me only more interesting, he added significantly, and there was still time to go to business school at their expense; if I should change my mind, he hoped I would remember this conversation and contact him. He discreetly pushed his business card across the table. I thanked him and put it in my wallet. But I knew deep in my heart that I would never take him up on his offer. The damned dissertation meant something to me after all.

I also had a letter from Paul Friedrich, one of my academic advisers. It was he more than anyone who had encouraged me to study Yemen's tribal poetry. As I gazed over Sana'a, the whitewashed, crenellated rooftops seemed to blur into the gray, gargoyled towers of the University of Chicago, and I remembered a conversation we had had one wintry afternoon. I had expressed some reservation about going to the Arabian Peninsula, claiming that I had had my heart set on working on creole languages on a warm island in the Caribbean, preferably with beautiful beaches. I could see my breath rising ghostly in front of my face. Friedrich, who was far from a humorless person, sternly refused to recognize the levity in the remark and admonished me in no uncertain terms that he would resign from my committee if I were to change my mind. If I went through with the project, by contrast, he would do everything in his power to help me succeed. Look, he said more sympathetically, I know you're fighting the odds. It's a difficult place to work in, the academic job market is weak, and your topic makes you vulnerable to criticism for being "non-scientific." I know better than anyone how much contemporary social science marginalizes the study of figurative language. But you've spent a lot of time learning Arabic and you've just come back from Saudi Arabia: this is an opportunity to make all that pay off. Being a poet himself, he may have had too much personally invested in this topic, and I wondered whether I could trust his advice. Friedrich's letter included a list of some books he was sending to me by separate shipment. Gary Snyder, *Turtle Island*. Theodore Roethke, *The Far Field: Last Poems*. I supposed he had it in mind that I should try to become a poet in my own right.

I spent the rest of the afternoon writing up the last batch of field notes. I opened up the spiral notebooks that contained little bits of information—mostly mnemonic—I had jotted down in the course of a conversation or an event, then proceeded to convert these into fuller, more layered accounts. These were written down on multiple carbon copies of eight-and-a-half-by-eleven-inch paper. It was important to write this set of notes soon after the initial recording in the notebook, while the fuller conversational text or social context was still fresh in my memory. I wrote quickly but fluidly. I had to. There was not enough time to stop to think whether I had chosen the best word or caught all the nuances of the encounter. I hoped I'd have time to fill those in later, from memory.

In those pre-PC days, there wasn't enough time to rewrite the note later, after more reliable information was gleaned or my mistaken understandings were cleared up; the most recent information had to be scribbled above the line or in the margin. In time, a page could end up looking like a palimpsest. Here is what I wrote in February about what had happened a month earlier, from the notebooks I had filled with information in the sanctuary. The text reproduced here in square brackets is what I added after the first recording of the field note.

January 19, 1980

A big uproar in the sanctuary [I remind myself that I must change the name for reasons of confidentiality] over an alleged abduction of two young girls (10 and 14 yrs. of age) by one of the sada [again the names of people must be concealed]. The girls are from Sarkhan [again the name of the village must be changed], only 1/2 km. due west of the sanctuary—the elder is the daughter of the sheikh (also the sheikh of the tribe of al-Dhubayyinah, a branch of the Bani Dhubyan). The boy was supposed to have circled the village in his car early in the morning as if he were spying on it. He then came across the two girls, who were gathering firewood (hatab) on the hillside and somehow lured them into his car, a white taxi. Some say he went off to Sana'a, others suspect Hodeida [the truth, of course, was that he took them to Taiz]. A note about the boy. He's in secondary school in Sana'a and was visiting the sanctuary on vacation. He has a reputation for being a bad character, so what he did may have shocked but not surprised the people of the sanctuary. Apparently, he hadn't come back to the hijra since he was a baby. When I asked what would happen to him if he were caught, I was told that if the gov't got ahold of him, he'd be sent to prison. But if he fell into the hands of the girls' family, he'd have his throat cut. (As it turned out, he was taken by the people of the sanctuary and held for several days there, where he was interrogated as to the whereabouts of the two girls and then handed over to the tribes for eventual execution.) [This was another mistaken impression on my part, for not only was it the sheikh of Royshan and his party who eventually apprehended the boy but "interrogation" is too mild a word for what they did to him.] I was chatting with some boys at the time that the war broke out who were appalled by what Abdullah the Culprit did. They called him a dog—and said that he would have his prick cut off in addition to having his throat cut. The crime is indubitably a big embarrassment for the hijra, which is also potentially in great danger because of it. It is ironic that just a few minutes before the hubbub started the people of the sanctuary were laughing over the reported abduction of two girls from Sarkhan by gabilis [tribesmen]. They pointed out this incident as an object lesson to me; see how dirty these people are, completely indecent and immoral. Every day something will happen among the tribes—a beating, a killing, an argument—there's never a moment's peace. Such things, however, rarely occur in the sanctuary, which is after all a hijra *and is orderly, peaceful, and above all civilized. They kept referring to the state of political order among the tribes as chaos,* fawdha, *in the middle of which the* hijra *stood as an island of civilization and order.*

Recall that my diary entry of January 19, 1980 (quoted in chapter 2), focused on the dramatic entry of Sarkhan's sheikh into the sanctuary's souk, a moment to which I allude in my field note as "a big uproar in the sanctuary." The difference between the two illustrates my tendency to keep personal reactions out of my field notes, reserving them for my diary, and mentioning in the notes only what was necessary about myself to recall the physical and social circumstances in which something was said or observed: a date of communication, the person conveying the information (with the names often coded, to ensure a modicum of anonymity in case the notes fell into hostile hands, which in fact some of mine eventually did), interlocutors present, et cetera. The field note, after all, has a status as a scientific genre and has been subjected to critical scrutiny, though to the uninitiated this remains a mystery. Field notes are rarely published or even seen by other anthropologists, and they are considered "private," which is why they are often left in the anthropologist's personal papers—if they are not destroyed. Ironically, they then take on the status of diary entries.

No teacher of mine told me that I should distinguish diaries from field notes, but I assumed it from the shoptalk I heard, and I also was influenced by the functionalist, or perhaps Aristotelian "cathartic" explanation that anthropologists sometimes give—namely, that one wrote a diary to vent one's frustrations, leaving the ethnographic note for the more dispassionate recording of objective knowledge. One well-known anthropologist explained to me that I had missed the point entirely about Malinowski's Trobriand field diaries when I observed, rightly, that they revealed his racism. "The diary just shows how good he really was, because one is bound to think those thoughts in the field and feel guilty about them later." Apparently, one didn't question the effect that the great Malinowski's secret, illicit thoughts might have had on his ethnographic reporting anymore than he did himself, though a later generation of anthropologists did precisely that with regard to their own fieldwork.

These genres reify a distinction that ought to be blurred in practice, I think—the distinction between the objective and the subjective, between knowledge scientifically arrived at and the particular life circumstances and emotions of the investigator—but I'm still inclined to agree that using them is the right way to proceed. As one's fieldwork progresses, topics begin to emerge as long-term interests, and there has to be a way to get to the commentary on them conveniently; even if it has a complex cross-indexing system, a diary would not be appropriate for this. I tried to keep a record of both, so that I could consider the one in light of the other, which literally doubled the amount of time I devoted to writing. And yet, as far as the troubles in the sanctuary were concerned, my diary entries inevitably bled into my field notes, and now, years later, I see that the two were deeply implicated in each other. The strategy I have adopted in this book, interweaving the diary entries and field notes, may have rendered these two genres more visible and once again reified the distinction between them when I wish to do just the opposite. In writing this ethno-memoir I have wanted to bring these two narratives in closer proximity to each other, hoping they will interact and produce something other and greater than either or both of them alone.

While I was writing up my field notes and diary in Sana'a, I was disconcerted to realize that the dispute was taking up more and more of my attention, given that the main reason I had come to Yemen was to research the poetic system of the tribes. In hindsight, this seems like a strange reaction, for it also was clear to me that because the mediation of the dispute was generating so much poetry, I could not separate the historical event from the poetic performances. Perhaps I resented the dispute as yet another intensive problem that threatened to make my fieldwork untenable. Guilt was coupled with resentment, not because I seemed to be "exploiting" the miseries of others for my own "career" ends (a silly criticism of anthropological fieldwork if there ever was one) but just the opposite: because anthropology had not taught me to take events of this kind seriously enough. The dispute was not part of the everyday, the mundane, the ritualized, the conventional—those objects of social-scientific description since Emile Durkheim at least— and so I tried to ward it off like some evil spirit. But it continued to cast its spell over me, and I have not shaken it off to this day.

Although the researchers affiliated with the Institute had access to their own kitchen in the hostel, Janet often invited us to join her family for a potluck dinner, especially on the first night back, when we hadn't had time or energy to buy groceries and cook our own meals. A couple of researchers joined us that evening. Mary was back from Taiz, taking a break from fieldwork on a fascinating group of enterprising women with strong public personalities who controlled the local markets there. She was by now one of the Institute's old hands. Barbara was a more recent arrival, like me, a historian who was attempting a cultural portrait of a town in the Tihama, a semiarid coastal region of the country that had been famous three hundred years ago as a center of Islamic learning. Sort of a *Montaillou* of Yemen, she explained partly in jest, referring to the work of the great French cultural historian Emmanuel Le Roy Ladurie. She was an eccentric, as the expression goes, conspicuous for being so even among Yemenis, who adored her all the more for that reason. She always wore black, with a scarf wrapped around her head to cover her blond hair, like an old Sicilian village woman or a devout Irish Catholic widow. She would sometimes decorate her hands in the dye used by women in Yemen, and she spoke the local dialect with an exuberant lilt, perhaps making up for the brogue she might have had in English. She was involved with a young Italian doctor who looked like a rock star, yet none of us could quite picture them together, he phlegmatic, she so vivacious. She sometimes got on my nerves, but I felt loyal to her because she had helped me get over my depression in my first months in Yemen, when I couldn't find a place to stay in Khawlan and was about ready to give up. "*Kef-ak, ya*

Seif?" (the equivalent in Yemeni Arabic of "How's it going, Steve?"), she had said then, imitating the distinctive intonation of a Yemeni greeting, and climbing the narrow stairwell to my room at the top, she had sat with me and chewed *qat*, cheering me up and talking me into giving it one more try. Mary and Barbara had known each other as graduate students at Harvard and had become friends, though they could not have been more different. Mary was precise, thorough, and literal-minded. Barbara said affectionately of her once, "Yeah, Mary can kill you with the details." In turn, Mary noted that Barbara was incapable of being on time for an appointment. "She's always seven minutes late. You know something"—she chuckled—"when her plane landed in Yemen, it was exactly seven minutes late."

Janet brought a big pot of spaghetti to the table. Heath had prepared the pasta. It was his specialty. He knew without using a timer precisely how long to cook the noodles so that they would be al dente.

"*Kef al-Haal, ya Heath,*" I said to him.

"*Mabsut, al-hamdullilah. Kef al-Hal, ya Seif?*" He grinned just enough to show his slightly buck teeth. He had become something of a neighborhood celebrity. On walks in the city the family might be stopped for inquiries about him. Because it was easy for an eight-year-old to learn the local dialect, people thought he might be a Yemeni boy from the United States and were then astonished to discover that he was the adopted half black son of Americans. Knowing that he was mistaken for a Yemeni, the female researchers sometimes asked him to accompany them on their errands, for a woman chaperoned even by a male child, was less likely to be hassled on the streets. He put up with this in part because he was so good-natured but also because it made him feel grown up. And insulting as this may have seemed to the women, in a sense he was.

"Do you still play soccer with the neighborhood boys?" I asked him in Arabic. He nodded his head. I tried to grab and tickle him, but he squirmed out of my clutches and with a little squeal ran to the other end of the table. Heath and I got along all right, but I was not his favorite. That was Chuck, a researcher who was working in west-central Yemen on agricultural development and traveled about on a motorcycle. I noticed it wasn't parked in the courtyard.

"Have you seen Chuck?" I asked. Heath spent hours with Chuck and his motorcycle, watching him fix and clean it, or just sitting in the saddle, leaning over to hold on to the handlebars. I wanted to get him a cap, take a picture, and entitle it "The Wild One."

When Janet returned from the kitchen, I told her how well I thought Heath seemed to be doing. "Yes," she remarked, "he's adjusted well and is getting along with his teachers—for a change. Isn't that so, Heath?" She cleared her throat meaningfully and looked in his direction. She then silently mouthed words to me: "I only wish he'd do more R-E-A-D-I-N-G."

The two teenage girls, Allison and Cristin, brought an enormous salad bowl to the table. I knew I would relish the fresh greens. They were both good students and seemed to be enjoying the international school they were attending. Allison, the older one, had been a little concerned at first that she might not be able to prep well enough here to get into a good university back home, but in fact the school had a decent record in qualifying its students, and besides, there were few social distractions to keep her from her studies. Cristin, who was in junior high and could enjoy her stay in Yemen without that kind of scholastic pressure, took advantage of her more flexible schedule to read widely and most of all dabble in many interests she had always wanted to pursue at home and didn't have the time for, such as dance and painting. Both girls were studying Arabic.

"So tell me, Seif, what's happening in the sanctuary?" Barbara had heard the story from Janet about how I had gotten my Arabic name. "I understand there's been trouble."

"Whom have you heard that from?" I asked, startled that the news had carried so swiftly.

"You forget that I know your landlord because I'm doing a translation job in his ministry."

"There's now been a startling revelation. The boy who abducted the girls has been apprehended and has claimed that the older one, the daughter of the sheikh, gave him money to take her and her ten-year-old companion out of Sarkhan. There's even speculation that she was pregnant."

"How do they know that he's telling the truth?" Janet asked. "He could be trying to blame the girls. Did they ever find the girls to question them?"

"They've sent out search parties, but they're still missing. The presumption is that they're in hiding somewhere. But to make sure the boy wasn't lying, they applied electric shock. They said that he stuck to his story."

"Good God!" Janet exclaimed. "Torture seems a bit drastic, doesn't it?"

"Maybe. We used to do it too, though we had a more elegant name for it. 'The ordeal under oath.' "

Jon asked me whether the girls' tribe had gone to war. "They are still threatening to do so, if the girls aren't found," I told him. "We've had some shooting, but the sheikhs who have come to mediate the dispute have managed to keep a truce going. I don't know how long it will last, though. No one seems to."

"What does this mean for your fieldwork? Aren't you worried about your safety?"

"A little, but the fighting really isn't serious. They tell me it's more like a game. The sheikh and father of one of the girls has to show that he's ready to go to war to defend his honor."

" 'Anger be now thy song,' " Jon said.

"What?"

" 'Anger be now thy song.' That's more or less the opening of the *Iliad*. Another story about female abduction, male honor, and war, as you will recall."

"I hope it's not like the *Iliad*," exclaimed Allison. "That's the bloodiest book I've ever read. Men being disemboweled by swords, arrows piercing eyeballs, heads lopped off—."

"Please, Allison," her sister moaned. "We're eating." Heath sniggered.

"Well, those Greeks were a nasty bunch," Allison said. "I hope the Yemenis are not so bloody."

"Are they?" Jon asked me with a grin on his face.

"Not even close. At least not so far. If I remember correctly, Allison, isn't there also plenty about talking in the *Iliad* as well?"

"What do you mean?"

"I mean, men try to persuade each other, to move each other with words, not just war. Am I right?"

"Yeah, but those aren't the parts I remember. It's all the blood and gore. That's the heroism of the epic, isn't it?"

"A macho thing," Barbara volunteered a little facetiously and helped herself to more salad.

"I suppose so. Maybe it's harder for us to feel the drama in the word, so it doesn't appear as heroic. But that's what I'm really interested in, how the various parties are trying to work things out by a combination of word and war—mostly word so far. There are many poems being composed on the dispute. I've learned more new ones in a month than I have all year. Jon, you asked what this means for my fieldwork. It has *made* my fieldwork. My insights into the society grow deeper as things around me get all stirred up."

Mary, the only other anthropologist at the table, was alive to this point. "It's funny how we're taught this myth about fieldwork, that you go to some sleepy little island or isolated mountain village in order to learn everyday things by blending in. But then they're not so ordinary, and you never quite blend in."

But this was a tangent, and the rest of the company was getting bored. Heath had already asked to be excused from the table once it was clear I wasn't going to talk about the fighting. Janet reminded him he had homework to do and she would come up later to make sure he had done it. He trundled off to the Yemeni-style sitting room with his books and plopped down on the floor to begin work.

"Anyway," I continued, "it was said of the sheikh of Sarkhan that he was beside himself with grief when he discovered that his own daughter might have been pregnant and that's why she paid the boy to take her and her friend away. The entire tribe went into mourning. Fatimah, my upstairs neighbor, told me why soon after Abdullah's confessions became news: 'Now no one will want to marry their women, for fear that they are shameful.' "

"Has anyone said what would happen to the girls if they found them?" Mary asked.

"What do you think?" I asked her.

"Well, I suppose the daughter of the sheikh will be killed, if she is indeed pregnant. They may be lenient with the other one."

"I've heard of cases where girls have become pregnant out of wedlock and got away with it," Barbara said. "If her lover were a boy of whom her father approved, there might be a shotgun wedding—hmm, bad choice of words, sorry—assuming the boy was willing. But if the father did not approve or the boy refused, then she'd be in trouble. When so much of the father's honor depends on the conduct of the girl, which is especially true in the case of a sheikh's daughter, I suppose he can't very well overlook it if he can't conceal the facts. Not every father would even go along with such a ruse, no matter how much he loved his daughter."

"Do they practice patrilineal parallel cousin marriage in Khawlan?" asked Mary.

Allison and Cristin gave us a quizzical look. Janet chuckled and, turning to her daughters, said, "Anthropological shoptalk, girls." She looked at us with an exaggerated grin. "Do tell us what patrilineal parallel cousin marriage is."

Mary offered to explain. "There's a preference for marrying the cousin on the father's side of the family. Meaning *cousin* in the loose sense: first, second, or third cousin, several times removed even. As a rule, this kind of marriage is relatively rare, and some people think it's distinctively Arab. Do they practice it, Steve?"

"Yes, they do."

"If she's pregnant and the father is a cousin, that would make it easier for them to get married, assuming he's available," Mary reasoned. "So it's likely that the father is someone else, who either would not or could not marry her, and that she then feared for her life."

"What about an abortion? Or is that a naïve question?" Janet asked.

"Yes, that's possible," Mary agreed. "I know abortions are performed. But the girl has to find a woman to help her whom she can trust and who would be discreet, and that might be difficult."

"So one scenario," I suggested, "is that they paid the boy to take them to Taiz, where they hoped to get an abortion in a clinic."

"Still, how would they have explained their absence if they wanted to return?" wondered Barbara. "They would have been punished for going like that without a proper escort and not seeking permission."

"Punished, maybe," I replied, "but a punishment that was not worse than death. Who knows, maybe they planned to come back after the abortion was performed and blame the boy for having abducted them. It would have been their word against his, and I bet people would have been more likely to have believed them."

"Well, I'm not so sure," said Mary. "It would be an incredibly risky plan. Whatever the motive, it shows the desperateness of the girl's situation. The consequences of her action seem irrevocable and so tragic. It's hard to make someone understand them who isn't part of this culture."

"Oh, I don't know about that," remarked Janet after a pause. "Consider *Anna Karenina*." She glanced at the paperback on the windowsill. "In some ways the whole book is a commentary on arranged marriages, a custom of the Russian aristocracy. And it's clear that for Tolstoy the institution had its failings, to say the least. Take Anna. She marries a man out of duty, not love, ends up falling in love with a dashing army officer with whom she commits adultery, and all the while is torn up by guilt and, of course, the ignominy of divorce, not to mention the fear of losing her son because of it. She ends up living with the man she loves, but as long as she doesn't get divorced and remarry they do not have legal control over their own child. Meanwhile, she's not exactly ostracized in high society but certainly made to feel ashamed of herself. The two of them have the means to live above it all, but they are not unscathed. Her brother also commits adultery, but he hardly seems bothered by his infidelities. Anna, on the other hand, slowly deteriorates. True, she isn't stoned to death, but is she any less a victim because she throws herself under a train?"

It was now Cristin's turn. "What I don't understand is how young these girls are and yet one of them could be punished by death. She's only fourteen! That's my age. What can she have done at her stage in life that she should be punished so drastically?"

"Girls are expected to grow up faster here than they do in the

United States," observed Mary. "By the time she's twelve or so, a girl is no longer a minor. She knows more or less all she has to know socially in life, except of course if she's going on for a high school or college education. She knows how to cook and sew, how to take care of children, to run a household, and so on. And at your age she is probably engaged and will soon be married. That's why the pressure to maintain her modesty and decency is so intense at this stage in life. For this is the time when she must become engaged to a suitable husband in a marriage arranged by her parents."

"And it is important that her reputation for chastity appear spotless," Barbara added. "Otherwise a possible suitor will worry that the children won't be raised properly. In principle, the girl has to agree to the match for it to be sanctioned, and in practice she may choose someone else, someone who is not of the prescribed category, but that depends on circumstances—the particular personalities of the girls' parents and her social standing—and it's never assured. A daughter of a sheikh, especially a powerful one like the sheikh of Sarkhan, would probably be intended for a man who was himself powerful or came from a prominent family, and the pressure for her to consent to the match would be intense. That's the case with European dynastic marriages, too. Ironically, the higher the status of the girl, the less control she has over the choice of her spouse."

"But surely it's important that the couple fall in love before they get married," Cristin protested.

"You're talking to a teenager from the United States, Seif," Barbara warned.

"Of course, love is important," I almost shouted. "But does it have to come before marriage, or can a couple fall in love while learning responsibility toward each other and their families? For example, my friend Muhammad, the young carpenter in Sarkhan, and his recent bride, theirs was an arranged marriage, but they weren't permitted to consummate it until they had gotten to know each other, and until the bride seemed able to run a household efficiently and the husband in turn learned to respect her. Given that context, it was hoped they would fall in love, if they hadn't already. If there were problems, they'd be encouraged to work them out, and if they remained irreconcilable, then divorce was possible and not frowned upon."

"And can the woman divorce as easily as the man?" asked Cristin. "I'm learning in my Arabic class that the man can say 'I divorce you' one, two, three, and then it's all over, but that the woman can't do this."

"True," said Mary. "The woman doesn't have as easy a time of it. She has to have a male relative like a brother or father intercede on her behalf, and in the cities she might represent herself in the courts, if she's educated. Nevertheless, it's not impossible."

After a while I offered an anecdote as a way of illustrating all these themes. "Remember, Mary, when I first got here I was tutoring the daughter of that man from Taiz, the one you knew and said might be able to help me meet some poets from the south? The man was in many ways quite supportive of his daughter, and extraordinarily trusting of us, as we spent many hours alone together.

"Our English lessons took place at his home, but almost as if she was challenging his authority under his own roof, she'd wear casual clothes with low-cut necklines, all the time bending over her books with the utmost concentration. I became flustered and confused. Was she being a tease, or was she simply oblivious? On the one or two occasions when the father walked in on us while we were working together, he was somewhat taken aback by Waffa's appearance and made a remark, and she'd respond saying if he insisted that we work at home—presumably because no one would see us together and start gossiping—he could not object if she was just relaxing. Or did he want her to veil at home too? she asked sarcastically. Well, he said, can't you relax in something less revealing? Next time she wore jeans and blouse, both tight-fitting, hardly an outfit to appease him or to make me less nervous. But by then I realized what she was trying to do. She was saying, These are the clothes girls wear in America, isn't that so, Steve? And it doesn't necessarily mean that boys and girls are having sex with each other when they dress that way. Right, Steve? Look at the two of us: we're just studying. I had to admire her fearlessness, though I worried about her.

"Then the father issued a warning of his own. Do you know what my daughter's name means in Arabic, Steve? 'Trust.' It means 'trust.' It would be a terrible thing, Steve, if I found out that you and she . . .

"I decided I'd had enough of this chess game with me as pawn, so I quit the lessons on some excuse or other. But before I did, the tension between them exploded before my eyes. I don't recall now how the argument got started, but he wanted her to marry a cousin whom she found perfectly pleasant but did not love, while her father said that marriage was the important thing and love—of which he spoke rather triflingly—would come later. To Waffa, the issue was not love so much as her own autonomy. I'm not just a piece of clothing on some rack, she yelled, that you can take on or off as you like."

"It sounds to me like the girl thought it was important for two people to love each other before they get married," Cristin said.

I sighed. Who was I to gainsay an American teenager's belief in true love? I thought it wiser to retreat from this field of battle.

I had been in the telephone and telegraph office for about an hour. It was quite noisy in the main lobby, with people milling about and chatting while they waited their turn to be called to a booth where an operator would place an international call for them. Clerks from various business establishments were collecting reams of telexes. Finally, I heard my name called with instructions to go to a numbered booth.

"Hello, Dad?"

My father's familiar voice came on a second later. "Yes, Steve, I'm here. Your mother's at the other phone."

That was her cue. "How are you, Steven?"

"The miracles of satellite communication!" I said. "You sound like you're in the next room."

"That would be too lucky."

"We can hear you fine, too," said my father.

"How are things at home?" I knew I would hear news I had heard many times before, but this was a comforting ritual. I told them I was learning many new poems, making the acquaintance of many poets in the region, and satisfied that my work was coming along. We ended as we always did, with my inquiring only half seriously whether they might visit me in Yemen. Although they had been intrepid travelers in their youth, a flare-up of my mother's colitis at the time of my father's retirement had curtailed their travel plans. They weren't even sure they would make it to Europe, where they had spent much of their youth and where my mother's family still lived.

"Wait a second!" My father rang the doorbell so that the dog would bark. "Did you hear him?"

We said our goodbyes. After a moment's hesitation, with both parties wondering who should hang up first, my father put down the receiver. My mother was still on the line and didn't realize I was, too. Then I heard a gentle click.

5

∽

MUHAMMAD THE MASWARI

I returned to a disgruntled sanctuary. The search for the missing girls had come up empty-handed. The trail had gone cold in the Taiz hotel, where Abdullah the Culprit had said, under torture, he had left them. Since the sheikh of Sarkhan made the settlement of the conflict contingent upon their return, the negotiations stalled.

Muhammad the Lame explained the new developments to me. The search party headed by sheikhs al-Qiri and al-Royshan swooped down like vultures on the Taiz hotel and threatened to burn it to the ground if the owner, Shahben, didn't tell them where the missing girls were. But Shahben insisted he had no idea they'd even been in his hotel, let alone what had become of them. On the night the girls had supposedly been there, his son and an assistant had been on duty, so the sheikhs' investigations focused on them. From the son's acquaintances, they heard rumors of nefarious business practices and suspected he might have sold the girls into prostitution. Such things were known to happen in Yemen, where young women were kidnapped by prostitution rings and then sold into sexual slavery. Perhaps the hotel owner's son had hired Abdullah the Culprit to procure them. The sheikhs kidnapped the son and delivered an ultimatum to the hotel owner: convince your son to return the girls or return them yourself, or you will

never see your son again. The North Yemeni government raised no ob-
jections to these vigilante actions, supposedly having been convinced
of the hotel owner's probable guilt but in all likelihood because it was
in no position to stop them. Yet again, however, the sheikhs came up
empty-handed. Now tragedy turned into farce. They would not release
the hotel owner's son, even if he was innocent, unless the father agreed
to pay a large ransom. The sanctuary was aghast. This was extortion!
My friends like Muhammad the Lame were fuming. *The sheikhs were
driven by motives of greed, not justice, he averred. They had lost all credibility. How
dare they accuse the sanctuary of moral degeneracy when they were acting no better than thugs?* The government may have been too weak to stop the
sheikhs but not the hotel owner's tribe, and so this whole terrible business took on another bizarre twist as Khawlan became embroiled in an
ancillary dispute with a tribe from the powerful Hashid confederation.
Of course, as soon as the Hashid became involved, Khawlan had to
call on *its* confederation, the Bakil, for support, and now two great
tribal factions of Yemen were very upset with each other.

A month later, Ibrahim the Beltmaker provided more context to understand why things went so wrong. My later field notes of April 12
recorded that he *said [the sanctuary] had made a big mistake in the very beginning [by] giving up the hostages to secure a truce with the Dhubayyinah [the branch
of the Bani Dhubyan to which the people of Sarkhan belonged] . . . Perhaps [it] particularly regrets having handed over Shabben into the custody of al-Royshan and the
tribes, for it is clear that he is a valuable pawn, which they have lost and is now being played against them at every turn. The tribes have everything to gain and nothing
to lose by prolonging the dispute, milking [the sanctuary] on the one hand and extorting money from Shabben on the other. If [the sanctuary] had possession of Shabben,
they could have (1) secured the whereabouts of the girls, who are still missing but are
generally assumed to be in Shabben's possession, and (2) exchanged the life of the son
of Shabben for the two girls and at the same time gotten money out of him to pay for
the damages levied on [the sanctuary] . . . It has, by the way, been assumed that
Shabben does have the two girls. He does not want to give them up until he can secure
a deal with the sheikhs to guarantee the safety of his son, who is their prisoner. If the
deal hasn't been made, it's because the Khawlan sheikhs want to squeeze more money
out of him, or so [the sanctuary] believes.*

Soon I had some encounters in the sanctuary that deeply disturbed me.

February 21, 1980

Yesterday, Ali [the Bird] came to say that he could not meet with me inside my house—on his father's orders. I asked him what [his father] meant, but Ali couldn't or wouldn't tell me the reasons . . . I was furious and frustrated. How should I interpret Ali's father's injunction? Does he think of me as a child molester?! Has there been talk about us around town that his father is reacting to? . . . Last Friday a tribesman in the sanctuary stopped to talk to me. He's from al-Ghars and knows all about my project. Come with me, he said; we have some poetry. At the same time he accused me of being a *siyasi* "politician" and warned that if I stepped foot outside the *hijra* someone would shoot me.

Siyasi can have the meaning of "political agent," so the man was implying that I was working for the U.S. government (or at least some foreign power) to stir up trouble—though to what end wasn't clear to me.

"How did he say it?" I later recalled Muhammad the Lame asking me. "Did he say it as though he meant it?"

"How should I know?" I answered testily.

"Well, you are supposed to know. Sometimes it's just talk and means nothing. I think, Seif, it really did mean nothing. And what did you say to him?"

"Nothing that I recall. I just walked away."

I decided Muhammad the Lame was probably right. It was just a provocation to see how I would react. Still, I was perturbed by the fact that the man said he came from al-Ghars, home of the poet Muhammad al-Gharsi, whom I'd interviewed in Sana'a for my poetry research. Was this a coincidence, or had he been talking to the poet, and had the latter expressed suspicions about me? Or had this man acted independently? Did he want to frighten me into leaving for reasons having to do with the ongoing dispute? Or was he just being a jerk?

Because of the cold shoulder people had given me, I decided to make good on my resolution to visit places outside the sanctuary where I might hook up with poets. Ordinarily, I would have sought protection from the *sada*, but the so-called troubles made that protection futile and even undesirable. I first tried to make contacts with immediate neighbors of the sanctuary.

February 10, 1980

I went yesterday to Bait al-Mahjari to see the poet Ali (the same who had been maligning the sanctuary in the dispute). By chance we happened to meet in the sanctuary souk that morning and arranged to chew *qat* together at his place, where we would discuss poetry.

So in the afternoon I packed my tape recorder, organized my thoughts for the interview, and bought some *qat*, but when I arrived at Bait al-Mahjari I found Ali working in his fields, not apparently expecting me to show up. I was embarrassed, he was embarrassed. But we talked a little while he planted some *bisbas* [fennel] and onions and puttered around in his fields.

The most striking impression I had was of his very strong dislike for the *sada*—as a class, not just the ones in the sanctuary. He told me that they belong to another *madhhab* [religious sect], having been brought in by the Persians when they conquered Yemen before Islam. Their hierarchical view of society, he claimed, was heretical to the true teachings of the Prophet, who emphasized the social equality of all men within the Muslim *'ummah*. As far as he was concerned, Christians and Jews are closer to the true spirit of Islam than the *sada*.

He told me this with complete conviction. The *sada* are our enemies, he said. We despise them. There was no hatred or fanaticism in his voice, simply a firm and very steady belief in the rightness of his own views . . .

I would like very much to get to know him better. But I sensed that something was restraining him when I was talking to him yesterday. Perhaps it was only the fact that he hadn't eaten lunch and was ashamed to eat when I was his guest for the chew. So I excused myself, saying that perhaps we could talk again some other time on the subject of poetry . . .

The [people in the sanctuary] are not happy that I go to see him because they know his views on the *sada*. Some of them have told me point-blank not to visit him. The majority, however, couldn't care less, and so I will risk a diplomatic crisis.

February 24, 1980

Went to see Ali, but he wasn't at home. His daughters greeted me—politely but very suspiciously. I said I would try to see him another time.

I never saw Ali again—in the sense of actually working with him. When I happened to pass by his village, I would occasionally see him working alone in his fields. My upstairs neighbor Ahmed, an ancient firearm slung from his shoulder as he patrolled the sanctuary, warned me that Ali was a troublemaker who had fomented anger against the *sada* in the tribal assemblies and that if he didn't shut up he'd be killed. Cooler heads prevailed. Nevertheless, Ali became silent after a while, and whether this was because he was threatened or bought off, I never did find out.

Perhaps I could cash in my chips with Hussein the Servant and ask him to try once again to set up a meeting with the poet from al-ᶜAin. That is exactly what he did. It wasn't just the famous poet Salih bin Gasim al-Sufi whom I met but also his sheikh, the sheikh al-Royshan, whom I had encountered earlier and who had left such a sour impression. He and his entourage joined al-Sufi and me while we were working on some poetry. The room started to fill with people curious about Seif the American, and before long I, not the poet, was the interviewee. The sheikh said very little as I recall, but one of his henchmen proceeded to ask me the same questions I had answered dozens of times. Where was I from? What was I doing in Khawlan? Why was I studying poetry? Who was giving me money for this research? The grilling made me nervous, and my stomach started to churn. I had an intuition that I was suspected of something but did not know what. (I did not learn until later that al-Royshan was keeping the hotel owner's son and his assistant hostage, and that he may have thought I was trying to find out something about that.) Eventually, I was asked what I had collected in the way of tribal verse. Luckily, I had memorized several poems and could recite them, much to the approval of the poet, who until then had been quiet.

Salih was in his late fifties or early sixties, with white hair and weathered skin. A reserved man, scrupulously polite, he was nevertheless friendly without being particularly warm. He had spent years in the army (which may have accounted for his somewhat stiff and formal demeanor) and was now more or less retired and living in the village. He seemed pleased with my knowledge of poetry and started to recite poems he knew, some of which were familiar to me but a good many of which were not. I took out my notebook from the pocket of my jeans (what possessed me to wear jeans instead of the more comfortable *futa*, I do not now recall) and began writing as quickly as I could. I was concentrating so hard that I didn't even notice the sheikh quietly leave the room and his attendants slip out behind him. I was aware only of feeling elated, not because I had passed a test—if indeed I had—but because for the first time in Khawlan I seemed to be deeply engaged in the subject I had come to study.

Then, suddenly, I needed to excuse myself to go to the toilet. I was getting sick and sicker. As I sat on my haunches over the latrine, I had a feeling that something was terribly wrong. At the precise instant that I looked down, the notebook slipped out of the pocket of my jeans and fell fluttering like a wounded bird into the hole. Its descent was caught in a thin ray of light that made it seem as though it were falling in slow motion, an effect that magnified my fascinated horror. Then I could see it lying in the muck. I vowed never again to wear jeans at a Yemeni gathering. For a moment, I actually contemplated retrieving the notebook, even if it meant getting a village servant to help, but I managed to collect myself, knowing this would be too embarrassing. I shuddered to think what my new nickname might be. Then I began to laugh. The first time I had collected poetry of any range and substance, and it ended up in a shit hole!

When I came back, I retrieved a fresh notebook from my backpack, hoping that my acquaintances would not catch on as to what had happened to the one in which I had been writing so furiously. But I was so disheartened I could not go on. I said it was late and I would have to go back to the sanctuary. As I got up to leave, I told Salih the poet that I hoped to return, and if he would permit it, we might discuss his own poetry rather than other people's.

"*Inshallah*," he replied and shook my hand. "I am here in the afternoons almost every day. Come and chew *qat* with me, and we shall go over as much of my poetry as you like."

On the way back to the sanctuary, I thanked Hussein for what he had done. He was obviously pleased that he had finally acquitted himself with me.

Sensing my despondency and wanting to help me out on my work, Muhammad the Lame suggested an outing.

February 27, 1980

Reports are that Sana'a had snow, which actually stayed on the ground for a day. A meter deep, supposedly. Jabal Nugum is as white as the Matterhorn . . . [Muhammad the Lame] invited me to come along with a group of people who were going to Shalalah to buy *qat*, and I tagged along. A pleasant little village not more than 3 km. from [the sanctuary] in ENE direction. Collected a few *zamils*.

February 28, 1980

Spent the morning doing my chores around the house. My digestion has been poor lately, which caused me not to want to eat too many foods, and consequently I've lost weight and feel sluggish. Taking vit. B tablets again. I think one reason for my lack of appetite is that the food I prepare is so unaesthetic looking. Perhaps if I made it look more attractive I would want to eat it.

I also miss meat. Most of my protein comes from chicken (once a week) and tuna with beans and rice as a supplement. My iron comes from the *gushmi* "horseradish" leaves and *kurath* "leeks" that I occasionally mix in a salad with hard-boiled eggs, some pieces of mackerel or tuna added. Breakfast is a big meal of oatmeal with fruit or pancakes or bread & butter. Lunch is usually soup and some fruit. I've run out of cheese, which I miss . . . Despondent. I think a lot about X's return to Yemen this March, which I look forward to very much, while not overly optimistic about our future. What can *two* academics do in life together?

One night I think I had a sort of nervous breakdown. For several nights I had been awakened by something running lightly over my body and then scuttling away. I wasn't sure if I was going mad, and of course, by the time I had turned on the light, the rat was gone. I knew it would be back, so I wedged strips of cloth tightly in every crack of my bedroom door. When I woke up in the morning, the strips of cloth looked undisturbed and I presumed they had kept my nocturnal prowler at bay. Not for long. When I inspected the door the next night, I saw the strips had been shredded as if by scissors and nearly torn away. What amazing strength and tenacity the animal had. I pictured a Godzilla. I spent the next few days doing little except plotting to dispatch him. Getting a cat seemed impossible. I asked Muhammad the Hunchback if he had a rat trap. Then I asked him for rat poison. Finally I realized I would have to improvise. I went into the kitchen and carefully sprinkled food in one corner. I then proceeded to the bedroom and sealed the cracks in the door as usual. Later on that night, I was awakened by a clawing sound around the edges of the door that grew louder and more frenetic. The door actually rattled as the animal pulled on the strips of cloth to loosen them. I reached for a knife in case the rat breached the defenses. Suddenly there was quiet. If I had guessed correctly, he had become enticed by the odor in the kitchen. In the morning I found that the food I had left in the corner had been eaten. I repeated the same routine for several nights in order to condition the rat to go to the kitchen. I had become the B. F. Skinner of highland Yemen.

I suppose we could have coexisted in this way indefinitely except that the house wasn't really mine but that goddamn rat's, so I vowed to get rid of it. One night, as I heard it rustling in the kitchen, I quietly got out of bed, opened the bedroom door, and walked stealthily toward the kitchen. I took a deep breath and opened the kitchen door, quickly closing it behind me. I placed a flashlight on the stone floor, its beam projecting in a large cone on the whitewashed ceiling. Particles of crystal in the plaster reflected the light, making the room seem as bright as day. I knew I had to act quickly. I assumed that the rat, startled by the flashlight, was cowering somewhere in a corner, so I quickly began to plug up the cracks in the kitchen door. Then I turned around to face my opponent. We were closer than I realized, and I saw it staring at the two huge bloodshot eyes staring back at it; I ran at it with the knife and began chasing it around the room. It tried running over the wall toward the door but found no exit. I lunged after it, the point of the knife buried in the door just a fraction of an inch from its belly. Do rats squeal? I wondered. As it darted across the wall again, I stabbed at it, the point of the knife chipping off plaster flakes that seemed to fly in the air like sparks of electricity. Around and around we went. Its fur was brown and sleek, its body tautly muscled, its movements lithe and agile, like those of a finely trained athlete. My hatred for the animal began to drain away, and I stopped chasing it. I opened the kitchen door, collected the strips of cloth, went back into my bedroom, and sealed myself in my tomb. I was never bothered by the rat again. I laughed to think that it must have warned its friends there was a lunatic in the house who got his kicks from torturing animals.

My health continued to deteriorate. The next day I was in a taxi to Sana'a.

In mid-March the sanctuary held a big meeting in the Citadel. Hussein the Servant had put forward a petition to buy property in the sanctuary as compensation for all he had done in the first twenty-four hours of the conflict. If granted, it would mean that he would finally realize his dream to own land and build a grand house. Since many descendants of the Prophet from out of town were present for the mediation of the dispute with Sarkhan, this seemed like an opportune time to get a consensus.

I waited outside the great house along with my friend Muhammad the Maswari to find out the outcome of the deliberations. Hussein the Servant was holed up in his home with his sons. Hours passed before there was a word. Finally, the Hunchback emerged, looking grim and weary. Hussein's petition had been denied.

"But why?" I asked.

"Only descendants of the Prophet who have the same name as the inhabitants of the sanctuary can own property here" was the answer. Instead of land, Hussein would be given a generous cash gift in recognition of his services.

I expressed my doubts that he would accept it. "Why give a rich man a subsidy when what he wants is a little respect?"

"It cannot be, Seif," said the Hunchback, solemnly. "If Hussein were a really good man, then perhaps an exception might have been made."

"How can you say that?" I asked him in astonishment. "He saved you, didn't he, from certain attack by the sheikh of Sarkhan when you were badly outnumbered?"

"Yes, we acknowledge his help, but that's why we want to pay him. There are other things about Hussein, Seif, things you would be better off not to know, that make me say he's unworthy." I was never able to get a straight answer from him or anyone else about why Hussein was deemed "unworthy."

A week later I noticed a new tent pitched in the floodplain and was told that it belonged to the great sheikh Hussein Ali al-Gadhi, of the Bani Suhman tribe, a member of the parliament-like Shura Council, which the nation's president regularly consulted. He had come to mediate the dispute at the request of the president, supposedly. It was hoped that a man of his stature and influence could bring the deliberations to a swift conclusion. "Now we may get somewhere," said Muhammad the Hunchback. The sheikh's tent was pitched exactly at the halfway point between the sanctuary and Sarkhan, a location meant to be symbolic of his neutrality. I learned also that he had brought with him two of his own daughters, whose presence would serve as a painful reminder of the two women who were still missing. That he too had daughters, that he too could understand their vulnerability, that he too could sympathize with the horror and pain of their father—these were all meanings he hoped to convey by this gesture. But above all, it symbolized his sincerity in wanting to mediate and his trust in all parties concerned to negotiate in good faith—otherwise he would not have exposed his own women to risk of public insult or worse.

March 24, 1980

Muh'd the Lame is now back in the center of things. I see him entering and leaving the tent quite frequently—more than perhaps any other sada. Ali al-Mahjari, the scrappy little poet from down the way, was stirring up trouble again. He urged the following settlement [for the sanctuary]: two sada girls to be handed over for execution in place of the missing tribal girls. But this idea was denounced by the sheikhs as unjust and has, apparently, been dismissed.

Once Sheikh Hussein Ali al-Gadhi was on the scene, Sheikh al-Royshan and his supporters decided to stay away. Sheikh al-Royshan, the one who was extorting huge sums from Shahben to make sure that his son was kept alive, was suspected of trying to prolong the dispute, insisting that the two girls had to be found and returned, in order to shake this money tree as long as possible. Therefore, Sheikh al-Gadhi decided to place the hostages in government keeping in Yarim, a southern city that had no connection to Khawlan. Al-Royshan was furious. *Al-Royshan has been exceedingly inflammatory in his rhetoric against [the sanctuary], contrary to the more moderate stand he took in the beginning of the dispute. Of course, [he] technically belongs to the Bani Dhubyan, . . . which would dispose him to a pro-Dhubyani stand. But his position has become ambiguous or at least self-interested . . . [since] Shahben began to ply him with money, hoping to convince the Bani Dhubyan not to demand the life of his son (which indeed they have not, for they've been saying that they don't want either Shahben or Abdullah the Culprit but only the two girls of their tribe).* Although people could see through his game, al-Royshan boycotted the mediation and called for the resumption of war in the name of his tribe's honor. The sanctuary was hoping to avert this outcome by a last-minute legal maneuver. They said it was unfair for the opposition to hold up the settlement until the girls were found because no one knew where they were or whether they would ever be found. Let it be presumed, they said, that one among them, Abdullah, was responsible for their disappearance. *The Bani Dhubyan would decide what the penalty would be. Then the tribes would check with a man called Sayyadh, who is of the Bani Jabr and is supposed to be in possession of a "Book of Judgments," a sort of law book for the tribes of Khawlan. Its sources are reputed to go back to the pre-Islamic period. Sayyadh would be able to tell whether the judgment of the Bani Dhubyan is too great or too little for the given offense. The tribes would then adjust the penalty until it is equitable according to the codebook.* Although the sanctuary did at least get a judgment from Sayyadh, they failed to persuade al-Royshan and the Bani Dhubyan to go along with it.

Meanwhile, the *sada* bore the expense of hosting the mediation sessions that seemed to go nowhere. Lunch had to be provided by the wealthier families, such as the one to which Muhammad the Hunchback belonged. And for the afternoon assembly there had to be *qat*, which came as a "gift." Local *qat* suppliers were busy day and night trying to meet the demand, roaring into the sanctuary in trucks laden with the stuff. By mid-April the sanctuary was groaning under the burden of its expenses. On April 12, I wrote, *With regard to expenses incurred by [the sanctuary], I've been told the total amount so far has come to approximately 1.5 million YR [about US $333,000 at that time] measured in guns, sheep, and cows slaughtered in hospitality for the mediators and no doubt also bribes (though this, of course, was not mentioned to me). Each adult male is expected to pay 4,000 YR [about US $900] to meet the expenses [i.e., about 375 men]. Approx. 40,000 YR is coming from Sana'a and another 60,000 YR from outside the country, among the [sada] of the sanctuary who emigrated . . . Note that the burden of paying off these [expenses] falls only on "true" [members of the sanctuary]—which is to say that Hussein the Servant and others like me who live [there] are not considered its "citizens" . . . [and] are exempted. This does not mean that Hussein, who is thought to be a multimillionaire, will not contribute something as a "gift," but he is not obligated to do so . . . One has to feel sorry for the poorer sada—Ali the Bird's family, my upstairs neighbors Ahmed and Fatimah, Ahmed's brothers, and many others—who can't afford to pay the expenses. The richer houses have advanced large sums with the understanding that they will be paid back by the others . . . Little things reveal the plight of the poor: giving up qat, borrowing money, desperate search for work, etc.* But the wealthier *sada* had to give up things, too. Muhammad the Hunchback told me that he would not go on the Hajj this year because he couldn't afford it.

———

I was quite aware by this time that important poetry was being produced on the crisis in Khawlan. I wrote in my diary,

> Today Salih al-Sufi sent a *qasida* to al-Gadhi, which the latter is
> replying to. Apparently, a great deal of poetry is being produced,
> but I cannot, of course, be privy to it for political reasons until the
> negotiations are settled.

But when would that be, if ever? I thought if I showed too much interest in what was going on, people might think I was prying; yet I had to
make sure that I collected and translated enough poetry before the
texts and their various allusive references were forgotten. I had a faint
hope that Sheikh al-Gadhi might be the solution to my dilemma. One
day I saw him in the sanctuary walking to a luncheon. He stopped, we
were introduced, and he smiled. "Oh yes, I have heard of you, Seif.
You're interested in our poetry and would like to collect some."

"And who has not heard of the great Sheikh al-Gadhi?" I replied. "It's
an honor for me to meet you. I have heard that you are a great poet."

"It is you who honors us. Why don't you come to lunch?" I knew
better than to accept such an invitation. It would have to be offered
more than once before I could do so. And he was probably on his way
to a business lunch, where my presence might have proved awkward.
"Well, some other time, then." He was still friendly and charming.
"Come and visit me if you can't come to lunch. I will give you some
qasidas. Come this afternoon, if we are not having a big meeting."

I was on cloud nine for the rest of the day. But it turned out that he
was busier than he had perhaps anticipated, and every time I inquired
as to when I might see him, one of his assistants politely told me, "Tomorrow, God willing, might be a better day." The same thing happened for the next three days. On the fourth day I was told that the
sheikh was terribly sorry but perhaps when this was all over we could
get together. Just as I had suspected.

I remember all this but did not record any of it in my diary, because the demoralization brought on by not having a talk with the sheikh was too much to cope with. Only now, more than twenty years after the fact, *can* I remember it, and of course I wonder whether I have re-membered it correctly.

May 1, 1980

If I could not learn new poetry directly from the sources, I might do so indirectly. I've been making very good progress on my fieldwork largely because of the conflict between the sanctuary and Sarkhan, which has proven to be a good case study of the way poetry is used in disputes. For one whole week tribesmen have been coming to chew *qat* in my *mafraj* and giving me *zamils*. I befriended a young man, Muh'd Qasim al-Hizam of Wadi Maswar, whose hobby is collecting poetry. Unsolicited by me, he volunteered to collect *zamils* for me, writing them down in one of my notebooks (at his request).

An oddity of the diary entry is that it makes it seem as though I met Muhammad for the first time in late April, but this was not the case, for I distinctly remember him approaching me much earlier. Why was he absent from the diary until then? I suspect that when I first met him, I still thought of the sanctuary as my primary field site and the *sada* as my principal informants except when tribesmen came to visit me. Among the latter Muhammad was not so much a poet as an aficionado, and I did not at first take his talents seriously. By March I had changed my mind, not only about him but about my whole strategy for study-ing tribal poetry, and had begun my forays into Khawlan, visiting Salih al-Sufi in al-ʿAin. It was then that Muhammad the Maswari took on added significance. It's as though a figure who'd been in the back-ground now emerged in the foreground, catching me unawares. I went on to write about him in the same entry in a startling way which I now read with what I can only describe as chagrin.

Muhammad Qasim is an interesting guy. Bright and sensitive with an excellent analytical mind, he makes a wonderful informant. He's also a good friend and I enjoy his company. There's not the slightest hint of sexual attraction between us, which is also refreshing. When he professes such warm feelings of friendship, I know it's the real thing.

In truth, I was attracted to Muhammad but had repressed my feelings for him, and for good reason. I thought they would not have been reciprocated, and the last thing I needed was to have my life made complicated—even perhaps endangered—by such a relationship. What troubles me now about what I wrote is its implication that other Yemeni acquaintances were coming on to me, which was far from true. It betrays what some of the people in the sanctuary, like Ali the Bird's father, did, projecting a completely false sexuality onto certain behavior. To be sure, once in a while an acquaintance or stranger alluded to the possibility of sex with me, but this was rare, and I was always prudent enough to claim ignorance of what they were saying (the advantage of being a nonnative speaker), no matter how attractive the possibility might have seemed. In hindsight, I think I viewed Muhammad as the "pure" friend precisely because he seemed to have no other motive for working with me than intrinsic interest in my project. He once remarked to someone, "You think I have to want something from Seif in order to help him on this thing, don't you? Money for *qat*, a trip to America, whatever. It doesn't occur to you that we might both like poetry and each other's company, and that that is enough." I think I was not alone in needing this Platonic ideal of friendship.

It was a friendship largely forged in work, which was both a source of its exhilaration and a strain. The occasions when Muhammad and I got together were dedicated to the work of recording poetry and understanding it, and little else. The intensity and dedication of our engagement made possible a bond between us that was the strongest I experienced in Yemen, whether with Yemeni or non-Yemeni. At the same time, however, because the work became connected to a disruptive, even dangerous event, those were not the most relaxed or happy circumstances in which to enjoy a friendship.

For me to understand the poetry that we listened to, Muhammed

had to give me information on the ongoing event and its various political contexts. As a result, I saw it largely through his eyes. We became
chroniclers of it together. How much and what kind of information to
give me, without compromising certain parties, were always his deci-
sions, and though it was sometimes hard for me to fathom how he
arrived at them, I respected them. I knew it was important to keep
sources anonymous.

You have to imagine the scene, he would say. Here in the wadi is
Sheikh al-Gadhi in his tent, ready to receive the various mediators. One
by one they come, the head sheikh from each tribe along with his escort,
and they chant their poems to him. Here's the *zamil* from the poet ad-
Daba from the ʿArush. That's al-Ghadir's Tribe, a subtribe of the Garwa:

> O Gadhi, know my words and my plea, O towering peak.
> If there were still powerful tribes left, they would not abandon the
>   lords of Qureysh.
> The tribes of Khawlan have been ground into the dirt since the death
>   of Naji [bin Ali al-Ghadir]. They've become weaklings, O Merciful
>   One.
> Their dynamo, machine, and spark plugs are busted! If tribalism were
>   to ride, it would soon be finished [pronounced fi-nesh].
> If Naji were still alive, he could have driven it sideways and filled the
>   countryside with the might of the army.
> A gloomy night has fallen on politics, and wisdom is obscured. O
>   tribes, woe to you.

Immediately Muhammad would launch into a fluid interpretation. "You
see, Seif, the poet is complaining that the tribes cannot solve their
own problems because there is no strong leader like the legendary
al-Ghadir to steer the negotiations. Of course, the poet is from al-
Ghadir's own tribe, and so he's celebrating one of his own. But there's a
certain truth to what he says. Ever since the end of the civil war—really
from the time that the several sheikhs from Khawlan, including al-
Ghadir—were assassinated, there have been no effective leaders. Look
how he makes use of the metaphor of the car, suggesting that Khawlan is

like an automobile and that a leader has to know how to drive it." He laughed. "And al-Ghadir was effective enough to have driven the automobile sideways, if necessary, to keep the region on the course to peace."

I chimed in. "I like the way he uses a variant of the English word *finish* to rhyme with the Arabic word for army [*jesh*]. Did you know that that word came from English? But, Muhammad, tell me, what was happening in the dispute that made the poet doubt the efficacy of the Khawlan leadership?"

"Well, the Bani Dhubyan, who as you know are backing the sheikh from Sarkhan and his grievances against the sanctuary, refuse to settle until the girls are found. But no one now knows their whereabouts, and they may never show up. So the mediators are saying that the Bani Dhubyan have to give up their demand and settle anyway. The trouble is, no one is persuasive enough or powerful enough to convince them, not even Sheikh al-Gadhi."

"Why won't they drop their claim?"

"Nobody knows for sure. In some ways, they are honor-bound to fight until the girls are retrieved, even though they may never be. But there comes a point when any reasonable person has to give up hope."

"When does one know the point has been reached?" I asked. "Who decides?"

"The Bani Dhubyan insist that we are not there yet," Muhammad explained. "They insist that the search must continue. Others are saying the search has gone on long enough and that we must try to settle our differences by other means. It's up to Sheikh al-Gadhi to persuade the Bani Dhubyan to settle peacefully."

"But I thought that unless the girls were found there could be no solution. I thought this was a point of honor for the Sarkhan from which they could not back down."

"Even honor can be carried too far, Seif. Search parties scoured the countryside and came up empty-handed. The boy was tortured, and he insisted that he didn't know what had become of the girls after he left them in the hotel room. The sheikhs confronted the hotel owner in Taiz, as you know, and still they found no trace of them. Now we have to assume that they'll never be found and get on with it."

"What do *you* think happened to them?"

"Maybe they were sold into prostitution, or they sought protection from a powerful sheikh who agreed to shelter and hide them."

"Or maybe, Muhammad, someone found them after all, but whoever it was decided to kill them."

"And why do you suppose that, Seif?"

"Oh, it's not my theory so much as the talk I hear. In the sanctuary they think there are people in Khawlan who want to make trouble for them by prolonging the dispute."

In another *zamil* poem Sheikh al-Gadhi concurred with the view that the national leadership of Yemen was weak, which was why the dispute would drag on interminably, but his solution, put forward in one of his *zamils*, was different.

> The sanctuary is unjustly treated for the driver and the two girls.
> Everyone has swung an ax at them.
> God, the Judge and Knower of Innocence, understands who is vile and
>   base.
> Security has left with the sada Hamid al-Din. Those who came after
>   are like the skinnings of animals.

When he said, "Security has left with the *sada* Hamid al-Din," he meant that the ability to impose a general peace on the tribes departed with the last royal house of Yemen. Whether it had in fact been able to do so and for how long is a matter of debate, but the belief that it indeed had had this power served those who were sympathetic to the former monarchy. By contrast, it was often said that the present government of Yemen was weak or, as the poem suggested, no more than "the skinnings of animals"—a ringing rebuke, to say the least. The last line is a daring one, given the sheikh's position in the parliament, and I wondered whether it had been added to the poem without his knowledge or permission. Whereas the previous poem had decried the lack of leadership among the tribes, here it was the lack of leadership in the country as a whole that was being criticized. The poem could have ended with a paean to the former president al-Hamdi, widely regarded as a powerful and effective leader, assassinated in his prime, but that it didn't and that it invoked the royalists instead made it implicitly condemnatory of the republic as a form of government in and of itself.

The ⁛Arush were not the only Khawlan tribe to weigh in, and Muhammad was not the only one to share their opinions with me. Here is a poem that Muhammad the Lame picked up at one of the negotiations with Sheikh al-Gadhi, a *zamil* from the Bani Jabr:

> My greetings to you, says a Jabri, O people who exert every
>   conceivable effort.
> Revenge killing has been fixed by custom since ancient times.
> If the murderer is killed in revenge, then the custom of the
>   grandfathers
> Dictates that the victim's family be satisfied. If the victim's family fails
>   to take revenge,
> Then the murderer's family can kill the guilty one [to end the dispute].

No wonder Muhammad the Lame recorded this poem and passed it on to me, for it made the argument that the *sada* had been urging all along: that Abdullah the Culprit be handed over for a revenge killing to cancel the crime he had committed against the girls and their tribe, which would end the matter. Muhammad the Lame was intrigued not only by the poem's rhetoric; he was one of the few *sada* who could savor its uncommonly elegant construction. With unbelievable compactness it squeezed a fairly complex legal principle into a metrically tight-fitting structure of only a few lines. I would come across him in the marketplace reciting it to me, tripping over its clotted syllables but relishing its meaning.

A poem of such brilliance would inspire a garland of replies, and it is not surprising that Sheikh al-Gadhi, himself a great poet, composed a reply. Muhammad the Maswari supplied me with the text:

> Double greeting, O lock and pillar of Khawlan, greeting as strong as
>   the army's pride in black Mount al-Tiyal.

Loyalty is alive. But the one who is wronged is unable to render
    judgment. We have crippled the one born to leave the tribes weak.
If the adversary has been strengthened and has given "an eye for an
    eye," then his obligations have been fulfilled.
If he has been demolished, then he will have to endure his throat being
    cut with a sickle.
An eye for an eye! The bully is resisted even by the Jews, O
    al-Saalami, al-Jalud, and al-Qudri ᶜAbdul-Hakim.
The demand has been made. The judgment is in nine clauses. You look
    for the missing girls, and Shahben has been taken to Yarim.

I had to work hard with Muhammad to unpack the references of this
complex poem. Sheikh al-Gadhi is implying that the plaintiff in the
case, the sheikh from Sarkhan, cannot make a decision even though the
"one born to leave the tribes weak"—the culprit Abdullah, whose deed
brought the tribes to their present impasse—had been "crippled" (in
other words, tortured). He then lays out the options for the plaintiff.
The sanctuary has been "strengthened"—defended by the tribes of
Khawlan—and so cannot be pushed around. Besides, the *sada* have
handed over the culprit for revenge killing. As for the imbroglio with
the Hashid, it, too, has been cleared up. Sheikh al-Gadhi has made al-
Royshan hand over the son of the Taiz hotel owner, Shahben, to be put
in government custody in Yarim, where he awaits his fate after his guilt
or innocence is determined. Now that these conditions have been met,
it is only right that the plaintiff try to negotiate in good faith. For the
sheikh of Sarkhan and his supporters to refuse to negotiate now is to go
against the will of the majority and to act like dictators. These are mentioned by name: Sheikh al-Saalami, of the Bani Dhubyan; al-Jalud, one
of history's most infamous tyrants; and al-Qudri, a former leader. As if
to mock their challenge, the sheikh reminds the Bani Dhubyan that the
bully was "resisted even by the Jews." Muhammad went on to explain
that no tribe could act against the will of the majority, for doing so
would risk the autonomy of the entire region by placing it in the hands
of a potential tyrant. The tribes' freedom had to be protected against
such threats, even if it meant going to war against the Bani Dhubyan.

Sometime in April, Hussein al-Gadhi replied to the *zamil* by the poet ad-Daba from al-ʿArush.

> Welcome as great as the wind that whistles around the canyon bends,
> As great as the rain clouds that mass to launch their attack.
> God will know, as will the lads in the bulwarks:
> The seven tribes are there to strike down the enemy with hammer blows.
> If there is war, the beautiful-eyed ones will wax proud and ululate for the masterful lads.
> The seven tribes are in the position of outsiders and emigrate to lower Yemen.
> Woe to the sada, if there is no cure, after their sheep have been slaughtered and their bread eaten.

It was clear—rain clouds gathering in the storm, young men at the bulwarks—that war was imminent. "The sheikh warns that if Sarkhan and its allies remain obstinate and refuse to negotiate," Muhammad continued with his commentary, "then there will be war to punish those who go against the consensus." Thus, if the plaintiff were to act against the will of the consensus slowly building in favor of the sanctuary, he would have to be resisted by force. The most interesting line to me was "The seven tribes are in the position of outsiders and emigrate to lower Yemen." I asked Muhammad, "What does that mean?"

"It means that if Khawlan loses the war with Sarkhan and the Bani Dhubyan, the defenders of the sanctuary will be like emigrants who must leave the country."

The *sada* had been vociferously complaining about all the *qat* and food they had provided the mediators on their visits to the sanctuary during the endless dispute, so Sheikh al-Gadhi decided to move the negotiations to another venue, a marketplace, al-Hadharim, at the foot of Mount al-Tiyal in central Khawlan, the traditional meeting place of the tribes at times of crisis.

The Bani Dhubyan stuck to their old position. Here's a *zamil* composed by one of their main sheikhs, al-Damani (the other paramount sheikh being the alleged dictator al-Saalami):

> The host said, "Welcome, O hijra of the seven tribes."
> I say that there are conditions in this case.
> Three of them: you arrest those present, the one who transported
> them, and grab the greedy one.
> All that because of the girls.

I failed to indicate in my field notes what "you arrest those present" might have meant, and I may have even forgotten to ask Muhammad the Maswari. Did it mean the sanctuary as a whole should be held accountable, according to the tribal legal principle of collective guilt? I'm afraid I will never know the answer. But "the one who transported them" could be none other than Abdullah the Culprit, and the "greedy one" was the hotel owner in Taiz. Nothing had essentially changed in the Sarkhan position. "All that because of the girls," the poet concludes, as if everyone agreed about what had happened to them, though their fate was in fact being hotly contested. Had they been abducted against their will, as the Sarkhan assumed, or had they paid Abdullah the Culprit to take them out of their village, as he maintained? Some argued that he must have been telling the truth, since his confession was extracted under duress. Others suggested just the opposite: that to exonerate himself in the eyes of the sanctuary, he had lied about the girls *even* under such circumstances in order that the judgment would go easier on the *sada*.

By this point, news of the dispute had spread across Yemen and even abroad. A poet from Wadi Maswar, Muhammad's turf, said at al-Hadharim:

> The news is in Bajil, and I fear they will put it down in the register.
> A broadcast with the details leaving honor degraded.

Bajil is a town in Yemen; the poet could have chosen any other, for the point is that the event in Khawlan was being noted everywhere. And because people were talking about it, the honor not only of the Sarkhan but of Khawlan as a whole was being besmirched. This "talk" threatened the reputations of everyone concerned, thus increasing the pressure on them to act "honorably" (as so viewed by the participants). That is why the poet continued:

> O al-Saalami, fighter, he who is killed will obtain martyrdom,
> Until the baskets are returned from the side of the watercourse, even
>   if dead.

The poet is not advising Sheikh al-Saalami to fight—far from it, since he is also exhorting him to accept the fact that the girls will not be returned; he is saying that he can understand why al-Saalami thinks his honor is at stake and therefore persists in fighting until the girls are returned.

Not everyone was convinced, however, that the poet's motives were pure. After seeing how prosperous the sanctuary was, with its rich agricultural lands and imposing stone houses, Sheikh al-Damani wanted some of its wealth. A poet siding with the sanctuary and its supporters noted:

> Individuals of Khawlan al-Tiyal say, "There's no excuse for us not to
>   plunge into battle."
> If al-Damani wants to fill sacks with the sanctuary's gold,
> Then let him have it! (Shoot him.) Why still this delay?

Muhammad the Maswari and others spoke disparagingly about the Bani Dhubyan as "Bedouin" and about their predatory history of raiding agricultural settlements. Greed more than honor was motivating the Bani Dhubyan to go to war against the sanctuary, it seemed, and nothing al-Gadhi could say would change their minds.

6

∾

WAR

At the end of April, Sheikh Hussein Ali al-Gadhi left the sanctuary in disgust. I assumed he was peeved by the Bani Dhubyan's refusal to settle, but Muhammad the Maswari shed a different light on his departure. *[It] is supposed to be a "deep secret" that the Bani Siham have been fighting the Bani Dhubyan over tribal boundaries for the past five months. About forty people of the Siham tribe have been killed, and al-Gadhi is their sheikh. Now it stands to reason that the Bani Dhubyan would doubt al-Gadhi's impartiality . . . Another point worth mentioning is that the Bani Suhman are allies of the Bani Siham in the tribal boundary dispute, and the Bani Dhubyan may fear that the sheikh is trying to forge an alliance against them. In his stead, the al-Giri sheikhs and the houses of Wadi Maswar (my friend Muhammad's clan) became more prominent in the negotiations. For my fieldwork, this had the result that I could see more of Muhammad, which allowed me to work with him on the poetry of the dispute.*

That I would see mainly the mediator's and sanctuary's sides in the dispute should come as no surprise. I did not learn until much later the Bani Dhubyan's view, and it went something like this: Ostensibly mobilizing its forces to defend the sanctuary, Khawlan was in actuality threatening the capital, trying to pressure the North Yemeni government into retreating from its policy of unification with South Yemen. The accusation cut even deeper, implying that Khawlan was working in concert with a foreign power—unnamed but probably Saudi Arabia. This thesis sounded fantastic, but it gained plausibility by the following occurrence. Sometime in April a truck filled with Saudi riyals was found abandoned by the side of the road in Khawlan. This much even I knew at the time. The inference drawn by the Bani Dhubyan was that the anti-unification party in Khawlan was being paid by agents of Saudi Arabia to oppose the government's policy. Of course, this meant that the North Yemeni state might have been covertly supporting the Bani Dhubyan so that it would have allies in case of an offensive against Sana'a launched by the Saudis or, more likely, their proxies.

It might help to understand the conflict, as it grew and changed course from January until April, by borrowing a term from physics. *Resonance* is a word used to describe vibration that passes from one body to another in such a way that the two vibrate synchronically and sometimes synergistically. A local tremor, for example, produces vibration along adjacent fault lines, which in turn can magnify the energy of the initial seismic event, possibly causing an earthquake. When one prong of a steel tuning fork is struck, it sounds a particular note, and almost immediately the other prong vibrates at the same energy to emit the same note, the two prongs now vibrating together to amplify the sound. As with resonating bodies, so with the initial event and the successive waves of tensions it produced. A local conflict over honor started in January between sanctuary and tribe, and immediately set off tremors along the ramifying fault lines of the political system: first in what might loosely be called competing ethnic groups (*sada*, tribe, and servant group); then in blocks at the regional level (the Bani Dhubyan versus the rest of Khawlan) and the national level (Hashid versus Bakil; Khawlan versus the North Yemeni government); and finally in adjacent countries (North Yemen versus Saudi Arabia). As a result of these perturbations, the event itself grew in scale, complexity, and volatility.

Around the time the truck was found, an older man in the sanctuary asked me, "Do you think you could give us some money?"

"What do you mean? For cigarettes?"

"No, I mean lots of money. For guns and other things?"

I was completely taken aback. I did not connect what he was saying with the incident of the truck. People knew I had worked in Saudi Arabia. Did they think perhaps I was an agent working with that country?

"I don't know what you're talking about. Do you think I'm the Bank of America?"

One can get a sense of the Bani Dhubyan's position by listening to a poem that Sheikh al-Saalami composed in April in response to the poem issued by Abu Talib several weeks earlier.

> I saw the danger encompassing the ranks of Khawlan, befalling the en-
> tire society, due to the scheming of the spinner,
> A danger that will put an end to the tribes, burn them up. And some of
> our wise men want it, indeed accept it.
> How many wretched men hope to benefit their own party by
> hardening the position of the sanctuary's sada.
> Souls [consciences] have died in order that others might profit. If the
> profiteers had not caused trouble, they would not have earned their
> bread.
> Patience is a virtue. We've been patient with the people of the
> sanctuary. Compassion [too is a virtue]. We are opposed only to
> those parties that try to spread the danger.
> A protector of Khawlan [are we], so that it will not disunite and lose
> its position of strength, its men perishing,
> So that the hypocrite's aim will not be implemented and he who is
> controlled by money will not cause problems.
> . . .
> You see al-Saalami, O [Salih] al-Sufi, distressed today by the tragedy of
> the Khawlan tribes.
> What is your opinion of the black, white, and blue? To me send your
> responses with an equivalent meaning.
> Inside souk al-Hadharim they are driving their cars. They sell and buy.
> He who pays, takes it.
> . . .
> Neither is a solution found nor reasons [for the dispute] unraveled.
> And the daughter is still absent from her father . . .

The poem is filled with allusions to "hypocrites" and "infiltrators," meaning that certain negotiators who claimed to be working solely for a good resolution to the dispute were actually pursuing their own political and financial gain with the help of outside powers. There is a premonition of bloodshed.

This poem more than anything would have unnerved me and sent me packing had I heard it when it was issued, but Muhammad the Maswari did not share it with me. I now find this odd. It is inconceivable that he was not aware of the poem. At the time I did not suspect a political motive in his friendship with me, yet I knew that he was opposed to Yemeni unification and therefore would have come under suspicion as possibly working against the state. Was he interested in me because of my project, or was he, too, trying to find out whether I was an American political agent working with the Saudis to destabilize the central government in Sana'a?

When al-Saalami said in his poem that his tribe was patient with the people of the sanctuary, he was being sincere, for he believed that the latter, not he, had been stubborn. According to his lights, the sanctuary, not the Bani Dhubyan, had needlessly prolonged the process by insisting on having the entire region agree to peace terms. And there was no reason to think that it would be fruitless to continue to search for the missing girls, he argued. Who decides, after all, how much time is enough? For his part, al-Saalami was patience personified, and as he reminded us with not a little irony, patience is a "virtue."

I never met al-Saalami, never even saw him or learned much about him. I only knew some of his poetry. Salih bin Gasim al-Sufi, the man to whom the poem was addressed, was a different matter. I had visited him in March and decided to take up his invitation to see him again. The fact that he was retired from the army and leading a more or less sedentary life was to my advantage, for the odds were that he would be at home when I called on him. This was an era before telephones, let alone cell phones.

For about an hour and without an escort, I walked across the ancient volcanic hills to al-ʿAin. Except for a shepherd tending his flock or a solitary man on his way to the sanctuary from a nearby hamlet, I seemed to be entirely alone. I was a little apprehensive at first, looking over my shoulder from time to time, for I would have made an easy target. I knew full well the extent of the animosity between the people of al-ʿAin and the sanctuary, and of course in the minds of the former I was not exactly a friend or ally. I remembered the man from al-Ghars who had tried to intimidate me with his veiled threat, but then I decided that my fears were exaggerated. I focused my attention on the desolate but beautiful landscape, hoping it would calm me—gullies choked by giant boulders, here and there a succulent plant thrusting its stalk through the fissures, its prickly leaves drooping like the ears of a bloodhound, no sound except the wind. Fear soon gave way to forlornness, and I hastened my step. I didn't care if I bloodied my toes stubbing them on a rock; I wanted to be among people again so badly that I almost ran down the hill toward al-ʿAin as soon as it came into view.

Though Salih al-Sufi had no visible means of support apart from his pension, he seemed comfortably well-off, if not well-to-do. A man getting on in years by Yemeni standards, he was vigorous and lithe in body and very sharp mentally. His craggy face was handsome, with gray stubble for a beard. I remember best his clear, resonant voice, to which I would listen with all my powers of concentration. I could not describe him as jovial, though he was not without flashes of humor either. When we went to sleep that first night in his sitting room, he gave me some bolsters to put under and next to my head, saying he would be "on the other side of the bulwarks," a sly reference to the sanctuary dispute and our respective positions on it.

I asked Salih if he could show me the *qasida* he had composed for Sheikh al-Gadhi. To my surprise, he agreed. I could follow the outline of his recitation but not the details. For those I would have to get Muhammad the Maswari's help.

> Tribes of Saba, the seven tribes! The day you mobilize with right
> against wrong, long life to you!

We know the one drowning in greed for money. His soul is vicious,
    lost in straying [from the path of righteousness].

There are a few persons clamoring, signaling to the Ba^cth party, asking
    their hand in marriage.

Khawlan does not yield to someone who comes to incite. Even if he
    comes with Ba^cthist money and gives it all.

He who has lost his honor cannot hurt [Khawlan] through the
    deception, stratagems, and trickery he has built for it.

A graven image will be with us if we do not block the pass to every
    cunning person who denies its nobility.

O Saalami, stop the flowery talk and let our tribes march as directed.

Already your friends and Ahmed Ali Salih are sympathetic toward the
    hijra of Khawlan, surrounded by tribes.

A place of great learning, of progress, it is patiently bearing everything
    that has happened to it.

Their youth supply the hotels with grapes from vineyards no one may
    enter.

They took to Taiz clusters of razigi grapes, and they notified one who
    buys and sells them.

Let them return, if they are still unused, in a box, and to the good people
    give recompense for patiently bearing the problems.

How many times did we meet before the branch sprouted leaves in
    order to make right the moral positions, which have become
    unclean.

We arrived when all of you were still mobilizing, and we said that it
    might still happen that God would correct the state of affairs.

The machine guns of every one of you were in position, a secret target
    erected whose bull's-eye they hit.

Khawlan incited its army, and it gathered, setting up its tents and
    occupying the hills.

Magsa^c [head sheikh of the Sinhan, the president's tribe] the noble
    one, came, the immediate neighbor of Khawlan. His intention was
    to lift tribalism from its servitude.

He saw the tribes convening in the floodplain. He knew their politics
    and its intricacies.

His people were with him the day the guns were received [as
  guarantees of the truce].
With him were the leaders of Khawlan, to whom he gave justice
  in full.
He made every sacrifice for the two sides. He encountered only
  ignoramuses and losers among the people.
He left the politicians, who were going around in circles, and
  abandoned all the evil ones and their followers.
Valiant men came from the Bakil like flashes of lightning who wanted
  to solve the problem by transporting it.
It is true that there is no solution they can agree to. I regret that the
  problem solvers seem to be biased.
Already tribalism has been divorced from its people a thousand times.
  It has departed the land of Yemen.

The poet was clearly criticizing al-Saalami for being out of step with
the rest of Khawlan. I was somewhat surprised by this, but I was learning that the position of the Bani Dhubyan, while it might have been
united, was not uniform. "Already your friends and Ahmed Ali Salih are
sympathetic toward the *hijra* of Khawlan, surrounded by tribes."
Ahmed Ali Salih was the sheikh of Sarkhan, and the line suggested that
he and others who were allied with the Bani Dhubyan thought the dispute had gone far enough and should be settled.

"It was really al-Saalami who was holding out, not the fathers of the
girls," Muhammad the Maswari later explained.

Al-Sufi did not cast aspersions on the sanctuary, as others had done,
instead calling it "a place of great learning, of progress" that was "patiently bearing everything that has happened to it." Yet at the same
time, he held not just one individual responsible for the abduction but
the sanctuary's youth as a whole. "They took to Taiz clusters of *razigi*
grapes, and they notified one who buys and sells them" (i.e., the youth
of the sanctuary took the girls to Shahben, the hotel owner). The implication was that they were nothing better than pimps. I was shocked
by this accusation. I asked Muhammad whether the poet literally
meant that the sanctuary youth were involved in some sort of prostitu-

tion ring. Not directly, no, was his surmise, but their "loose morals" contributed to a climate such that a perverse act of the sort Abdullah had committed could be possible. He elaborated: "Many of them did-n't grow up in Khawlan but lived in Sana'a or even abroad, where they learned all kinds of immoral things from foreigners, or so some people, like the poet of al-ᶜAin, think. What Abdullah did any one of them is capable of." I already knew the claptrap about the *sada* youth having been corrupted. The Bani Dhubyan even made a threatening demand at this time for the removal of the sanctuary's *hijra* status on the grounds that it had lost its moral authority, but Muhammad assured me that this would never happen.

"Muhammad, what does the poet mean by 'the branch sprouted leaves' in the line 'How many times did we meet before the branch sprouted leaves'?"

"It means the thing with Shahben."

Muhammad also explained that Magsaᶜ was not only sheikh of the Sinhan but a state agent working with the Khawlan leaders to bring about a settlement. According to the poet, a settlement hadn't been reached because the mediators were "biased." Again Muhammad came to my rescue. "He's talking here about Sheikh Hussein Ali al-Gadhi's tribe having had disagreements with the Bani Dhubyan, which suppos-edly made them unfit mediators. But others have mediated, too, who have had no such history with the Bani Dhubyan, and they haven't succeeded either. It's because al-Saalami has a different agenda."

"And what is that?"

"Some say that when he saw the mighty houses in the sanctuary and the green fields around them, like his colleague al-Damani he decided he was going to hold out for more money."

"Is it possible that he could have a political agenda as well?"

Muhammad looked at me blankly.

Changing the subject, I asked what the poet might mean by the line 'There are a few persons clamoring, signaling to the Baᶜthi party, ask-ing their hand in marriage." The Baᶜthists were the ruling party of Iraq, but what did that have to do with anything?

"He really means South Yemen, a socialist state like Iraq. And when he adds, 'Khawlan does not yield to someone who comes to incite. Even if he comes with Baᶜthist money and gives it all,' he means that we won't be bribed into agreeing with the state's southern policy."

"So, the poet is against this policy?"

"Absolutely."

"Well, let me ask you then, might al-Saalami have an agenda in regard to this policy?"

"Like what?"

"Could he be taking money from South Yemen to advance a pro-unification government? Is that what the poet means when he says that Khawlan will not agree even if it is bribed by Baᶜthist money? Meaning money from the South?"

"Seif, you have to decide for yourself what it means."

"True, but I also want to know what you think."

Muhammad simply shrugged his shoulders. I realized I ought not to push the question further.

Like so many of the other voices in this dispute, the poet's was ultimately critical of "tribalism," "divorced from its people a thousand times." Tribalism was not working in Yemen, then, I said. "Well, that remains to be seen, doesn't it?" was Muhammad's response.

Events in Khawlan were mirroring what was happening elsewhere in Yemen. I communicated as much in a letter to my father, though in order not to worry him I did not mention that the sanctuary was being attacked.

April 8, 1980.
Dear Dad: . . . North Yemen is almost certain to be in another war this year. Not that I am speaking with any authority other than personal opinion, but tensions are building everywhere and nothing in sight to defuse the situation. SA [Saudi Arabia] is becoming aggressively militant on the northern border, the south is only biding its time for a "golden opportunity," and we poor bastards in the middle

are waiting and holding our breath. It seems increasingly clear (again my personal opinion) that SA [Saudi Arabia] with U.S. encouragement is preparing for some grand scenario of confrontation with its southern communist neighbor, but it will, of course, be NY [North Yemen] that will be caught in the squeeze play.

All of which does not bode well for my research. I'm working like a fiend to get my basic data collection finished so that I can start writing a preliminary draft of the thesis. If real trouble should start on a serious scale, I hope to get out in a hurry and salvage my dissertation.

Fortunately, my prediction of war did not come true, but why was I convinced of its likelihood in 1980? We already know something about the tensions between North and South Yemen brought on by the cold war. Let us now look more carefully at relations between North Yemen and its neighbor to the north and east.

There was a long twentieth-century history of animosity between Saudi Arabia and Yemen, starting with war in 1933 over the ᶜAsir, the mountainous region to the north of the present-day Yemen-Arabia border that was incorporated into Saudi Arabia in 1934 but that Yemen claimed for itself on what were fairly legitimate historical, cultural, and political grounds. Among the issues left unresolved by that dispute, besides a festering sore over regional claims, was the delimitation of a border, which up to this day has been the cause of periodic armed skirmishes. (In the 1980s, with the discovery of oil in Yemen's eastern Marib Governate, the lingering question over the border with Saudi Arabia has, if anything, grown more acute and acrimonious.) The Yemeni civil war in 1962–74, with Egyptian military assistance for the republican side, was viewed by Saudi Arabia as a serious threat to its national interests, for now the Soviet Union seemed to have gained a toehold in the Arabian Peninsula. When South Yemen became a militarily powerful communist state with strong ties to the USSR, the threat to Saudi Arabia grew more ominous. Though the kingdom steadily expanded its army and increased its purchase of military equipment, it mostly flexed its economic muscles when attempting to wield power and influence, as it did during the oil embargo against the United States and Europe in 1973. In Yemen, its influence took the form of financial aid, ranging from the direct payment of government bureaucrats' salaries to the funding of covertly pro-Saudi groups such as Wahhabi religious schools.

Besides this long history of conflict, the other factor I thought made war conceivable in 1980 was the relative weakness of the Yemeni state. If by mid-April the North Yemeni government had seemingly neutralized the threat from South Yemen by agreeing to unify by decade's end, this step had angered the Saudis, fearing as they did the formation of what they (and everyone else) assumed would be a Marxist country united against them, and they were determined to do anything to stop it. Anything short of direct armed conflict, that is, which is why events such as the one in Khawlan were so dangerous, because in them the kingdom might be able to induce others to do its dirty work—for a price, of course, and in a shared ideological cause. Armed conflict subsidized by Saudi Arabia could successfully destabilize Ali Abdullah Salih's regime, leading to the formation of a government presumably more in line with Saudi interests. Add to this mix world historical events, such as the Iranian Revolution, the invasion of Afghanistan, and the takeover of the Haram Mosque by Muslim extremists—all in 1979 and all exacerbating Saudi Arabia's sense of vulnerability—and it is quite plausible that the kingdom might have planned a move in the country nearest to it and most subject to its influence.

By the end of April, the sanctuary had the look of an armed camp. Men whom I had ordinarily seen unarmed were milling about with weapons strapped to their shoulders. One day an older man with a Kalashnikov greeted me solemnly. "Isn't there somewhere you can go, Seif? It might be safer if you went to Sana'a for a few weeks and took a vacation." I should have taken the hint, but I was making headway on my project, and I wanted to see what other poetry on the dispute I could gather. I still had not prepared a chronicle of the events that had occurred since early January to which the poetry was connected, and I wanted to work on it *en place*.

Then the first tremor of war could be felt. In my diary I wrote,

> Last night, May 5, shooting broke out again between [Sarkhan] and the [sanctuary]. My house seemed to be the target, and a few bullets apparently entered the upper story, but I never was in any real danger. It lasted only a few minutes, and the rest of the evening was quiet. No one knows who started it. Nevertheless, tonight I'll sleep in my *mafraj*.
>
> Salah al-Qiri [the poet I met in the sanctuary souk and a son of Muhammad al-Qiri, one of the main sheikhs of Khawlan] has been very helpful in my research.

I wonder now whether it was literally true that my house was the target or whether someone was trying to scare me into leaving. If the gunfire was intended to intimidate me, it obviously failed. If my house were to come under further fire, I reasoned that it would simply be because it was so prominent, being the second building in the village, and not because I lived in it. I seemed to think my fieldwork could proceed unhindered.

Once shooting broke out, the mediators—from Khawlan, these now included only Muhammad al-Qiri and his son, the two sheikhs of Wadi Maswar along with my friend Muhammad, and the paramount sheikh of the Bani Bahlul tribe—negotiated another truce. Meanwhile, I learned that Sheikh Hussein Ali al-Gadhi had issued a response to the poems by al-Saalami and al-Sufi.

> [Welcome] to Sufi and Dhubyani, covering the towering peaks, from people of nobility and generosity. Long life to the tribes!
>
> Welcome to the poems from the two astute ones. May the welcome cover Mount al-Tiyal, whose call we rush to answer.
>
> [Welcome] from your brothers of Khawlan, the standard-bearers. Their generosity is everlasting, sacrificing themselves for the good cause.

Why are you accusing them of being a [political] party and of being
thieves? Khawlan is far from being either. It is loyal.

It is al-Saalami who has laid a foundation for the gallows. It is he who
has adopted [a party] and sown the seeds [of divisiveness].

Without the broadcasting system, he has fabricated rumors. And as
for his lie, a proverb says, "God has cut the throat and caused it
to die."

Enough pain! Lock the door! If there is a remedy, it is daylight.

How many men are living off money from the Sholagi Bank [a
well-known moneylender in Sana'a] and accumulating wealth from
American imports?

If you still lust for war, then make an appointment and we shall
rendezvous. God will not protect everyone who lights the brand
of war.

Promises of compensation have been made to you, and you are still
angry, along with four hostages whose internment is wrong.

. . .

There are those who are taken in by deception and lies. No one is
paying back wheat with corn.

Abu Nayif [al-Gadhi] listens excitedly to your speech. And I was ready
to abandon the *qasida*.

My nature is not to praise by my speech and my logic. I speak frankly
when the time has come to mobilize for war.

We hope all poets will poetize on this problem. Honor is one [i.e.,
there is no difference between us], O magnificent horned ones!

The president of Yemen is pure and honest with our people. He
contains all noble characteristics.

He who lies will become weak and come to nothing, like the person
who makes a slip of the tongue when he prattles.

He is a dead loss in the assemblies and valueless, like the girls who
card the wool in place of the girls who spin it.

And in conclusion, pray for the pious and pure one who lived in
Medina and embellished its beauty.

I want to focus for a moment on the line "Without the broadcasting system, he has fabricated rumors." Unbeknownst to me, BBC Radio had recently issued a report about Yemen, its Arabic Service had broadcast it, and it had been heard by some tribesmen in Khawlan. It was rumored in Khawlan that the report mentioned the dispute in Khawlan and said it was threatening the stability of the central government. Also unbeknownst to me at the time was the suspicion that I or someone else in the foreign community had been talking to the BBC about the dispute and its consequences. Years later I had a chance to consult the Bush House News Index—a summary of topics covered in specific news broadcasts of the BBC—for Yemen for this period as well as a copy of a report on Yemen issued by its correspondent Bob Jobbins on May 23, 1980, entitled "Yemen Contrasts." But neither of them referred to the dispute in Khawlan, let alone any possibility that the central government was threatened by it. (I was unable to obtain information from the Arabic Service to see whether it had made any other reference in another of its broadcasts.) So the line in the poem was suggesting that these rumors had been started by al-Saalami and al-Sufi and spread before they were broadcast to the outside world.

The poet vehemently denied that Khawlan was using the dispute to mobilize political opposition to the government's unification policy—forming a "party"—though he did seem to concede that money was changing hands (how else could one interpret the line "How many men are living off the money from the Sholagi Bank"?) and that perhaps this money was coming from America (the sly reference to "American imports"). It was al-Saalami who was acting disloyally, al-Gadhi insisted. For a long time I pondered over the line "No one is paying back wheat with corn," until Muhammad the Maswari clarified it for me: "He is claiming that his tribe, the Bani Suhman, are not trying to use the dispute with the sanctuary to get back at the Bani Dhubyan for their border disagreements." It is interesting that toward the end of his poem the sheikh invited other poets to "poetize" about the dispute, as if to suggest that words had not yet run their course. But on the whole the poem was pessimistic; there was little prospect that the "problem" could be solved without war.

By the middle of May, it was clear that the Qiris and the Maswaris were not making the progress they had hoped for. My field notes of May 24 more or less tell the story: *In the middle of May the tribes of Khawlan met in Jihana [Khawlan's capital]—about 20,000 of them—to try to settle the dispute between the sanctuary and Sarkhan. It was decided that they would send a delegation of about 10–15 sheikhs from Khawlan to the president in hopes that he would settle the matter. He received them but did not come up with any viable solution, so now Khawlan is back where it started . . . The president has been helping the Bani Dhubyan with money (about 40,000 YR) and food (two huge loads of grain of about 300 sacks). Public opinion attributes a twofold motive to this help: (1) he's concerned that the western branch of the Bani Dhubyan, or al-Dhubayyinah, will attack Bait al-Ahmar, his home; and (2) in case of another war with the South, he will have to count on the support of the Bani Dhubyan on the eastern border, where fighting usually breaks out. He cannot, therefore, afford to alienate the tribe.*

People are convinced that the girls are still alive and being kept secretly by Sheikh al-Royshan. AR is supposed to have received 20,000 YR from the sanctuary and Sarkhan to look for them and claims not to have found them. But if this is true, what exactly is his game? And could he really keep the whereabouts of the girls a secret from the Bani Dhubyan? Or do the latter know where they are and are scheming with AR to prolong the dispute in order to inconvenience the sanctuary as well as get more money from Shahben and the president?

Incidents keep occurring to terrify the sanctuary. A couple of weeks ago bullets were fired into a house of al-Mudir, even though a truce was in effect at the time and still is at this writing. Then a haystack was set on fire on the hills overlooking the sanctuary. Yesterday, two cars and their owners were taken into custody by Sarkhan, who demanded two women from the sanctuary in exchange for their lives. But they were returned soon thereafter unharmed. Now a complaint is being lodged against Sarkhan for its action.

What happened next was open to controversy. On June 4, men in a brown Toyota pickup drove to a point halfway between Sarkhan and the sanctuary and let off several rounds of automatic rifle fire on Sarkhan, then drove back to the sanctuary. The question was whether they had started at the sanctuary, thus making it responsible for the attack, or whether they came from somewhere else. It turned out that the driver of the car was Yahya bin Muhammad al-Qiri, one of the sheikh's sons. The sanctuary claimed that he acted in retaliation for an attack a few days earlier on his brother Salah al-Qiri, who had been fired upon by unknown assailants from Sarkhan. But Salah later denied this to me, asserting that Sarkhan had done nothing to provoke the incident and that his brother was simply drunk out of his mind and didn't know what he was doing. This was nevertheless interpreted as a blatant terrorist act against Sarkhan by its staunch defenders, the Bani Dhubyan.

June 6, 1980

Last night a very fierce war broke out in [the sanctuary] between Sarkhan and sada, with the Qiris helping them. I had been anticipating an outbreak of hostilities but assumed they would take the form I had experienced previously in [the sanctuary], but this war was much more violent, leading to at least three deaths.

Shooting started around 8:00 p.m., when the electricity was cut . . . I was sitting in pitch darkness and debated with myself whether I ought to crawl into my bedroom to get my flashlight or perhaps light a few candles in the kitchen. It was then that I heard the sharp twang of a bullet entering my bedroom and I immediately changed my mind about going after the flashlight.

Footsteps were audible above my head. Marksmen were positioning themselves in the rooms on the second floor to return the enemy fire. Occasionally someone ran through the yard only a few steps away from my window.

I remained fairly calm, primarily because I still supposed that this was not a very serious skirmish. The pressure on my bladder was more discomforting than the rattling of my nerves. Finally, I stepped gingerly into the bathroom and squatted to take a leak—fear of having my head blown off keeping me from standing. I was looking up into the night sky, seeing [what I thought were] falling stars until I realized they were streaming bullets emitted from the guns pointing out of the upstairs windows. And from the hills around could be seen the flash of answering gunfire.

I was now certain that this was a serious confrontation. I decided I would sleep in the kitchen and tried very quickly to move my bedding from the bedroom. I grabbed the flashlight along with the mattress and sheets that were entangling themselves in my feet as I scurried with my load into the kitchen. Even in the kitchen I wasn't completely safe from bullets ricocheting off the garden wall into the room, so I crouched for over an hour in a corner . . . waiting for the gunfire to abate before I moved about. But the sound of battle seemed to get more intense as the night wore on . . .

I tried to read a little with my flashlight beamed on the book (Boys of Summer [!]) but either I could not concentrate—my thoughts wandering to the eerie sounds of fighting around me—or else reading with only a flashlight proved to be too uncomfortable, and eventually I gave up. I turned off the flashlight and huddled under the covers. It occurred to me that this is what civilian victims of war must go through in places like Beirut— . . . the interminable waiting for the letup in gunfire, the suspense that grows as the menacing sounds come nearer and nearer, the anguish that goes out to some poor soul who screams in the night during the middle of it all, the brain-draining fatigue that eventually saps one's will and even one's fear so that one doesn't care anymore about one's safety—relief means an end to that relentless rat-a-tat-tat.

The Bani Dhubyan entered the yard to my house at some point in the fighting. I remember a knock on my door and my shouting " Man? [Who is it?]." The knocking continued more loudly, and I responded, "I'm an honored guest in Khawlan. I have nothing to do with this fighting. Go away!" There was no answer, but the footsteps retreated. Much looting and vandalism took place that evening, and so it may well have been that someone attempted to break into my house but was deterred by the knowledge that I was a foreigner.

. . . At one point I hear voices yelling in the village. From the semihysterical tone I can tell something ghastly has happened—probably a death—though I cannot understand clearly what is being said. What can I do to help? I'm almost grateful I'm not a doctor, otherwise they'd bring some bloody, mutilated body into the house for me to try vainly to bring back to life. I fall asleep again—too tired to feel much pity for the dead man. My only prayer is: Dear God, I hope it's not anyone I know. I don't want to be haunted by a face I'm always expecting unconsciously to meet but know I will never see again.

I don't know what time of night it is that I next hear the muezzin chanting in the mosque. At first I think it's the dawn prayer, but then I realize that it's a hymn of praise to God. I learn later that they were carrying on a funeral service for the dead man. Still dark outside. The lone faltering voice of religion in a mad counterpoint with the din of war.

At eight in the morning I woke up to find the world outside very still. I got up and got dressed and suddenly heard the unmistakable sound of zamil-chanting in the village . . . The mediators had arrived . . . [Intermediaries] in the form of the poet Salih al-Sufi and others intervened in the early morning hours, managing to bring about one day's truce. I saw and heard them sing a zamil when they marched from the big mosque in the center of [the sanctuary] to the sela [watercourse] and then proceeded to [Sarkhan]. Late in the morning other cars arrived bringing representatives of tribes from Khawlan to act as intermediaries.

[The sanctuary] helped the Qiris in this fight, though reluctantly, because they didn't, I think, want this war, which they realize drives the solution to their problems further down the road of protracted and complicated negotiations. But [the sanctuary] had little choice in the matter. They long ago had struck up an alliance . . . to the extent that people now say they "are one group." [The sanctuary] may have discovered that its allies have proved to be more of a hindrance than a help . . .

The Sufis [the poet and his relatives the Royshans] are now [back] in a position of strength. The Qiris are out of the running as intermediaries, and [the sanctuary], which now sees them as a liability rather than an asset, may try to bargain with the Sufis in spite of their reservations. There is certainly no one else with the same clout to turn to for help—but what a "friend" to have to rely on! As the poet Salih al-Sufi remarked to me in another context, "The people of [the sanctuary] really are poor bastards!"

As it turned out, five men died, three immediately and two others from their wounds later that day, and one was Yahya al-Qiri. It was for him, apparently, that the nighttime service was held in the mosque. The rest of the dead were from a branch of the Bani Dhubyan, one of them a young man who had given me a zamil poem in the marketplace some weeks earlier. Muhammad the Hunchback sadly told me the news. "Remember him, Seif? He was from Sarkhan." People in the sanctuary told me it was a miracle that none of them was killed. "Our best defense," they told me, "has always been God and the Qur'an." Gimme a break, you self-righteous jerks, I thought to myself. You had a helluva lot of tribesmen helping you.

In the morning I tried to get to Sana'a, but every vehicle leaving the village was already occupied with women and children and their assorted baggage. I expected pandemonium, but while people were obviously worried they weren't panicking. The men stayed behind to help defend the sanctuary in case the truce did not hold, and they were saying goodbye to their families calmly.

I was determined not to spend another night in the sanctuary if I could help it. If I could not get out by taxi, I would walk out, perhaps to a neighboring town. I went back to my house to pack what I could carry on my back—tapes, tape recorder and camera, notes, a few documents including my passport, and a change of underwear. I spent the rest of the morning writing in my diary. Or was it my field notes? The stories of my life and of the event were now fatefully intertwined, and I could hardly tell them apart. When I finished and looked out the window, the *hijra* was almost deserted. Not more than thirty men could have been counted on to defend it at that point, but the mountains all around were occupied by the enemy. "If no reinforcements come to the *hijra* soon, the enemy will have no trouble overrunning it," I wrote in my diary. The truce would run out in the evening of the next day. Fear clawed at the insides of my stomach.

And then Muhammad the Maswari appeared at my doorstep. He had come with a number of tribesmen to defend the sanctuary, but in the meantime he and his friend, named Salah, were going to help me get out.

"That must have been quite a scare you had last night," he said, grinning from ear to ear. I told him about the knock on the door and someone's attempt to break into the house. "Salah and I will take you to our village in Wadi Maswar, where you'll be safe. You can stay there or go back to Sana'a—as you like, Seif—until things quiet down enough here for you to return."

I needed no coaxing. "I'm packed and ready to go," I said, holding up my backpack.

Muhammad looked around and shook his head. "Oh no, we're not going to leave anything behind, in case the enemy should break into the house. We're taking everything with us." He had an air of determination that I had learned not to challenge.

With the afternoon's rush of *qat*-induced adrenaline, we packed all my household furnishings and personal belongings, leaving not a single tin can or bread crumb behind, and early the next morning we piled it all onto a pickup truck. I sat in the front, sandwiched between the driver and Salah, who rode shotgun, the barrel of his Kalashnikov propped upright next to my head. I kept wondering whether the safety was on or whether the gun might go off accidentally with the bumps in the road. Muhammad and a younger boy sat behind, on top of the lumpy heap of my furnishings. Because we had been in a rush to leave, we'd loaded everything sloppily, with the inevitable result that things came loose and slid off. I would look into the side-view mirror and see a cushion, say, kicking up dust as it rolled down a hillside.

I laughed with my companions. "See, we should have just taken my pack here on my knees and forgotten the rest of it. It will be strewn all over Khawlan before we're done, if not ripped to shreds."

"Stop the truck!" Muhammad would shout from his perch, pounding his fist on the roof of the cab in case we couldn't hear him.

"Leave it! Leave it!" I would plead, but he was adamant. He would jump off—the front of his skirt tucked inside the waistband—and scamper down the hill to retrieve the item. Without a rope to secure the baggage, Muhammad decided to form what I can only describe as a human clamp, with himself and his friend straddling my earthly goods, their trunks and limbs stretched over the top, hands clasping each other's and the sides of the truck. I was mortified and deeply touched.

We arrived in al-Hijla, Wadi Maswar, our destination, about an hour later, passing transports of cars and trucks on our way loaded with rifle-toting tribesmen and bazookas destined for the "front" in [the sanctuary]. There were even people on foot or donkey, some of them unarmed and carrying only a shepherd's stick, looking rather feeble or inefficacious judging from their age and strength. They all seemed to be going to [the sanctuary] as either fighters or mediators.

When we got to Muhammad's house, I could tell from the reaction of his mother and wife that my appearance was unexpected.

"This is Seif. He's my friend from the sanctuary. He will stay with us for a few weeks," Muhammad announced to his assembled relatives. I greeted them all in turn, and they received me graciously.

"A friend of my son's is like a son of mine," Muhammad's mother said grandly. "You're welcome to stay in our house as long as you like."

Muhammad, his friends, and I unloaded my possessions from the truck and stacked them by the side of the house. Miraculously, nothing was lost or broken, not even the water pipe, with its fragile leather hose. After he instructed the women of the house in due time to move all my belongings to one of the upstairs sitting rooms, Muhammad showed me the house and the *mafraj* where I would be staying, urging me to make myself at home and arrange my things as I had done in the sanctuary. I became uneasy, wondering just how I should interpret his splendid gesture of hospitality, for he seemed to have envisioned a more permanent arrangement than I had in mind.

"I can't put your family out like this, Muhammad. This space belongs to them, not me."

"Oh, there's plenty of room," he insisted. And then he was gone.

7

∾

AN IDYLL

Muhammad had gone to join the fighters in the sanctuary. Like a couple, we had set up house, and now the man was off to war!

While I stayed in Muhammad's village, I didn't have time to write every day in my diary, but I kept scribbling in my little spiral notebooks. It took a full month after I left the sanctuary before I wrote in my diary again, and when I did, it was in one sitting, during which I jotted down everything I could remember of my stay. As I reread it now, I discern moments of misplaced concreteness when I seem, for no reason, to have dwelled on certain details and skipped over others that I should have elaborated, but such is the errant nature of memory.

> With Muhammad gone, I decided to spend the rest of the morning exploring the village, which I did in the charming company of some of his cousins. One is the ten-year-old Muhammad Hussein, who goes with me everywhere. In the afternoon I lunched with the sheikh [brother of Muhammad's mother] and his sons. I already knew the oldest boy, Hizam, from the sanctuary—I had met him and Muhammad there several months ago when the conflict . . . first erupted, and we had all three become good friends . . . I also knew Ahmed from those

days, though he had always been the quietest of the three and I never felt that I had gotten to know him very well. It was the second oldest son, Muhammad, whom I met for the first time at lunch (as well as the youngest, Salih). He is the handsomest of the four brothers with perhaps also the greatest natural charm but without Hizam's intelligence (which I felt was matched only by Salih). Slight of build but [with] sturdy, regular features in a square face that lights up occasionally in a radiant smile. I had the thought of giving him a comb; his hair, though clean, was always unkempt and matted, but it curiously suited his looks by setting them off even more—that is, the regularity of his features against the wild extravagance of his hair.

The sheikh was quiet but nonetheless outgoing . . . And his answers to my questions were, I thought, informed and incisive. Besides local questions of geography, history, et cetera, I also asked him his opinion on the problems in [the sanctuary]. He told me that the conflict had now entered the stage of "tribal competition," where the various parties in the dispute were testing each other's power and strength. A view on the issue which I had not heard from anyone before and I tend to think is to some extent correct— though this is only one aspect of a most complicated affair. After lunch we all chewed *qat* together, though the sheikh by this time had excused himself to join the other men from Wadi Maswar who were going that afternoon to [the sanctuary].

I spent the evening with Muh'd's father [Qasim], talking about religion, the Qur'an, America, et cetera. He's a quiet man who mumbles a lot in his beard, but kindly. Later we were joined by Muh'd's wife & mother, who sat at the foot of the *mafraj*, asking me the same sorts of questions I had been answering all day. The novelty of sitting with women in the same room who, moreover, made no effort to keep their faces thoroughly concealed, as is the custom among females in [the sanctuary], took me aback at first. Then M's wife started to breast-feed her baby girl [Fatimah] in plain view of me, which again came as a surprise. Never had I seen anything like this sort of behavior among [*sic*] the sexes in [the sanctuary]. I tried to ask them about the disappearing girls and what they thought might have happened to them, but they only shrugged and shook their heads as if they didn't know.

When we all retired for bed around midnight, the father & I both slept together in the sitting room. It was hot and stuffy and the air swarming with flies. In such uncomfortable quarters I didn't [have] much hope of sleeping that night even though I was exhausted from the last several days of fighting and moving.

We got up early the next morning—Muhammad's father having risen at dawn for prayers and then returning to listen to the radio, a religious program so soothing to his soul that he went back to sleep while I tried to read a little. Breakfast consisted of stale bread so hard one had to dunk it in tea before it was palatable.

Soon the neighbors' children arrived who had kept me company during most of the previous day. They took me into the fields, where I saw women cutting clover, which they wound like strands around a few dried and slightly mashed cane stalks and then fed to the draft animals—cows or bulls, donkeys and camels. Men and boys were struggling with plows in the fields . . . Other fields were being irrigated, the cool, clear water feeding into them by way of hundreds of small channels extending from the wells . . . I loved being out in the open air, under the sun, smelling the sweat of the animals. One of the men working in the fields was Dahhan, Muhammad's uncle (his father's brother), who taught me how to steady the plow and shout out commands to the bull.

"Yisrah, Yamin!" Left! Right! *"Gu!"* Stop! *"Mi-mi-mi-mi-mi,"* Right!

It was a delicious feeling, to have one's feet sink into clods of moist earth, to see a spurt of silvery water gush from the well pipe and splash onto the smooth, satiny stones of the cistern. I spoke to some of the men about the conflict between the sanctuary and the Bani Dhubyan. It seemed to be engulfing more and more tribes as each fails in its mediation and joins one side or the other. An old-timer gave me a wonderful proverb for the situation: *Al-musiba taᶜumm w-al-rahma takhuss,* "Catastrophe spreads and mercy contracts."

194 ~ Steven C. Caton

Later in the morning I was introduced to Muhammad Muhsin . . . a big man, jolly, with a Santa Claus face. But his affable demeanor ought not to fool one: he's extremely shrewd, well-educated (entirely self-taught), and very capable . . . USAID selected him to carry on an experimental poultry farm in Wadi Maswar after he received training . . . He's had a string of jobs in the Cable and Wireless Office (having been the first Yemeni to learn how to tap Morse code), in the Information Ministry, and elsewhere. Being from the tribe of Sinhan, he has the ear of the president . . .

We had lunch with Muh'd Muhsin in his house. With him were friends of his from the Sinhan. Throughout the meal he directed his comments toward America, saying what a great country it was, how outstanding its technology, how excellent its people, et cetera, I grew tired of his hollow flattery and responded somewhat mockingly to it . . . I might have offended him. He told me he'd do anything I wanted. Did I want to go to Marib? He would arrange it. Did I want to see the president? Tomorrow I could be talking to him. (He was making me feel uncomfortable. I felt once again that I was being tested.) No, I wasn't interested in seeing the president, I said, but he might try to get me in touch with al-Shanbali, the great poet from Khawlan, the only person I was interested in seeing. The rest of the party sniggered, knowing I was making fun of him.

After lunch we chewed *qat* and were joined by a large group of people. A heated discussion or should I say complaint developed with Muh'd Muhsin. It revolved around his chicken farm, abandoned now these several months, which had attracted flies to the wadi in quantities not witnessed before in living memory. People complained that he ought to do something to kill them off now, as it was his chicken farm that had attracted the flies in the first place. He hemmed and hawed, never promising any positive action on the matter.

That same evening someone started a fire in the abandoned chicken farm. It went up in a stupendous blaze in only a few seconds because M. M. had been storing hay in it. The fire caused quite a commotion in the village, which turned out to inspect damages & discuss the case. In the meantime, thieves were busily stealing *qat* while the owners of the fields were away tending to the fire. I doubt that the fire was started by thieves . . . rather they took advantage of what was for them a lucky break. But who started the fire and why are not known. Perhaps it was intended to frighten M. M. into doing something about the flies.

My friend Muhammad returned to Wadi Maswar the next day. He had promised to come back in time to attend a big wedding at which we could record lots of poetry. I wrote up a summary of what he had told me in my field notes. *Truce had been in effect for several days through the intervention of the Sufis. But the situation is very tense, and everyone is resigned to the fact that another war is imminent. Convoys of tribesmen arrived in [the sanctuary] by the hundreds to take up positions in and around the* hijra. *They have come from Garwa, al-ᶜArush, and Suhman. At least 2,000 of them. Tribesmen have also been brought in from surrounding villages to prepare the meals for the fighters [presumably because the women in the sanctuary had fled] . . . The road . . . to the beginning of the Sana'a highway is entirely in the hands of sanctuary supporters . . . The Sufis have now given up trying to mediate the dispute and have joined the side of the Bani Dhubyan. They are also being helped by Bait al-Shadeg. Rumor has it that Bait al-Mahjari has joined the Bani Dhubyan as well . . . The uncle of the president is supposed to have visited the Bani Dhubyan and offered them full military assistance, if they need it, including troop reinforcements. The Sinhan-Khawlan border is also said to be heavily manned by government troops, who have been put on alert to enter Khawlan in case the Bani Dhubyan need them. The conflict has now entered a new phase. It is no longer a local engagement between the [sanctuary] and the Bani Dhubyan. There is a possibility that Khawlan might end up fighting the central government.* Depressed by this news, I asked about some of my friends. Muhammad the Hunchback had reopened his store. He had asked where I had gone and, when Muhammad told him, asked that his greetings be relayed to me. Muhammad the Lame had apparently fallen victim to exhaustion and was resting, and Ibrahim the Beltmaker was as reclusive as ever. Muhammad had seen neither of them.

That day we went into Jihana to buy things for the wedding. Accompanying us was a very sweet young man who is a blacksmith in al-Hijla [Muhammad's village], the son of their best butcher [*muzeyyin*]. Muh'd wanted a new sports coat, which I paid for. [His taste ran to bold patterns—polka dots, wide stripes, snowflakes. He was full of good cheer, and I had never seen him so relaxed.]
I bought some perfume for the groom. The three of us had lunch together in Muhammad's house, and then we joined the whole family to go to the wedding. They took my water pipe along to smoke at the *qat* chew. Muh'd's father was wearing my Tihama shawl, the red, gold, and green striped cotton cloth with tassels at the ends draped over his shoulders. A mule preceded us, bearing foods as gifts for the wedding, and Ahmed, Muh'd's little boy, was sitting astride it, holding on bravely to its neck . . . I kept getting thorns in my flip-flops, which jabbed painfully. Or I would lose my footing on the sharp little stones that lay in the wadi bed and sometimes disconnect the sandal straps, which I then had to stop to fix. The old woman, Muh'd's mother, was in the rear, balancing a basket on her head, containing God knows what, and not once stumbling under her load . . .

The sun was out, but visibility was poor because of all the dust blown about by the wind . . . The haze gives to the air a peculiar milky sheen like the surface of a pearl.

When we arrived at the groom's house, I tried to take pictures of the group of celebrants, but suddenly a man stepped forward and motioned me to stop what I was doing. "No pictures," he said. "This ceremony is not something for tourists to gawk at." Alarm and anger suddenly seized me. I was afraid he might try to break the camera. A drunken fanatic, I thought to myself (that he had been imbibing was only too evident from his breath). "I'm not a tourist," I snapped back. "I'm a researcher from America who is studying your customs." I put my camera safely back in its case and walked away. Almost at once people were upon me, telling me it was all right to take the pictures as long as I didn't photograph any women. They were trying to soothe and reassure me. Once again,

the man lurched toward me and attempted to interfere, but he was
put in his place by one of the senior members of the crowd.

Muhammad vehemently defended me before the man and would
not let the matter rest unless I was allowed to continue taking
pictures. For nearly an hour the argument raged while the wedding
party was in the midst of its celebration. It nearly ruined the occasion.
I told Muhammad I had plenty of pictures from other weddings
and I didn't need these. I tried to prevail on him to keep calm, but
this only succeeded in irritating him. He was duty-bound to defend
my honor, he whispered to me fiercely, but I think it was more than
that. He felt bad for me as a friend. And I, who may have seemed
in the eyes of my companions to be lacking in pride, I wanted only
to ignore the insult and get on with the celebration . . . I felt
caught in a dilemma. Either I offended Muh'd by refusing to help
him save face or risked the possibility of wrecking the wedding.

Gradually I began to take pictures again. It was what Muh'd
insisted that I do. If I was discreet, it might be less noticeable. A
snapshot here of dancers, a quick freeze of the groom coming out of
the mosque, a still of the wedding bouquet, et cetera. In one or two
frames a figure might be seen darting madly out of the way—that
would have been the man who had accosted me . . . Muh'd in the
meantime was taping the *zamil* poems. The man who had objected
about the pictures came over to me again and started a diatribe
about America being the greatest enemy of Islam, et cetera. A number
of people pulled him away and reprimanded him. Something like this
had never happened to me before in Yemen, and I was quite shaken
by the experience, though I knew I had to keep calm.

We finally made it back to the [groom's] house . . . The *qat* chew
was relaxing and uneventful. I tried to collect & calm myself so that
I could enter into the joyous mood of the wedding.

I forget to mention in this diary entry that in the course of the afternoon
my water pipe got broken. It was no one's fault in particular—if I recall
correctly, Muhammad's father had accidentally stepped on it—and it was
not a very good one to begin with, but Muhammad was mortified.

"Seeeif! I'm so-o-o sorry. I'll have it fixed. You'll see. I know some-one."

"Don't worry about it, Muhammad. It's a piece of junk anyway."

Toward sunset, when men were filing one by one out of the assembly room to do their ritual ablutions before praying in the mosque, I went outside with Muh'd [who stayed behind to keep me company] and some of his younger friends . . . Muh'd knew I was tired of answering the same questions, the answers to which he had heard so many times before that he could recite them verbatim, but whenever he tried to relieve me by subbing for me, so to speak, my inquirer took offense. Why should Muh'd answer for me when I could do so myself in Arabic and it would, after all, come straight from the horse's mouth? Muh'd tried to explain that I had grown weary of having always to answer the same questions. I winced at how "put upon" this explanation made me seem . . .

After the sundown prayer, we joined the procession from the mosque to the groom's house, with *zamils*, gunshots, firecrackers, et cetera. Muh'd had by this time become quite adept at taping the zamileers, so I was content simply to follow the crowd on the outskirts, where I would be safe from exploding firecrackers.

Before we entered the room in which dinner was to be served, Muh'd motioned for me to follow his example and put my flip-flops inside my jacket. When we left the sitting room late that evening, I understood why. With the dozens of pairs of shoes cluttering the hallway, all looking very much alike in any case but even more so in the dark, it would have been impossible to have found ours. The meal was bounteous and delicious, and afterward we carried on with *bala* poetry and dancing for the rest of the evening.

> O bal, Saalami did wrong to go to war—facing him are the men of
> Habab. And the time is full of evils; there is no proper conduct in
> this time.
> O bal, and now we shall plow and the seed will be in the ground.
> O uncle, O nice one, you are mighty and young.

O bal, O Hajji, may God save you. How can we be threatened by
flies? And as for the groom, from me to him sweet basil.

Bala poetry is meant to be a gift to the groom, as the last line says—
"from me to him sweet basil." Basil not only is aromatic but is thought
to have healthful properties and to bring good luck to the person who
wears a ceremonial sprig of it.

Muhammad had my Sony tape recorder hanging by a strap from his
shoulder and held the microphone close to each of the poets as he broke
into the circle of linked arms to deliver his verse. The intrusion made me
cringe and laugh at the same time. Usually I kept farther back, hoping the
mike would be powerful enough to pick up nuances from the audience.
But Muhammad even had the temerity to tell them to raise their voices or
to articulate more clearly when he felt the delivery wasn't up to standard.
I have to confess that, after getting over my chagrin, I was relieved he had
taken over the recording, for it meant I could take more pictures as well as
join the chorus and participate more fully in the performance.

As with the *zamil, bala* lines are composed on the spot, but the performance differs in other respects. A circle of men forms the chorus,
their arms around one another's shoulders or waists or holding hands.
A poet steps into the middle of the circle, cups his hand to his mouth
like the muezzin calling the prayer, and shouts his gift in a high-
pitched voice, all the while slowly walking in a counterclockwise direction. The first line sets the meter and rhyme to which all other
offerings have to conform. If they do not, the chorus or audience
shouts, "A broken line!" and the poet must scramble to come up with
an alternative or cede his turn. When he is done, he leaves the circle,
and the chorus chants the line over and over again until another poet
or the same one is ready to deliver a new offering. Meanwhile, audience members might exclaim, "God is great!" at a beautiful line or
laugh at a funny one, but mostly they converse in low voices—not always about the poetry. So the performance would continue, sometimes
for thirty lines or more, sometimes for only a dozen, sometimes with
only two poets, sometimes with a half dozen, until it was time for the
groom to go on a final procession to meet his bride. In the depths of

the village, one could, if one listened carefully, hear the women performing their poetry for her. I told myself to ask Muhammad's mother about it when I had the chance, but I never did.

One can discern the spontaneity of the poetry in its references to people and things in the *mafraj* where the *bala* performance took place, as well as to events happening at the time, including the dispute between the sanctuary and Sarkhan. The first line, for example, chastised the head sheikh of the Bani Dhubyan for going to war and warned him that he would face the men of Habab—presumably the poet's village—should hostilities continue. The next line celebrates the plowing and planting season at its height, the poet hailing and praising his uncle, who was in the room. The final line refers to the pestilence of flies that had plagued the wadi because of Muhammad Muhsin's chicken farm, the argument over it being still fresh in people's minds.

The next day early in the morning, after another breakfast of dry bread & tea (Muh'd had kindly fixed me a separate pot of tea without sugar because I had told him a long time ago that I drank it without and he had remembered), I went out into the fields to help with the clearing . . . in preparation for plowing. Muhammad and I pulled out the roots of sorghum stalks to be used for fuel in the kitchen—because of the scarcity of firewood, nothing is wasted.

A wonderful old man actually did all the plowing with the help of an enormous ox that munched on its *gadhb* [alfalfa] and cane while pulling the plow in arrow-straight furrows. The air was cool and still crisp at this hour, the valley cast in shadow except for a few stray patches of cultivation illuminated in brilliant greens and purples. In some fields dogs were tied up, mostly where *qat* was grown, which they guard. They'd bark furiously and yank fiercely on their chains as we went by, curling their lips so that their canines would show. Few people were about—mostly women who were cutting *gadhb* and piling it up in bundles, which they carried on their heads, their hips swaying gently under the load. Or a few boys struggling with the harness on a donkey, which is a far less satisfactory draft animal than an ox, sometimes pelting its hide with little nodules of earth that exploded in puffs of dust in order to get the beast to do what they wanted . . . Eventually Muh'd's wife'came to the field with little Ahmed . . . I played with him for a while. He would stand on the wall skirting one side of the field and then jump into my arms, whereupon I'd lift him high up in the air and whirl around . . . Ahmed never once evinced the least sign of fear or timidity. His sparkling eyes would look excitedly into mine, his tiny arms waving up and down as though he were trying to fly, and then he'd gurgle with glee as soon as he'd landed safely in my arms. I could have played with him all morning as far as he was concerned.

In that afternoon's *qat* chew, Muhammad announced that he would probably be going back to [the sanctuary], where fighting seemed likely to break out again. I was disappointed to see him go and worried that he might be injured in the war, but I knew there was nothing I could say to persuade him to remain behind, especially when it was expected of him as a young man of the village and close relative of the sheikh . . .

He was not, of course, the only one to go . . . The conversation in the *qat* chew, as it had in previous ones of that week, centered on the topic of the war and the problem of how to get the Bani Dhubyan to agree to a peaceful settlement . . . The young were exhorted by their elders "to go out there and fight," and one by one they responded by getting up from their places in the *diwan* [large assembly hall], their cheeks still bulging with *qat*, . . . taking their rifles off the pegs on the walls, and going out to pile into the cars that were heading out to [the sanctuary] . . . Not all the men left without grumbling. Some were clearly put out at having to fight when they were very busy during the plowing season. And then it never seemed to lead to a lasting settlement because the B.D. would always threaten to attack after they had agreed to a truce and the tribes [had] left the *hijra* to return to their own settlements. It was clearly frustrating and galling.

So I spent the evening by myself taping the *bala*, which was not up to par because of the absence of so many of the men. Nevertheless, those of us who stayed behind tried our best to make it a festive occasion, the troubles in Khawlan notwithstanding.

I left early, as soon as the dancing started. Another little boy named Muh'd [Hussein], who is my friend Muh'd's nephew (sister's boy), accompanied me on the way back and carried part of my equipment. Had the *mafraj* to myself, as the old man was sleeping in the guardhouse by his *qat* fields.

The truce in Khawlan held after all, and so Muhammad returned. Soon he took me to another wedding in a village about a kilometer away, and took the broken water pipe with him. We stopped along the way to visit one of his dearest friends, who was also a renowned poet.

Ahmed al-Sharegi was at home, mending the leather tube of a water pipe, work which he does professionally to earn a living. The long spring of the tube lay coiled on the floor of the sitting room, a snake that had shed its skin, and a large skein of string, which would be wound around it, was nearby. A strange guest could not be in a village for very long before he would be joined by curious onlookers, and this occasion was no exception. Soon the room was filled with Ahmed's relatives and friends. Sharegi was in his early thirties, with a pleasant and open face, a charming conversationalist. "I remember when Muhammad got married," he said to me, his eyes twinkling. "He seemed so young and so tiny. No bigger than this branch of *qat*," and he held one playfully in his fingers and then tossed it to his friend, who was red with embarrassment but grinning from ear to ear. "He was so young, we didn't think he could get it up." The room filled with laughter.

When we headed off to the wedding, it was nighttime. There was a full moon . . . but without a flashlight the walk would have been tortuous. One of the most difficult places to cross was the climb over the rocky outcrop called ʿUgab, where there is a Himyaritic inscription on a rock face. I passed it that evening without being aware of its existence.

The land looked as if blanketed in snow, an effect of the moon's illumination. The air was cool but not crisp—enveloping one like some wonderful fabric that brushed delicately against the skin.

Except for our desultory conversation and the occasional bark of a fiercely vigilant dog, the night was completely still.

We could see the groom's house lit up by strings of lightbulbs. In the distance it glowed like a spark in a cold grate. When we got within fifty yards, Ahmed [al-Sharegi] started to compose the *zamil*. Having grasped his words and the melody, our voices rose like a flame that pops in the burner and surges . . . Our voices were high and nearly shrill but powerful and manly. Now we did not seem small in this vast and silent distance, swallowed up by the night . . .

We marched toward the house in two lines, one line chanting the first line of the poem, the other the second, and then alternating back and forth, back and forth.

> Good evening, friend of mine. In matters of the bride price and
>   marriage contract,
> O son of Hatim, we desire the oath of marriage. Don't get out of step
>   with our marching.

Our poet was referring to the fact that at many weddings the father of the bride decides at the last minute to increase the "bride price," much to the consternation of the groom and his family. So exorbitant had the amounts become (sometimes as much as the equivalent of US $30,000) that the young men were complaining that they couldn't afford to get married, which of course fueled resentment against the older generation.

> Eventually, figures stirred and scurried in the light that grew more
> expansive as we approached. I could see drums being carried as
> well as rifles, and when we finally arrived at the house door, men
> saluted us with rounds of gunfire, exploding firecrackers, and a wild
> beating of drums. We were hustled upstairs and soon were greeted
> by a room full of men . . .

This is when, to the best of my recollection, I first saw the man who was to cause me a great deal of trouble and anxiety. He was probably one of the groom's relatives or close friends. I remember very well his smiling face with its straight, regular features. I did not know it at the time, but he was an informant who worked for National Security police. I was much taken by another man there by the name of Ali al-Fagih. He was in his late sixties at least, with white hair and a wizened face; his eyes would twinkle when he had a humorous thought, of which I was glad to find he had many.

The time had come to start the *bala*. The poets were Ahmed al-Sharegi; Ali al-Fagih; the man from National Security, whom I will call Salih; a member of the *sada* who lived in Jihana and was a friend of the groom; and two others whose acquaintance I never made. But Ahmed dominated the performance. Ali al-Fagih would have been just as good, but he no longer had the stamina to deliver verse after verse in the high-pitched tone his younger companions could still master. The young man of the *sada* was also surprisingly good, surprisingly because this art form was not one his status group practiced very much.

I now have a confession to make. The performance presented a severe problem of comprehension for me because the chant stretched out the syllables to the point of unintelligibility. I've had that problem with songs in English, too, being unsure of the lines until I consult the printed lyrics. It was as hard for me as it would have been for Muhammad the Maswari if I had taken him to the opera for the first time. Only later, when I listened to the tape with him, could I make sense of what I heard. He would repeat each line in a plain speaking voice, and I would write it down in Arabic on the ruled pages of a child's school notebook I had borrowed from one of his cousins. It was not always easy for him either, and sometimes we had to play a passage over and over again until he finally thought he grasped the line. Occasionally he never did. "Dear merciful God," he would mutter and shake his head. "Never mind. Let's get on with it."

At the performance itself, most of the time I hadn't a clue what the poets were chanting, though I dared not look dazed or puzzled. When the audience laughed, I would laugh. Someone would look at me significantly, I would look back knowingly. To vary this repertoire a bit, I might look shrewdly at the poet, as though I knew his number all right. Otherwise, I listened to the poems with what I hoped appeared to be rapt attention, my brow wrinkling with the effort of concentration, my head tilted slightly to one side (perhaps with one eyebrow raised), as though I might be straining to take in every word. *Jesus, what a bloody faker*, I kept saying to myself, and when someone asked me if I understood, I would nod, yelling over the din, *"Jesus, what a bloody faker."*

"Ah, I thought so!" my appreciative neighbor would shout back.

Anyway, Ahmed began.

> O Lord, have mercy upon [the sanctuary], for the tribes are camping
> over it.
> It is said of the sheikhs that many of them are dictators.

Enemies as well as supporters had positioned themselves on the mountains around the sanctuary. The poet asked for God's mercy because it was outnumbered and in danger of another attack. Which of the sheikhs were dictators was ambiguous: the reference might have meant any number of men jockeying for power in Khawlan—Sheikh al-Royshan, inciting the Sarkhan to fight; al-Damani, refusing to go along with the consensus because he wanted to sack the sanctuary; Hussein Ali al-Gadhi; and so forth.

Ahmed's critique was answered by Ali:

> Good evening to you, sons of the defenders. O victors over the
> opponent!
> Woe to him who is the antagonist.

He addressed the assembly with a greeting and conventional epithet, "sons of the defenders," and invoked a key tribal value, defense of the borders. In context, this had added resonance, since the tribesmen at the wedding were actually deciding on whether to leave that night to defend the sanctuary. The antagonists were the Bani Dhubyan, who would have to face these brave, fierce warriors from Wadi Maswar.

Now it was turn of the young man from the *sada*:

> [The sanctuary] is free! It won't put up with threats.
> If the enemy comes, then with the howitzer they will shoot him
> in two.

Freedom or autonomy is another central value of tribalism, and the poet appealed to it. Freedom must be defended—with military arms, if necessary—and the poet suggested that the sanctuary had enough fire-power to deal the enemy a mortal blow.

This turn was followed by a poet whom I did not know:

> May God grant everyone long life and preserve you!
> Khawlan has already surrounded it. Verily, you will also see the
> doorway in shadow.

As Muhammad the Maswari later explained, "Khawlan has already sur-rounded it" was ambiguous for everyone: it could have meant either that Khawlan was coming to the aid of its embattled sanctuary by sur-rounding it in a protective girdle, or that it had surrounded and was planning to attack Sarkhan. Preparations for such an attack were al-ready in progress, but I did not know this until later. The hint of im-pending war gave a dark and ominous tone to the end of the line, "you will also see the doorway in shadow." The attacker's shadow seen on the threshold was an image very real to me.

Now Ali took another turn, aiming his verse at Ahmed:

> [The sanctuary] has been ransacked, O Ahmed, its mouth tied shut.
> And the sheikh has failed to do his job, listening to the voice of [the
> singer] al-Simah instead.

The image of the sanctuary being gagged, a metaphor of the *sada*'s de-fenselessness, raised a laugh from the audience. But Ali's line was also about the ineffectualness of the tribal sheikhs, humorously conjuring up a picture of a man of power lolling about in his sitting room listen-ing to pop songs instead of trying to resolve his tribe's problems in words and deeds. Yet again sheikhly power and authority were held lightly, if not actually ridiculed, and in that sense the line was a retort to Ahmed's comment that the sheikhs had become dictators. Ahmed's riposte was swift:

> Already the problem has sprouted wings, the turmoil of another battle
> to come.
> There are some people outside the fray and others who have dropped
> it.

The dispute had now become more complex and threatened to embroil all of Khawlan in a general war. But there was hope, for although some people like Sheikh al-Gadhi had given up mediating, others had remained neutral and could continue to arbitrate.

The next line came from a poet I didn't know:

> They have agreed to the truce, and we shall settle the issue.
> Verily, men of Khawlan have come to invade the enemy.

This seemed contradictory. The poet sounded first the note of conciliation and peace, then the alarum of war. But Muhammad later explained that perhaps the argument was that the enemy could be persuaded to press its claims through peaceful means once it saw the size of the army opposing it. The threat of force could be crucial to the successful outcome of negotiations.

By now Ali al-Fagih had had enough time to respond to Ahmed's challenge: His voice was beginning to break in the higher register, but the verse was still perfectly intelligible.

> Hamud, I am your brother. In the middle of the road is a great boulder.
> As for Nasir Ahmed [al-Saalami], you will see him trounced.

Hamud is a variant of Ahmed (chosen in this instance, I suppose, because of the meter), and it was clear that he meant Ahmed al-Sharegi.

The image of a stone in the road was an allusion to Sheikh al-Saalami of the Bani Dhubyan.

Once again, Ahmed came back with a caustic reply:

> Tell me why, O companion, tell me why,
> They pounded their heads and left them bashed in.

The audience tittered. I thought Ahmed was referring to the deaths the Bani Dhubyan had suffered at the hands of the sanctuary's defenders, but Muhammad disagreed with my interpretation. As a retort to Ali's line, it could only mean, he thought, that the Bani Dhubyan had been strong enough to break through the sanctuary defenses even though it cost them lives. Therefore Ahmed was warning the group that removing the "boulder" would not be as easy as people might suppose. The foe was redoubtable.

The young man from the *sada* begged to differ:

> They will come to us, fighters from the capital.
> Sons of Bani Hashim [the *sada*] and the mighty of the tribes will
>   demolish the opponent.

At this point Ali al-Fagih decided to try a different tack:

> Our friends, the people of Nahd, say they have put in the sprig of
>   sweet basil.
> The days have passed, you say, when the word of the *sada* was law.

The sprig of basil is often stuck jauntily into the folds of the tribal headdress, especially on ritual occasions, such as Fridays or wedding celebrations. The Nahd, a string of villages in the near vicinity whose inhabitants claimed to belong to the Bani Dhubyan, were fighting against the sanctuary and its supporters. That the Nahd "put in the sprig of sweet basil" meant, according to Muhammad, that they were celebrating their "victory" in having overrun the sanctuary. Gone were the days of the Imamate before the 1962 revolution, when "the word of the *sada* was law" and what had happened to the sanctuary would have been unthinkable. But nostalgia was expressed for the rule of law, often regretted when neither the tribal leaders nor the central state could contain a conflict.

Now a rough-looking man, his cheeks bulging with *qat*, delivered a line of verse in a voice so hoarse that it was unintelligible. "What did he say?" people asked irritably. The chorus was no longer in unison, and the performance threatened to break down. "If he can't enunciate clearly, he shouldn't join in," someone whispered fiercely. Later, when Muhammad listened to the tape over and over again, he gave up with a shrug and laughed.

Ahmed jumped in to keep up the momentum. Like Ali al-Fagih and the others, he had been prowling on the sidelines, pacing back and forth like a hungry lion. He was at the peak of his form, his voice clear and strong, his mind alert and agile, his imagination inspired.

> By God, he who attacks, he is heroic.
> They have surrendered like the bull led away by the ring in its nose.

He consistently interpreted the attack on the sanctuary as a victory for the Bani Dhubyan, and so the Bani Dhubyan were "heroic" because they attacked rather than waiting to be attacked, whereas the *sada* were passive as a sacrificial bull "led away by the ring in its nose." But Ali disagreed.

> They did not overwhelm anything, because there were reinforcements.
> Listen, in the morning al-Saalami had swallowed the war for breakfast.

The next poet, one of the two I didn't know, had grown impatient with all this talk:

> Why this hemming and hawing? Truly, we'll give the skull [kill them].
> Let's go, Ali [al-Fagih], and may God's blessing be upon you.
> Shorten the sprig of sweet basil [cut short the celebration].

Ahmed had a swift comeback.

As for al-Damani, we tell you, he strikes a blow against his opponent.
Murmurings of the heart and idle boasts no longer do good.

Mention of al-Damani, the other Dhubyani sheikh as powerful as al-Saalami, reminded listeners that their combined strength was formidable; against it the assembly's saber rattling was an impotent gesture.

Until this point, the cultural routine of challenge-and-retort had been carried almost entirely on the shoulders of Ahmed and Ali, so it didn't much matter that the number of performers was dwindling so long as the performance was heating up—which it clearly was. It was now Ali's turn to respond. During the *bala* performance some young men had gotten up, grabbed their weapons, and exited. It may have been that they were tired and wanted to go home, but the poet decided to interpret their gesture otherwise.

As for now, Ahmed, we are at the conclusion. See the leopards come.
We shall hear them attack.

Ahmed's reply to this was beautifully veiled:

They [the *sada*] have a *seyl* [floodplain] which has swept away the
    protective wall,
Swept it away in the middle of the wadi, where the property wall
    burst.

Muhammad worked with me a long time to clarify the subtle meanings of this complex metaphor. When it rains, water runs down the mountainsides and fills the plain below. Villages like the sanctuary, situated next to the plain, have irrigation channels leading directly to the fields, and when the plain floods, there is always a danger that the walls protecting the fields may break and the crops be destroyed. What I didn't understand at first was that the protective walls in question belonged to the Sarkhan and the crop-destroying flood came from the sanctuary, but the poet was alluding to the taking of the two girls by Abdullah the Culprit. This indirection, requiring one to read between the lines, is, as we have learned, highly prized in Yemeni conversation. But that is not all: the protective wall is symbolic of male society guarding a woman's *ʿirdh*, or chastity. Ahmed's rhetorical strategy, then, was to justify the attack on the sanctuary because Abdullah's heinous crime had breached (or penetrated) male honor and violated (or raped) it. I asked Muhammad why he thought this interpretation was possible, and he answered, "Because of the verses that follow. One can see how the other poets took up that meaning."

The hoarse poet's ineptness had become so comical that when he stepped into the circle for another turn, smirks appeared on audience faces, but this time he delivered the goods.

> Verily, and God is the Knower. He says and He knows.
> Filth has entered the *hijra*, which knows it.

The "filth" in question was obviously Abdullah the Culprit, but it could also refer to the alien ways that had crept into Yemeni society via its young men. Surely I, too, would be implicated in this circle of corruption, I thought to myself.

Ahmed intensified this sentiment.

> Say to Abu Hashim [descendants of the Prophet], Get rid of the snot.
> And al-Gahirah [the Citadel] was sealed off in the best possible way.

The filth of the previous line became more vile and more personal, more intimately associated with the *sada*. They could not so easily disassociate themselves from the culprit as they had been trying to do. And in reply to Ali's assertion that the sanctuary was well-defended, he pointed out that the largest house in it, the Citadel, had been taken and ransacked.

It was Ali who had the last word.

> Ahmed, and I am your brother, already the jaw of the Bani Dhubyan is broken.
> And in conclusion, pray for the Chosen One, father of Fatimah.

It was getting late, yet the men who remained, even the hoarse-voiced poet, wanted to continue. Ahmed still dominated. Though the evening's rhetoric was repeated, new elements were introduced from time to time. For example, by Ahmed al-Sharegi:

> O Salih, today I say to you: hand out the perfume,
> From the time that Khawlan said, "Lower the *mahr*!"

Mahr is one of two payments made to the bride's family at the time of marriage, and Khawlan had held a special meeting to get the tribes to lower these excessive payments. The poet was cautioning the bride's father to be reasonable, but the broader interpretation was that the line was a cautionary tale for Khawlan as a whole, that bridal payments were a contributing factor to Abdullah the Culprit's mad behavior when he absconded with the two girls and allegedly sold them into prostitution, for he was trying to raise money to get married.

One of the poets unknown to me spoke:

> O place of the *bala* which is in progress.
> The *bala* this night is created for the disobedient girls.

I had a hunch that this poet was disagreeing with Ahmed al-Sharegi, since he characterized the girls as disobedient or unruly, the types of girls who could have paid the criminal to take them out of their village, which shifted the blame back on them. Ali al-Fagih disagreed:

> The marrow has gone, nothing remains but the stalks.
> O Ahmed, and I am your brother, already they have dragged him off
>   to the vultures.

What a wonderful and frightening metaphor in the first part of the line, so powerfully suggestive of the terrible fate that had befallen the two girls, seen less as willful agents than as hapless victims. The real criminal, al-Fagih insisted, was Abdullah, who was already as good as dead. And then, as if from left field, came this salvo from Ahmed al-Sharegi:

> Ali Muhammad [president of South Yemen] has made the visit early.
> Aden and Sana'a will last the ages.

Why did he bring up this reference to the unification of North and South Yemen? A reasonable explanation is that he saw the crisis in Khawlan as having to do with national politics more than with local honor. The hoarse-voiced poet picked up this challenge and replied:

> It's one nation, from Wayilah to Hadhur.
> O scourge of God, how can money matters enter into affairs of honor?

He was confirming that the two countries had become "one nation" but suggested other reasons for the troubles in Khawlan—perhaps the sordid, drawn-out, extortionate affair between sheikhs like al-Royshan and the hotel owner in Taiz, or the efforts made by Saudi Arabia on the one hand and South Yemen on the other to bribe the sheikhs into taking sides on the unification issue.

And then, the agent from National Security uttered this line:

> Welcome to Seif, who has come to collect *zamils*.
> From Camp David and Washington [he has come] and has not tired.

My being mentioned was not just the innocent execution of a poetic convention—as an honored guest, I should have been praised during the performance. The security agent was implying that I had come to spy on Khawlan, and was more interested in collecting information than in learning about poetry. But the evening had been long and I was exhausted, so I was not paying close attention and completely missed the possibility of this interpretation. Just as well, for I would have been upset all over again after the incident over the camera. Ahmed al-Sharegi came to my defense:

> And Seif has come from America and has kohl around his eyes.
> He records the *bal* in collections of poetry, O *bala* of the *bal*.

A straightforward defense, but once again, I had been implicated in the events.

Muhammad and I stayed long enough for some of the dancing. I had a go at it with one of the older tribesmen, the kind who is patient at teaching the steps. The informant for National Security took my picture, the first time anyone had done so, and I later realized why. But shortly before midnight I signaled to Muhammad that I wanted to go. We quickly darted through the crowd and out the door.

It was a dramatically beautiful night. There were no clouds in the sky, and the moon hung above us like some brightly burnished shield. But for the bark once or twice of a lone dog, the night was still, and getting stiller as the voices of the *bala* faded behind us.

I had hoped we could walk home—in spite of my fatigue, the velvety air refreshed me after the stuffiness of the sitting room—but Muhammad wanted to hitch a ride, and for that we had to walk in the floodplain.

Muhammad was brooding. Was anything wrong? I asked him. A shake of the head as he trudged ahead in silence. Well, to hell with you, too, I thought. He'd been somber all morning and hadn't talked then either. I suspected that it was because of some tension in his marriage. He and his wife were in that stage of their relationship when they ought to have been settling into their own quarters rather than living with his parents. But Muhammad had no means of supporting his family as far as I could see and in fact seemed quite idle. Still, I knew he was not lazy or lacking in ambition. I suspected his eagerness to help me was in part because it gave him something to do. Yes, I gave him money to buy *qat* and to cover other expenses, but these were piddling sums, hardly worth his bother. If he harbored hopes of coming to America for work, he never mentioned them.

Sometimes I wondered whether Muhammad didn't welcome the prospect of fighting as an escape. If he distinguished himself as a soldier, that might make up for any sense of failure now. If he were killed, his family would be provided for—might even be better off, was the terrible truth. His pretty young wife would no doubt return to her father's family and remarry after a year. She would take their daughter, Fatimah, with her, leaving Ahmed to be raised by his grandparents, so that he might grow up within his own lineage. They would be too young to remember their father or to grieve his death.

To distract himself, Muhammad turned on the tape deck and listened to the *bala* as we walked.

I had wanted to leave all those raucous sounds behind, to steep my soul in the soothing depths of this wonderful night, and so I snapped at him. Did he want to wake everybody up with that blasted tape recorder? Did we have to listen to all the dogs between al-Hisf and al-Hijla yapping at us? He switched it off, but not without a surprised protest. And not right away either. It was as though he were waiting just long enough that it would appear that he was not so much responding to my request—or command—as he was growing tired of listening to the tape recorder himself . . . When we came up to one village, loud, quarrelsome voices became audible. I was all for marching ahead, but Muh'd stopped to eavesdrop and stayed that way for several minutes . . . Finally in a loud voice, and not caring if anyone heard me, I shouted for him to get a move on. He jumped as if startled and then quickly proceeded to catch up with me. I interpreted this as another sign of obstinacy.

Reading this now, I think how ungrateful I was. After all that Muhammad had done for—and gone through with—me, how could I have treated him this way? Could I not put aside my own vexation so that he could enjoy himself a little? Was it because I was tired that I was so crabby? Or was there something deeper, a need on my part to reassert my control over the project, which I felt had been slipping away from me for quite some time? Probably all were true. The truth was that I myself felt at loose ends about my life in Wadi Maswar, since I had persuaded myself that I was not accomplishing any fieldwork there. And since I wasn't able to do any scholarly reading, either, I wasn't always the most gracious of guests. Muhammad noticed my anxieties but was intelligent enough to interpret them in the right way—not as a slight to his kind hospitality but as an expression of my need to settle back into an orderly, productive life. Who better to understand my situation than someone who was also at loose ends but hoped for an orderly, productive life? I still didn't realize that I *was* in fact doing fieldwork, even though it was not as I had imagined it to be.

We never did catch a ride. But when I got home, I had no trouble falling asleep. Muhammad left the next day to go back to the sanctuary. I told him I would go to Sana'a to pick up mail and see friends.

While I was away, war broke out. Khawlan had apparently forced this outcome, and the poetry had prepared us. Angered that the Bani Dhubyan would never carry out what it had agreed to do under the terms of the latest truce, Khawlan preferred to fight until the tribe had no choice but to capitulate. The fighting had been fierce and covered more ground than in the previous combat. Sarkhan was overrun, and Hajbah's convenience store on the road to Sana'a was ransacked, too— both in retaliation for what the Bani Dhubyan had done to the Citadel. Even so, the casualties were lighter this time. One man was killed, and a woman who had shot at people from her upper-story window was killed instantly by a bullet to the forehead. Supposedly the marksman found out only afterward that his target had been a woman.

I had been in Sana'a for about a week when I heard from reliable people there that a one-year truce had been signed and that this time it would last. So I decided to go back to the sanctuary, but first I had to return to Wadi Maswar to pick up my belongings, which were still in Muhammad's house.

I brought back presents—a shirt for Hizam, the sheikh's son, who had kindly lent me his car when I moved from [the sanctuary], and a bottle of Aqua Brava for Muh'd. Unfortunately, Hizam had left for Saudi Arabia only a few minutes before I went to his house to deliver the present, which I gave to the sheikh, instead. Muh'd was much taken with his present and received my injunction "that it was not for drink" with a smile on his face.

. . . The upstairs *mafraj* had changed its appearance. It had been cleaned and straightened up, the carpets neatly laid on the floor, more back cushions brought in. The most important improvement was the daily spraying of insecticide, which got rid of the flies. No longer were we plagued all night by them.

Most of my belongings that Muh'd had put in the *mafraj* had been removed to storage. He had changed his mind about putting my furnishings in the place in order to make me feel "at home," perhaps because he realized that they might get broken or dirtied . . . The baby was likely to piss all over the blankets— Yemenis not believing in swaddling their infants . . . No doubt still mortified by the accident that had put my water pipe out of commission, he didn't want to court further embarrassment.

. . . In the evenings we hoped to work on the tape transcription, but the children would interrupt us with their playing or the adults would come to spend the evening . . . so eventually we abandoned the idea as hopeless. In exasperation he confided in me: "There's no order in this place, is there?" I explained that there was order but not one suitable for what we wanted to do and we couldn't expect these people to change around their whole lives to suit us. He agreed, and suggested that maybe we could arrange to work on the transcriptions in my house in [the sanctuary].

I only gradually became aware that Muh'd's wife had left him. They had quarreled, and Muh'd in a fit of temper had thrown some hot tea at her from a thermos, apparently the tea had soaked through her dress but had not, fortunately, burned her skin. However, it provoked her enough to leave the house that same evening and go back to her father's home. In the ensuing days Muh'd grew a bit more repentant and I guess also ashamed . . . His father straightened things out with his dau-in-law's father, and after about two weeks [Muhammad] sacrificed a sheep to appease the family. Muh'd's wife returned.

Perhaps some slight quarrel did precipitate the separation of Muh'd from his wife, but he seems to harbor a very deep "animosity" toward her, in spite of the fact that she's attractive and has a pleasant personality. He confided in me once that he loves another woman who is married to an older man and [that] they carried on an affair together in their adolescence. It may be that this love for this woman whom he has never gotten over prevents him from being very affectionate with his own wife.

This passage only alludes to a scene that was actually far richer than I had time to convey in my rushed diary notes and that had everything to do with our story. On either the first or second morning that I was in al-Hijla, Muhammad had decided to give me a tour of his village. He proudly introduced me to many people, but I remember only one of them vividly. She was working in a field, and her face was covered, so it was hard to tell whether she was attractive, but I found her manner quite charming. She did not come over to us but kept working, her eyes occasionally making bold contact with his. This look, along with her easy laugh and teasing banter, intimated that she and Muhammad were friends; anyone watching them from a distance, however, would never have been the wiser. For his part, Muhammad blushed like a schoolboy.

"What was *that* all about?" I had asked him later.

"She was my sweetheart, Seif," he had admitted shyly, and told me the story of their romance. I was deeply touched by this confidence, and he swore me to secrecy.

I asked him a provocative question. "Doesn't it occur to you, Muhammad, that you and your sweetheart could have been in the same situation as the girls from Sarkhan?"

"How do you mean?"

"Suppose, just suppose, mind you, that you had gotten her pregnant. What would you and she have done?"

He was taken aback. "Well, I didn't. She wasn't. We were careful not to get caught."

"But suppose you had. Gotten her pregnant, I mean. Could you have trusted your parents—and particularly hers—to have been understanding and forgiving if the two of you had come clean? I know that your mother has flexible views, but she's exceptional. What about your lover's parents: would they have set aside their own wishes for her happiness? I can't imagine, knowing you, Muhammad, that you would have deserted your sweetheart if she had gotten pregnant and let her face the wrath of God. No, you would have done something. Fled with her. Died with her. Anything but deserted her. Not like those girls from Sarkhan, left to take their chances in the world with that asshole Abdullah."

"Whoa, Seif, this is pure fantasy."

"Yeah, I know. I said just *suppose*." And I walked away from him testily.

He caught up with me and took my hand. "Look, we don't know what really happened, do we? The girls might still be safe. They might be under the protection of some sheikh and are in hiding. We just don't know."

I said nothing.

My diary entry about my return to al-Hijla continued:

I feel sorry for Muh'd . . . He appears to have little true respect for his father, whom he doesn't consider to be very intelligent. [Left unsaid was the fact of the father's lucrative *qat* fields, which would not come to Muhammad until the old man's death, and that rankled him.] He has little patience with children, and though he loves his son and daughter, I hardly ever see him play with them the way most Yemeni men do. And he has no occupation to fill his time most of the year, there not being enough work in the fields to keep him busy. One reason perhaps he hangs around his uncle the sheikh is that tribal politics can be interesting and engage his quick mind and talents. But what future is there in it for him? He's not about to become a sheikh himself, so there's little in his experiences that can be put to use . . . Lately he's been talking about the possibility of emigrating to Saudi Arabia to make some money in menial work—but he's so proud and so quick to take offense . . . that I fear he may do something rash there and get into serious trouble. The Saudis don't treat the Yemenis very well; the Yemenis in turn despise their employers as nothing more than mere "bedu."

It would be a shame if Muh'd were just to drift all his life, given his obvious intelligence, but the question is: what can he do? Does he show any demonstrable aptitude for a given profession or vocation?

I could feel the tension in my relationship with Muh'd and thought it best for me to get to [the sanctuary] as soon as possible in order to avoid bad words between us. And that very day we succeeded in finding transport for all my things.

. . . Then came the task of moving everything into the house. I told Muh'd that I preferred to do this myself as I wanted to follow a "system" (little snot that I am) best done by one person. In fact, I was just tired of him, though grateful for all the help he had given me . . .

When I went into the house, I found that the kitchen lock had been pried open. When Ahmed Hussein appeared, he said he didn't know who had done it, but Fatimah claimed it had been the work of the marksmen who had temporarily occupied the house during the war. I found a little child's book in the kitchen which was not there before, and inscribed on the title page was the name of Fatimah's brother. I suspect that Fatimah and he together had broken the lock to see what, if anything, I had left behind. But I decided it would be pointless to confront them with my suspicions and dropped the matter.

I spent the whole day thoroughly cleaning the rooms and then moving everything back into its former place. It was late evening by the time I had finished.

Muh'd left the following day with some friends who were heading back to Wadi Maswar. We agreed to meet in [the sanctuary] after ten days had elapsed in order to work together on my tapes . . . He never showed up.

8

⌘

PRISONER OF THE STATE

On one of my visits to Sana'a I found a tiny gray kitten all alone in an alley behind the American Institute for Yemeni Studies hostel. What possessed me to bring it back to the sanctuary with me I don't know— it would hardly have frightened away the rats. I suppose I missed the company of pets. There had once been a very sweet, three-legged mongrel bitch that had wandered by, and I had played with her, but she ran off as soon as the little boys came to torment her. They took to heart the Muslim belief that dogs are "dirty."

"They are also the creatures of God," I insisted, nearly in tears as they hurled stones at her.

"No, they're not, Seif," said one of them.

"Of course they are," I snapped. "Who else created them?" This was nothing more than casuistry as far as he was concerned, and he calmly walked away. Another example of how crazy I was, he was probably thinking. And when she stopped coming by my house, I knew they'd killed the poor animal. Crossing paths with a prime suspect in her dis-appearance, I yelled at him in English, "I just hope she died quickly, you sonovabitch."

A kitten had a better chance of survival. Cats were considered "clean," for reasons not entirely clear to me, and were tolerated in the house as rodent catchers. But the kitten I adopted seemed ill-fated and dim-witted, and I named it Dodo. It also was sickly. I fed it milk and occasionally solid food like canned tuna fish (someone had to like this stuff), but it only got weaker. Its yellow eyes were listless, glued almost shut with a rheumy film. It would lie on its soft little bed in the coolest corner of the house and sleep, not even purring when I stroked and petted it. It was the will of Allah, I sighed to myself.

People in the sanctuary were exhausted, but now that a truce was in effect, they were also determined to pick up their lives where they had been left off. The women had come back from Jihana and were thankful to have homes to come back to. Men returned to their jobs or, like my upstairs neighbor Ahmed, were busy looking for work. None could afford to be idle when facing the prospect of having have to pay a portion of the hefty indemnity in the dispute settlement. The sounds of children playing gaily outside my door seemed to bring life back to normal.

The one person who could not pick up the strands of his former life was Muhammad the Lion. When Muhammad the Lame became too tired to lead the sanctuary's negotiating team, the Lion took over and spent his days and most of his nights shuttling among the sanctuary, Sarkhan, Jihana, and Sana'a. He had a year to arrive at a final settlement, but everyone, and he most of all, clearly hoped it would be sooner, so the pressure was on. The Lion was filled with nervous energy, his bright eyes darting back and forth during a conversation, his hands always sawing the air. Though his face was haggard and drawn, his brilliant smile made him look less careworn and younger than his years. Yet, in spite of the hustle and bustle around him, he seemed a lonely figure, and I felt sorry for him on that account. Occasionally Muhammad the Lame would be at his side, but he didn't have the stamina to assist the lion all the time. Ibrahim the Beltmaker or Muhammad the Hunchback were also of some help, but for the most part the Lion had to shoulder his load alone. He was obviously a very bright man, but what most impressed me was his patience. I would see him as he walked briskly down the street, stopping every few yards to lend a sympathetic ear and then gently but incisively answer the petitioner before continuing on to his way to another appointment. People had to trust him if he was to negotiate a permanent agreement, and he knew that trust is built on openness and constant communication. Dressed always in his immaculate white robe and pillbox hat, which signaled his status as one of the *sada*, he was nevertheless on good terms with the tribesmen, who never spoke ill of him—not in my earshot at least.

The region had become so polarized that the Bani Bahlul was the only Khawlan tribe still neutral in the dispute, but they were not powerful enough to broker a settlement. The North Yemeni government called in the head sheikhs of the Bakil and Hashid confederations, notably the redoubtable Hussein al-Ahmar of the Hashid, one of the most powerful men in Yemen. Al-Ahmar was working not just for the regime in Sana'a. He had ambitions to become president one day, and if he could bring peace to a recalcitrant region, his political reputation would be enhanced. To complicate matters, he had to share the limelight with another head sheikh in the Hashid confederation, Abu Luhum, whose diplomatic skills Muhammad the Lion said were even more impressive. The two men seemed to be jockeying for leadership of the Hashid confederation, and their rivalry could have been a source of trouble, but like truly effective leaders, they worked harmoniously to resolve the dispute. The president's uncle participated in the mediations as well, so the state was now brought in directly. It knew that if the dispute were left to engulf an entire region hostile to its policies, the state would suffer. But the "state" in this instance was ambiguous. Was it al-Ahmar? Was it the regime in Sana'a that he represented? Were the two covertly at odds? There were more questions than answers.

I was not privy to any of the deliberations, of course, and I knew better than to ask about them, but through the poetry I came to understand their twists and turns. Salah Muhammad al-Qiri was my source. He enjoyed coming over to my house to relax in between bouts of negotiation. His brother Yahya's death in the sanctuary battle in early

June had subdued him and made him melancholy, though he was still friendly and outgoing to me. Perhaps because he knew that Muhammad the Maswari had enjoyed working with me on the poetry, he too decided to do so, but I could not honestly say his heart was in it. Fatigue and distraction were factors, but he also lacked Muhammad's clarity and incisiveness. Nevertheless, I owe more than twenty *zamil* poems in my collection to Salah, all of them composed in June, during the final phase of the dispute.

Among the most important were two by Ahmed bin Salih, sheikh of Sarkhan and father of the older missing girl. Ever since his initial outburst of anger, when he accused the sanctuary of responsibility for the girls' disappearance, he had been silent. As far as I know, these poems were the only ones he composed on the dispute.

> And now I have presented my view to the great sheikhs Hashid and
>   Bakil.
> I shall separate [from Khawlan] and go to him in the middle of Marib,
>   lest you think my people are few.

The anger is still there and the festering resentment. If the great sheikhs of the country dishonor *me* by not settling fairly, I shall go to Marib where I can seek the assistance of the ᶜAbidah tribe, a powerful nomadic group allied with the Bani Dhubyan. But, as Salah al-Qiri explained to me, that would only worsen the conflict.

Al-Damani, with al-Saalami the other sheikh of the Bani Dhubyan, struck a conciliatory tone.

> As for the women, we are no longer zealous on that point. Nor does
>   our honor depend on them.
> But I challenge you, O people of high office, Hashid along with Bakil.

This marked a breakthrough; the Bani Dhubyan were dropping the condition that the girls be found. Having made this concession, al-Damani challenged the intermediaries to resolve the dispute equitably. So it was the turn of the sanctuary faction to reply.

[The sanctuary] needs plaster of paris to set the bone.

O intermediaries of Khawlan, it is as if the cast were broken, and you
have let the condition worsen.

I remember how taken the sanctuary was by this poem, and no one more
than Muhammad the Lame. "What does it mean?" I asked him. He limped
over to me on his crutch and took a seat by Muhammad the Hunchback's
stall. "Don't you see?" he said excitedly, sweeping back one flap of his
headdress that had fallen into his face. "The sanctuary has been hurt and,
like a patient with a broken bone, needs to have a cast made from plaster
of paris. We have to settle this business once and for all. But the intermediaries broke the cast and prevented the bone from healing." And whenever he saw me those days, he would reiterate the statement as though it
were a slogan. "[The sanctuary] needs plaster of paris."

The intermediaries gave their opinion of what they had heard so far.

Beg pardon, O leadership of the Yemeni people. And you have shown
us the path.

We no longer want the proposals of [the sanctuary] or al-Damani. The
army is tiring of you.

This seemed to be expressing a pro-government position, but "leadership of the Yemeni people" is an ambiguous phrase, meaning either the
main sheikhs of the two confederations or the president or both. I am
not sure what the leadership's proposals were at that juncture, but the
second line clearly suggests that they superseded those of either side
in the dispute. "The army is tiring of you" unambiguously suggests
that the state would use force if the two sides wouldn't come to an
agreement.

But Ahmed bin Salih was not to be cowed.

O intermediaries, no one will fight at your back. As for fear, I am no
coward.

I hold my ground but say, out of much suffering: Right is not achieved
by might.

He was skeptical that the state, much less the intermediaries, would make good on their threats, but he wasn't a coward and wouldn't back down even if they did. He would only remind them that a settlement must be lasting, and it could not be secured by force alone. And then there is the allusion to his suffering, the only one I came across in the poetry, a reminder of the loss of his daughter.

Sheikh Muhammad al-Qiri, by contrast, questioned the ability of Sarkhan and its supporters to withstand the army assembled against them.

> It is not credible that the sea is diminished by a spoonful [of water], or
> that [the absence of] three individuals, O brothers, can decrease the
> power of seventy thousand [men].
> Tell the government and the tribes and the towering mountains:
> Millions will not disunite us even if we should be camped together
> in a cave.

A broad consensus of opinion considered this one of the best *zamil* poems from this phase of the dispute, indeed a minor masterpiece. Many people, including Muhammad the Maswari, heard and praised it. Salah al-Qiri, the poet's son, explained that the "three individuals" were the three sheikhly houses supporting Sarkhan and, more globally, the Bani Dhubyan: Bait al-Sufi (Salih's clan), Bait al-Shadeg, and Bait al-Royshan. "Khawlan" (in this context meaning everyone but the Bani Dhubyan) was like an ocean and the Bani Dhubyan no more than a drop in it. In other words, the sanctuary side was overwhelmingly powerful. "Millions" of riyals had surfaced at various points, either as money extorted from the hotel owner or in bribes offered by foreign powers. The incidents surrounding this money were moral troughs that Khawlan had sunk into at one time or another, but the region would make up for these failures by remaining united against all temptations and outside pressures, even if they squeezed Khawlan into a cave.

Other supporters of the sanctuary, in the voice of Sheikh al-Gadhi, struck a friendlier, more conciliatory note.

> A million greetings my tongue utters to you, O giants of the people
>   strong.
> I honor the guests by stretching out the right hand to our brother and
>   friend.

To which the intermediaries replied:

> Greetings, Khawlan, right shoulder, occupier of fortresses impregnable.
> O brother of ours in war and other times, we keep your blood from
>   spilling.

Recognizing and appreciating the friendly overture, the intermediaries
were honoring Khawlan as "[our] right shoulder," as a powerful ally of
the state. But the key phrase was the last one, stressing the benign
power of the state to defend and protect the people. The poem suggests that in the end the state alone can solve the dispute but can do so
only with the support of the people. Establishing the state's power was
what the dispute's final phase was about, even though *who* exactly was
the state was in doubt.

Ramadan was nearly upon us, and because nobody wanted to fight during the holy month of fast, the truce held. I was looking forward to
spending Ramadan in the sanctuary, where it would be particularly
poignant this year. Perhaps the intermediaries were counting on the
goodwill that the religious atmosphere would engender to settle finally
this endless quarrel.

On July 9, I was invited to chew *qat* with Ibrahim the Beltmaker and
then to have dinner with Rashid and Hamid, who were in from the
capital. Since we hadn't had a chance to spend much time together
lately, this was an opportunity to catch up. Ibrahim was his usual quiet
and reserved self. The two young men were as chatty and lively as
ever, though Hamid seemed strangely uncomfortable that evening and
asked whether I didn't want to stay over. I thanked him for his hospi-

tality and said I preferred to get back to my house, and when it was twilight and rapidly getting dark, I went on my way. From here on, I prefer to tell the story as I wrote it in my diary. Perhaps I lack the emotional stamina to re-create it.

I was walking along the main road [in the floodplain] when I saw two cars—a jeep and a pickup—parked outside the house of Y. H. . . . As I approached the jeep, men in the front seat called out to me. I went over to greet them and shook each person's hand, as one is supposed to do. One of them asked me where M. H.'s house was, and I replied that I didn't recognize the name and they had better ask someone else. What nationality was I? they asked. When I told them, they seemed very glad to have found me and said they had been hoping to get in touch with me. My "friends" in Jihana wanted to talk to me about the Khawlan war. This sounded suspicious to me, as I don't have friends in Jihana . . . I told them I didn't know which friends they were talking about. (Besides, I wasn't going all the way to Jihana in the middle of the night to talk about the goddamn war.) They then mentioned two names: al-Qiri and al-Baradah [the sheikh from Wadi Maswar]. (I still don't understand why *these* two names were mentioned. Obviously they thought they could lure me away by using them, but does this mean that al-Qiri and al-Baradah were involved in all this? Or did someone else, perhaps even a man from the sanctuary, at any rate a person who knew about my connections with al-Qiri and Wadi Maswar, make the suggestion to them as bait?) I was not about to leave for the sake of al-Qiri and al-Baradah and told them so. I started to walk past the car to go to my house when five men got out and began to struggle with me.

I shouted and protested, yelling, "I am a guest in this village, in this country. How dare you treat me this way?"

Someone hissed in my ear, "Shut up, you jackass, and get in the car!"

But I resisted. So now they fought me. I was boxed on the ears, strangled, gun butts were shoved in my ribs, my headdress was knocked off my head, my shirt was ripped. Together, they eventually hoisted me into the back of the car, with me still hitting out and squirming about. And then we were off. Not a single person in the sanctuary heard my call for help. Yeah, right. That's what they said at any rate. I suspect that some of them had advance knowledge that I would be arrested and either cooperated with the police or were told not to interfere.

I had no clue as to the identity of my abductors. I hoped and prayed they weren't wild and reckless tribesmen out to kill me because they hated Americans. I had heard enough stories from the people in the sanctuary, who said that it could always happen, though I had scoffed at the idea. Now I was horrified to think they might have been right.

I remember my feelings exactly. I was actually calm, concentrating only on what I could do to get out of this mess. Perhaps it was the *qat* that gave me this clarity of mind. I did think, My poor parents. How sorry I am for them, should anything happen to me. But mostly I thought about how to escape.

One man was holding my ankle, the other my arm . . . I thought for a moment that one of them looked familiar. Could it be? Yes, I was sure it was the same man who had accosted me at the wedding in Wadi Maswar, the one who had tried to prevent me from taking pictures.

The men in the front seat began to ask me questions. How long had I lived in [the sanctuary]? Where was I when the war broke out in the village? What was I doing here? How much money did I have in the bank? Did I take pictures and notes on the war? What did I do with them? Send them back to America? I answered . . . and they seemed to soften toward me.

"That son of a bitch!" I heard one of them mumble under his breath to his companion. They were talking not about me but about someone else.

I now suspected that my abductors were working for National

Security and had been ordered by the government to bring me back to Sana'a. I felt a glimmer of hope. National Security was certainly better than irate tribesmen.

But why? What did they think I had done? Or had there been an attempted coup in Sana'a that involved the Americans and we had been ordered to leave the country? I really didn't know what to think, except I was relieved that these men were not out to kill me.

They drove like maniacs, and I tried to make out where we were going. It seemed like the track to Jihana, but I couldn't be sure. One of the men in front kept nervously asking the driver whether we were still in Khawlan territory or Sinhan, so I thought perhaps we were heading to Bait al-Ahmar, the president's native village and stronghold. But why on earth would I be taken there unless the president himself wanted to interrogate me?

Once we arrived at Jihana, a car pulled up alongside ours, a pickup, but it was too dark to see inside. We stopped for quite a while . . . The men in the car got out to stretch their legs and passed around a drink of whiskey. They offered me a sip, but I declined. When they lit up a cigarette, they were careful to cover the match and the cigarette so that they wouldn't be seen in the night.

I wanted to spit out my *qat* and asked them for some water. Then I realized that I still had my spiral notebook wedged inside the waistband of my skirt and wanted to get rid of it. Even though it didn't contain anything incriminating, I didn't want them to find it on my person when they interrogated me in Sana'a. I asked them if I could take a leak. I squatted and slipped my notebook to the ground, where I covered it up with a big stone.

Suddenly, the contact they had been waiting for appeared. I was quickly hustled into our car, and the rest jumped in after me. Were they to take me in or not? was the question from our car. Yes, proceed, was the reply. We continued on to Sana'a.

It was now that I asked them point-blank whether they were the police. In a manner of speaking, yes, said the man who seemed to be their spokesman. Why hadn't they told me who they were in the very beginning? I asked angrily. Had I known they were the

central authorities come to take me in for questioning I would
never have resisted them, but they couldn't blame me for not going
willingly with total strangers in the middle of the night! The
spokesman saw the bruises on my face and half-mockingly scolded
his companions. "Now who was the dog who did that to you?"
Someone else said about me sympathetically, "Anyone can see
he's a nice guy. Why does that son of a bitch want him for
questioning?"

Now another car pulled up alongside ours, and a conversation
was carried on between the two speeding vehicles. HAD THEY
MANAGED TO PICK UP MUHAMMAD QASIM? was the
question that the wind took from our car and hurled into the night.
I didn't catch the reply. So, the Wadi Maswar connection was
important, though in what way I couldn't be sure. I think this was
the first time that I felt a real pang of fear. Were the people whom
I considered my best friends in Khawlan my betrayers? But in what,
exactly, was I being implicated? . . . Simply not knowing what I was
accused of became unbearable. As if to set my mind at ease, one of
my captors said, "Don't worry. If you haven't done anything, you'll
be back in [the sanctuary] in a few days."

They had brought it up, so I quickly asked, "What exactly is it
that I am supposed to have done?"

No answer . . .

We pulled into Sana'a around ten p.m. and . . . went to a large
walled compound. A man came outside dressed in an Adeni *futa*
and conferred briefly with my abductors. I was told to come out
and talk to him. He noticed I had no shoes on and asked me what
had happened to them. I tried to discern the features of his face,
but as he had the light behind him, most of his head was in
shadow. He seemed a relatively young man with a bit of gray in his
hair. About my height. Perhaps he was the high-ranking security
officer who, I later learned, had been put in charge of the
investigation. He asked me a few questions. How much money did
I have in the bank? Had I spent large sums in Khawlan? Had I been
sending my research out to America? Was there someone among

the Yemenis who could vouch for me? In answer to the last
question, I referred him to the Yemeni Research Center in Sana'a
and its director, Dr. Abdul-Aziz al-Muqalih. The style of
questioning was restrained and polite. And at the end, he told me,
"We'll meet again." (But I never did see him after that.)

Now I was driven to National Security. I asked the men in the
car who the person was I had just spoken to. You don't know? was
the surprised reaction. "Okay, he's just about the president," they
said. I presumed they meant the head of National Security. But
might he in fact fact have been the president's brother, a powerful
member of the government? Or could he have been al-ʿArashi, the
vice president? I later learned from the U.S. Embassy that some
people in Khawlan had complained about me to al-ʿArashi and he
had had me called in for investigation. But the man I saw that night
seemed much younger. To be sure, I did not get a good look at
him, but I had the distinct impression he was a younger man.
Whoever he was, he was a high-ranking member of the
government. It seemed ludicrous to me at the time that the state
should perceive me as a potential threat. At an embassy dinner
many months later, a Yemeni official who had known about my
case said to me sarcastically, "Your country has bombs. All we can
do is investigate." In other words, my detention could be seen as an
assertion of state power.

We arrived at this enormous, fortresslike complex, National
Security Headquarters, and I was ushered into the main lobby . . .
The men who had taken me from [the sanctuary] sat around
me . . . After about ten minutes I was conducted into a plush office
where I met my interrogator.

This man was to become known to me as the *mudir* [director].
Of course, this doesn't mean very much when almost anyone of
any importance is called *mudir*. (I think he may be one of the
deputy directors of N.S.) In fact, he may very well have been the
head of the entire operation, yet I was determined to downplay any
sinister construal of my presence in Khawlan. Though not friendly,
he was nevertheless scrupulously polite. He spoke to me in Arabic

the entire time, though I suspected he was fluent in English: if I was
who I said I was, it was important for him to determine how well I
knew the language. There were questions about my passport and
my residence permit. Who had given me permission to go to
Khawlan? To which I answered, "National Security! Since the
Yemen Research Center has to get its permission every time I ask
for a renewal of my residence permit." This was a simple matter to
check, he said. What was I doing out there? Was I *only* gathering
information on poetry and language? No, I said, I was also
researching customs, social structure, oral history, et cetera. Well,
what about the recent war? Had I taken notes on it as well? Yes, I
was collecting the poetry that had come out of it. That's innocuous
enough, but what about the notes on the politics of the war? Yes,
I was noting this down as well (a) because it wasn't possible to
understand the poetry without also understanding the politics of
the case, and (b) because it's the most important event in [the
sanctuary] in recent time. How could I *not* study it from the point
of view of its effect on the *hijra*? At this point, the *mudir* seemed to
be biting his lip, as though he realized a mistake had been made.
"Have you been to Israel?" A somewhat unexpected question, but I
said I hadn't. "How well do you know England?" The last question
was particularly pointed, as if to search out some connection with
the royalists.

The *mudir* then put a call through to the man whom, I presume, I
had met earlier that evening. He gave him a rundown of what I had
told him in response to his questions. Then they discussed what
should be done with me. Into security prison for detention, and the
next day we were to go to [the sanctuary] to bring back my
passport and everything connected with my research.

I failed to note in my diary, though I distinctly recall it, that after
he hung up, the director asked me whether I wanted to contact the
United States Embassy.

"What for?" I asked.

"To alert them as to what has happened."

"No, I'd rather deal with this directly than involve U.S. officials. I've done nothing wrong, and I'm confident I'll be cleared. This whole thing will be resolved much more quickly if we leave the embassy out of it."

"Very well."

Now I was taken in another police van to the detention unit . . . located inside the former National Security building near the American Embassy. My cell was a small room, not more than 3 × 8 m, but had a large bunk bed that took up nearly all the space and a set of large windows . . . Yemenia Airlines posters gave the stark white walls a touch of color, as did a ludicrously oversized and heavy red fake-damask curtain. Actually only one panel of such a curtain. I guess they still wanted to make sure they could see into the room. I happened to notice a section of rubber hose on the windowsill, and I couldn't help laughing sardonically at the thought that this might be *the* rubber hose one hears about in prisons where they "make people talk."

I had a nice chat with my guard, a young captain who is studying law at the university. He sat at the foot of my bed as we talked and reassured me that I had nothing to worry about. "This, in here," he said, looking around the room, "think of it as a vacation."

Hardly got any sleep that night, worrying about what would happen next and wondering just what I was accused of. Obviously it was some kind of spy charge or accusation of political activity aimed against the central gov't—that I was stirring up the tribes in Khawlan and supporting them with arms and money so as to threaten Sana'a's control of the region. It seemed fantastic that I should suddenly be in prison, but when I later thought about it, I could see that perhaps the possibility did not seem so absurd to the Sana'a authorities. Here was an American, in the middle of all the trouble that had been brewing in Khawlan, professing to be a "researcher" (a dubious profession to most people anyway), at the same time that a number of highly suspicious incidents had occurred—the BBC radio broadcast in Arabic, the taping of negotiations among the *wasitah* [intermediaries], evidence of large sums of money being passed around in Khawlan, murmuring of insurrection, et cetera. I knew I was innocent, but there was small consolation in that if I was being framed by someone and National Security believed the story. They could just lock the door and throw the key away, which has happened before . . . I also have to admit that I was afraid of being beaten or tortured, as this had happened to Americans held earlier on charges of espionage.

The combined confusion, panic, and fear was about to drive me mad. I resolved on one thing: that I would not lose my temper and always act respectfully to the guards and higher authorities. I figured the good behavior would speak as well for me as the lack of evidence . . . of political espionage. I also resolved [that] if after two weeks I was still in confinement, I'd try to escape. I was not to rot in prison for months when I was totally innocent of any wrongdoing.

Despite my anxiety I managed to fall asleep for a couple of hours, and around nine o'clock in the morning, I was escorted to a car in the courtyard at which stood an officer of National Security who was in charge of bringing my possessions and passport back from [the sanctuary]. He noticed how disheveled I looked and asked where my shoes were. He had a rather severe look on his face, which, however, gradually softened as we talked. Then we got into the car and drove to National Security Headquarters.

I was seated between the driver and this officer. I spoke amiably to the officer, even asking him if I could read the newspaper which lay on the dashboard, and when I found an article in it by [the poet] Muqalih [from the Yemeni Research Center], we discussed poetry a bit.

Upon arrival at HQ, we switched cars while the officer changed out of his uniform into civilian clothes. But we had hardly gone very far in Sana'a when we switched cars again—this time to a more comfortable jeep. "Especially for you," said the officer. I smiled even though I knew this was bullshit, for it was hardly *my* comfort they were thinking of; still, and true to my resolution of the night before, I pretended to be grateful. While the jeep was being serviced at the station, I bought a pair of plastic Chinese flip-flops. I believed I was almost elegant in them. The storekeeper tried hard not to give me strange looks. I was obviously a foreigner, but what was I doing dressed like a Yemeni who, moreover, looked as if he had just been in a fight, with his face bruised, his clothes torn, and his sandals missing? And what was I doing with officers from National Security? I knew there was no point in telling the man about my plight, and I was perversely amused by his confusion.

Now, we were finally off to [the sanctuary]. Besides the officer in charge of this mission, there was a driver, a guide who knew Khawlan, and my companion in the rear of the jeep, who was the same man who had squatted beside me in the back of the pickup when I was abducted, the tribesman who had accosted me in Wadi Maswar . . . There was something about him, a manner that I can't quite put my finger on, which reminded me of a serial killer. Except for him, we were a relaxed and chatty group. There was nothing "formal" or "official" in the way I was treated. Perhaps this was due to the way I acted with them, not reminding them that they had a "job" to do and a "prisoner" in tow.

There was nothing for me in Sana'a except prison, so I ought to have been pleased with this outing that afforded me a few hours of relative freedom. But I never dreaded anything more in my life. The horrible events of the past evening kept running through my mind, hard as I tried to put them behind me. And then there was the dreadful fact that these men would be taking all my notes—in effect, a year and a half's work—not to mention my passport, and I had no guarantee that I would see any of it again. To make the situation more awful still, I was helping them. Did I really have any choice? Besides, I hoped to show that I had nothing to hide by cooperating this way, which in turn I hoped would expedite their handling of my case . . . And I thought, perhaps misguidedly, I would at least know what they did or did not take and I might even be able to influence their decision. Furthermore, I might be able to pack my things safely so that nothing would be lost or broken.

We hadn't gotten very far when the car stopped on the Khawlan road, still within Sinhan territory, and we all got out to have breakfast. Some dozen or so prickly pears, which were then in season, were the temptation. That along with bread and beans was our meal. Sharing food is such a symbolic act of community, acceptance, et cetera among Arabs that I felt my mood lift. I learned that the head of our party was named Ali. He peeled a prickly pear and handed it to me dripping on the blade of his knife. It was delicious. Then he said offhandedly, "By the way, al-Muqalih knows you." This was by way of indicating that my identity as a bona fide researcher had been vouched for.

It was late afternoon by the time we arrived in [the sanctuary]. I opened the door and showed them in. Dodo, the little gray kitten, greeted me at a run—the most energy I had seen it display, poor thing. I had to leave it behind in the courtyard next to a dish of tuna and water before returning to Sana'a.

They started their search in the sitting room, where they retrieved my Yemeni song tapes as well as an English translation of the Qur'an.

When we went into the bedroom, which contained most of the things they were interested in, Ali told the others to stay outside. Into two large boxes I packed my poetry tapes, all my notes, Xeroxes of theoretical literature, my field tape recorder, my camera and remaining film with contact sheets, diaries, personal as well as official correspondence, my field notebooks . . . Lastly, I handed over my passport. Ali advised me to pack several changes of clothing . . . Meanwhile, I decided to change into a new shirt and a pair of pants. It was then that Ali came across the beautiful belts I had bought from [Ibrahim the Beltmaker] and greatly admired them. One, the smaller but also the nicer of the two, is missing to this day. As we were about to leave, Ali looked for the passport on his person but couldn't find it, and so began a long search among all my things before we finally came up with it. It had accidentally fallen out of his shirt pocket. A brief farcical interlude.

As we came out of the house laden with my notes and equipment, we ran into Fatimah's brother. He was shocked when he realized what was happening . . . He noticed the bruises on my face and asked how I had gotten them. I said that I had fallen the night before while walking home in the dark . . . Of course, he didn't believe me, but he got the point that I didn't want to drag him into the matter. The officer hustled me into the car, anxious to be off before any more nosy people came. "Is there anything I can do?" asked Fatimah's brother. I noticed Dodo wandering out the door of the courtyard. "Yes, ask Fatimah to take care of the cat while I'm away." He nodded. But I knew the kitten was not long for this world . . .

The misery I had felt on our way to [the sanctuary] was nothing compared to how I felt leaving it. For now, they had everything, and all I could do was wait. The box containing my notes broke because of the rattling and bouncing it had to take on the bumpy road, and I wondered anxiously how much of them would now be lost once they were moved from the car. I feared the vibrations would ruin my camera, and I was permitted to lay it on my lap. They took some of my *bala* wedding tapes and played them on the car radio, and someone laughingly suggested that they could play them back to al-Baradah [my friend Muhammad's uncle]. The remark instantly clicked with me. Once again this name—it could hardly be a coincidence. It meant that this sheikh, whom I knew well from Wadi Maswar, was implicated. But how? Was he also in their custody, and did they suspect and hope to prove some sort of connection between him and me, perhaps on the supposition that I had employed him as an agent or a spy? That they had been looking the night before for my friend Muhammad might mean that they were trying to round up suspects who were known to have had dealings with me. If they hadn't caught up with Muhammad, he might even now be on the run. On the other hand, could it be that al-Baradah had put the security police onto me in the first place and that they were hoping to question Muh'd about my activities?

Jihana. The officer in front tried to make radio contact with an agent. "Is Abu Hashim with you?" Jesus Christ, I had to laugh to myself. Abu Hashim? What a code name. It referred, of course,

to one of the *sada*, not necessarily from [the sanctuary] . . .
Nevertheless, I had a strong intuition that I knew this mysterious
Abu Hashim. Could he have been the son or nephew of Ibrahim
the Beltmaker, or even his brother? Or Muhammad the Lion?

On the outskirts of the capital, we stopped at a hole-in-the-wall
to have lunch. It turned out to serve very good *hilba*, along with
bread and meat. Then back to the former palace of the imam
where I had spent the previous night. I stood in its courtyard,
looking at my work piled at my feet, while Ali instructed one of
the guards to take me to my room. I was to be treated with kid
gloves, he said. "Well, what's going to happen to me, Ali?" He
stood squarely in front of me and looked me in the eye. "If you've
committed a crime against the state, then it's on your head. But if
you've done nothing wrong, all your things will be returned to
you." He gestured to the pile at my feet. So far he had been very
nice to me (aside from the fact that he had probably pinched my
belt, but I didn't know that at the time), and to show my gratitude,
I shook his hand and smiled.

"Can I take some things with me? A book or two and some
translation work to keep me busy?"

"Of course."

I started to retrieve some things from the boxes when my
nemesis piped up.

"What's that? That looks like a codebook."

Hans Wehr: A Dictionary of Modern Written Arabic was printed on the
cover. Ali examined it. "It's a dictionary" he said flatly. The little
man was obviously peeved. He'd been trying hard to find
something incriminating and had failed once again.

I smiled at Ali and said goodbye.

"Crimes against the state . . ." It was all so vague. Never having
been formally charged, I didn't know what I was accused of. And
apparently neither did they . . .

I was led to the cell I had occupied the night before. It was on
the third and top floor of this beautiful old building, near a
stairwell and at the foot of a fairly long corridor, at the opposite

end of which was a sitting room fully furnished in the Yemeni style. Occasionally I was to be let into this room, where the officers were having lunch, and they would invite me to join them. The bathroom was next to it. My movements were to be confined within this space, for how long I did not know.

The nice captain was not on duty. It was his night off. My warden was a much older man, decent enough but not very friendly. Just another political prisoner, he must have thought, like so many others that had been through here. He quietly closed the door behind me.

I flopped down on the bunk bed and retrieved from my pack a book, *Cider with Rosie*. A delightful volume but rather slim. It would hardly tide me over during my "vacation in prison." The most active part of my trials was over, but I feared that the worst was yet to come: the waiting, fighting the gradual ebbing of hope, the boredom of solitary confinement. If I was in for long, I had to ration my diversions over the stale succession of days.

Nervous exhaustion had left me weak, but I still had trouble sleeping. My thoughts flitted back and forth between home, my parents, my friends in Wadi Maswar who might or might not be in cahoots with the authorities, and my friends in [the sanctuary] who probably were . . .

A noise in the courtyard awakened me. I turned over in bed and pulled the pillow over my head to block out the light. I thought I heard the sound of the window opening in the cell door and could see an eye peer at me through a narrow slit, but perhaps I was dreaming. When I woke up again it was nighttime. My watch read eight o'clock. How long had I slept? Six hours? Thirty?

I got up and sat on the side of the bed. The neon lights from the courtyard lit my room in a sickly yellow pallor . . .

I decided to let the guard know that I was ready to eat. Someone new came to the door whom I hadn't seen the night before. They must shift the guards every day, I thought, so that they won't fraternize with the prisoners. There went my plan to befriend one of them as a possible ally—in what exactly, I wasn't sure.

I had been asleep only a few hours, he assured me. I told him that I wanted dinner but could wait to eat mine with him if he was having some later on.

"Fine," he said politely. "Is there anything else?" Might as well go to the toilet, I thought. Didn't know if I'd be able to rouse someone again to come to the door later.

When I got out of the bathroom, the guard was nowhere in sight. I caught a glimpse of him in the sitting room next door, apparently unaware that I had exited the bathroom. For an instant, my heart leapt with excitement. Had I wanted to, I could have made a mad dash down the hall right then and there but decided not to. Where would I have gone? How would I have gotten out? Instead, I went quietly back to my cell. When I got there, however, I couldn't open the door. I rattled the knob and lock, but they seemed fast, so I turned to go back and tell the guard, when I saw him standing in the doorway of the sitting room. Whether he had been aroused by the sound of my trying the door or had been watching me all along, I didn't know.

"Hey, man," I said in a somewhat condescending tone. "I can't get in because the door's locked." Here was the prisoner *wanting* to be let back into his cell and reprimanding the guard for dereliction of duty.

He came toward me nonchalantly. "No it's not. See?" And he flipped the lock and opened the door. We both laughed. His face was badly pockmarked, but he was otherwise good looking.

Eventually bread and beans arrived—not tasty but at least nutritious, and more than one person could eat. No thanks, the guard said, he had already eaten, and left me. I secreted one loaf in my backpack, in case I had to wait a long time for breakfast.

In the late hours of the night I was awakened by the chanting of the prayers from the mosques, but . . . I don't recall having awakened again afterward . . .

. . . It was such an odd sound. I had heard it before but couldn't identify it. The rustling of dresses, perhaps, or the wash of waves? I opened my eyes and looked out my window. It was dawn, and then

I realized—though I could hardly believe it—that what I was hearing was the sound of hundreds of birds stirring in their nests. The large, lone tree in the courtyard was alive with them, its leaves shaking, its limbs swaying, even though there wasn't a breath of wind, and now and then several of the birds would dart out of their rich green cover like tiny missiles hurled over the wall. Their chirping grew louder and more raucous, at times even ferocious, as if they were having an argument.

Got out of bed to do some calisthenics, dressed only in my underwear. A good time to do it, I thought, as none of the guards was probably up to watch me through the spy hole. Then, I sat back on the side of the bed and thought of ways to escape. Not that I would probably, but the idea gave me hope. I noticed that the window in the corridor outside my cell had been left open, and it could be reached through my window without too much trouble. I could crawl out my window and circumvent the locked door. I could make my way silently down the stairway and into the courtyard. Then it would be a matter of luck whether I could escape over the wall without being seen or heard . . . Since my room was on the top floor, an alternative route was through my window and onto the roof, which I judged to be only a few feet above my head. But once on the roof it would be a matter of luck whether I'd be able to find a way down the side of the building . . . The most direct escape was out my window to the courtyard below, but how to get down there? I couldn't jump three stories without a broken ankle or leg. Was there any means of lowering myself to the ground? Nothing as convenient as a rope, of course, so I would have to make something out of the materials to hand. The curtain perhaps, braided with strips of the blanket, which I could cut with my razor blade. [I had been allowed to take my toilet articles with me.] I would have to make my lifeline while everyone else was asleep. Even if it were strong enough to hold me, I doubted it would be long enough to reach to the ground, but maybe it would be long enough to allow me to jump safely. The distance was approximately fifteen feet. That would be possible.

Then it occurred to me in a shock that Ramadan had started. *That* was why I had heard the *tasbih* [special prayer] last night. That would also mean that the guards would be up most of the night. I would not be able to move around unseen, and surely there would be no cover in broad daylight. I had been almost exhilarated with planning my escape, but now I sank back onto my bed in despair.

I did some translation work. Concentrating on it, which wasn't always easy, relieved some of the anxiety. I read *Cider with Rosie*, read it again, and reread it. In the late morning I took a shower, as much to wash away the sweat and grime as to rouse myself from my lassitude.

Around one o'clock the officers and guards of the entire prison invited me to join them for lunch in the sitting room. My guard from last night was there too. He had been taciturn then; now he began asking me *why* I was here. I told him the whole story from start to finish, concluding that the security people had made a mistake, for I had not broken the law. I expected his reaction to be unsympathetic. Sure, sure, kid. How many people who get thrown in here say they're innocent! But he listened without expressing any judgment on the matter.

I became bitter and said, "They told me I might have to leave Yemen before I've had the chance to finish my work. Well, even if they don't find anything incriminating, I hope they deport me, because I'm fed up after all the problems I've had." I told him about spending the nine months looking for a field site and, when I finally found it, having to spend eight hundred riyals a month for rent, and no sooner had I moved in than a war broke out and eventually I had to flee, and as soon as I returned, I was picked up by National Security on charges of . . . well, I don't even know of what. This last experience has finished me. "I don't have the energy or the will to go on with the fieldwork. I want to go home."

I knew I was trying consciously to win this man's sympathy, but I wasn't playacting. I couldn't see how I could drive myself to finish the bloody dissertation . . .

One of the officers mumbled under his breath, "Bad luck is with him." He asked me brightly whether I'd been to the July 4 Independence Day celebration at the U.S. Embassy. The question took me by surprise. Perhaps he sought to change the conversation to a more cheerful topic. He apparently had attended the official function, a formal dress affair, and had enjoyed it very much. The picnic. The games. The fireworks. They were all great.

Soon I was back in my cell. The bloody dissertation . . . Surely I would not be allowed to finish my poetry research. But even if I were released and allowed to go back to Khawlan with all my notes and equipment, would it be safe to return? Someone in Khawlan had it in for me, and it was because of them that I was in prison. Even if National Security assured them I was innocent, would they believe it? There was always the possibility that those who were satisfied that I was not an American spy might now suspect I was an agent in the employ of the Sana'a government! . . . The dissertation would have to be theoretical, whatever it was, and that would represent a pleasant change from wallowing in treacherous fieldwork. I warmed to the prospect, as I did to the idea of going home. I spent most of the afternoon dwelling on such thoughts, if I wasn't desultorily working on the translations.

For dinner, the pockmarked guard got me a meat sandwich he had picked up at a local restaurant. I was touched by his gesture.

"I'm sorry that there isn't anything else to eat," he apologized.

"After bread and beans"—I laughed—"this is a meal fit for princes."

I was awakened in the night not by the mosque prayers but by what sounded like screams coming from deep inside the prison. They unnerved me, of course, but fatigue got the better of alarm . . .

The next day, Saturday, July 12, was the worst. My spirits sank when I heard a guard yelling to another man on duty, "Guess what? The American has given the whole rundown on the situation."

I presumed they were talking about me. Of course, I always knew they would read my notes, but I never expected it to come as such a shock, even more than when I was taken by force out of [the sanctuary]. I felt violated. They were reading passages I never intended another person, let alone bureaucrats of the state, to see.

And then, quite involuntarily, I thought about the two young women who had been abducted. Not that I thought at the time that I might be raped in this prison, but the utter loss of privacy and control was the closest I came to experiencing something of what they had been through. I burned with shame and resentment.

It is curious that I should have identified with the young women rather than with Abdullah the Culprit, who after all, was now in prison somewhere in Khawlan. But I had come, perhaps too lightly, to believe that he was guilty whereas they were not, and I thought I was innocent like them. I wonder whether I wasn't also suppressing a fear of being raped. I didn't then have the strength, as I might now, to acknowledge its possibility. It's not that I had heard stories about rape in Yemeni prisons; unlike our own, they are not dens of viciousness. It was, rather, the logical outcome of a certain train of thought that started with me in a conventionally female position—subordinate, passive, all but helpless. Had I been roughed up, would the torture have included some such humiliation as rape? It's something just to be able to ask the question, to shake up a complacent masculinity.

The prospect of indefinite incarceration depressed me. If I had "given the whole rundown on the situation," perhaps National Security would think that I *was* culpable. Nothing seemed to provide distraction, either. I was not in the mood to read *Cider with Rosie* yet again. And I was unable to concentrate on my translation work. What else was there to do except think of ways to answer certain questions that might come up in another interrogation?

I must have drifted off to sleep all that afternoon; at any rate, I cannot recall anything distinct that happened . . . At around ten o'clock in the evening, the officer who had spoken to me about the July 4 picnic came to my room and woke me up. He brought some fresh fruit—a banana and some grapes—and said something to me, though I was too groggy to register it. I do remember thinking at the time that what he was saying was a good sign. Perhaps the investigation was going well and he was trying to give me hope . . .

The next day [July 13] I was greeted with a surprise. In the morning I was conducted to the *mudir*, who was behind the wheel of a jeep parked in the courtyard.

He smiled for the first time. "How are you doing? Are you getting enough to eat? Well, we've just about finished our investigation. There are still some people we want to talk to—"

"Which people?"

"Oh, I'm sure you know who they are—in order to verify your story. After that we'll decide whether to let you return to Khawlan or to keep you in Sana'a or to deport you."

He paused to let that news sink in. "In the meantime, you're to be taken to the Sana'a Hotel to await our instructions."

"I have to stay there? Like a house arrest?"

He nodded his head.

After I gathered up all my things in my cell, I said goodbye to each of the guards. The young captain who had been so sympathetic on my first night in prison said without thinking, "I hope we'll see you again."

To which I responded laughingly, "Under better circumstances, I hope."

It was the pockmarked guard who drove me to the hotel. "You see! They didn't find anything. It failed." I was still too bewildered to think clearly about what had just happened. And nothing as yet, I realized, had been said about my notes and equipment. Would they be returned to me? And in what condition?

I checked into the hotel and said goodbye to the guard.

"Thanks for having been so nice to me."

"You're welcome. But it was easy, once it was determined that you were innocent. Take care of yourself, Seif."

My new quarters were an old Yemeni house converted into a cheap boarding hotel. I soon discovered that it was crawling with National Security types or their informers and concluded that it was a kind of halfway house for people like me, whose legal status in the country was in doubt. A lot of émigrés from South Yemen were there, waiting to hear whether they'd be granted an entry visa or would be deported. I was to await the verdict of my own fate with them. Once in my room, which was even less inviting than my cell in the palace, I lay on my bed thinking about what to do next. I could go to the embassy, but I had reasoned all along that it would probably be better not to involve the diplomatic types. The best thing would be to go to AIYS and see Jon Mandaville. Tell him what happened and confer with him on what to do next.

Jon was alone in his office. I was surprised to see how grim he looked and jumped to the conclusion that he already knew what had happened to me.

"No, I don't know what happened to you," he said, utterly surprised to see me. When I looked down at his desk, I realized the reason for his dismal expression; he was working on one of those tedious translations which brought in badly needed income to the Institute. I hurriedly told him my story. I didn't want to stay too long because I was hoping that National Security would call on me at any moment with news. It was rather a lot to lay on the poor man so quickly, and I don't think he quite took it all in at the time, but I said I would get back to him in the morning to see what advice he had about the matter.

"Does anybody else know what happened to you?"

"I'm certain that al-Muqalih does, because he was contacted by National Security to confirm that I was in Yemen to do research."

"What about the embassy?"

"I don't know. I didn't ask them to get in touch with the embassy. I didn't want to turn it into a diplomatic incident and complicate the issue."

I then handed him a handwritten list I had made in prison of all those items I could remember the agents from National Security taking [from the sanctuary]. I could account for about 95 percent of the material. In case I were immediately deported, he would have some knowledge of what had been taken from me, could inform the embassy of the items, and through them work to get it all, or as much of it as possible, back to me or to AIYS. Jon Xeroxed the list and gave me back the original.

Since Janet had spotted me from the window, I went into the main house to say hello to her. She immediately noticed the bruises on my face.

"Oh my God, you've been in a car accident."

I told her I couldn't talk about it now and Jon would fill in the details for her, but I was fine and she was not to worry.

"Well, at least stay long enough to have a cup of coffee."

"Ah, I've been dreaming about your coffee. And can I borrow some books from the library? I'm afraid I've exhausted the charms of *Cider with Rosie*."

The next day Jon and I went to the U.S. Embassy to have the list notarized—at the suggestion of Dr. al-Muqalih, whom Jon had contacted that morning. Muqalih promised to intercede with National Security to get the notes returned to the Yemeni Research Center.

This intervention was significant beyond what it might have portended for my research. The notes were no longer, if they ever were, mine. The point Muqalih was making, in asking that the notes be returned to the Center, not to AIYS or to me directly, reasserted the authority not only of the Center but of the Yemeni state, of which the Center was an arm. He was construing the notes as de facto as well as de jure property of the state. Yet the matter was not so clear, since I sensed that the Center and National Security, both state powers, were in discreet conflict. Muqalih, though appearing unruffled, seemed irritated that he—a man of national prominence—had not been consulted, let alone told in advance, about National Security's intentions to have me arrested and investigated. Having the notes returned to the Center would reaffirm its—and his—authority.

[The U.S. consul] told me that the embassy had been notified of my arrest by the Yemeni government just a few hours after it had happened. It had been told that it was a 'routine investigation,' prompted by a request from the vice president, who in turn was acting in response to complaints about me in Khawlan, that the

Yemeni government would handle it as fairly and as expeditiously as possible, and that I had specifically asked not to involve the U.S. government. When I made it clear that I still didn't [want to do this], unless I had to leave the country or unless my notes were not returned, the consul, in turn, implied that the embassy had no wish to [get involved], given that its relations with the government in Sana'a were already strained. He was referring, of course, to the negotiations over unification between North and South Yemen. Would it have intervened under other circumstances? I wondered.

And then, in a more casual, off-the-record tone, he asked me, "How did you do it? I mean, most of the time when these things happen, they lock you up and throw the key into the Red Sea."

"I suppose by trying to create some goodwill in the first place. But I have to assume that it was because I was innocent and in the end they knew that."

"Or perhaps you have more powerful friends in Khawlan than you realize."

"I like to think I was just lucky." Though he had a point. I was always wondering who was against me, not who was for me.

Back to the hotel I went. Like everyone else, I lolled about during the day, trying to work but too tired and weak to show much for my effort. I broke the fast in a local restaurant with other displaced souls in the city, urban migrants most of us, missing our relatives back in the *bilad* [home district]. It was not your usual scene. In order to be served water and food immediately after the muezzin's call to prayer, one had to reserve a place at the table, and that meant coming to the restaurant several minutes beforehand. There we all glumly but patiently sat, these anxious few minutes before the fast was broken being the hardest to endure. As soon as the sounds of the microphones could be heard to start up in the minarets, men would pour water or tea in their glasses and take their first sip of the day. One could see in their eyes how satisfying it felt.

"Are you fasting?" a neighbor asked me in surprise. "Are you Muslim? No? Then why are you fasting?" A good question. To have a vaguely felt experience of community, I thought, but I was too exhausted to give an adequate answer and tried deflecting the question. "I don't mean any offense."

"None taken, none taken. To your health!" And my curious interlocutor cheerfully raised a glass in salute. The others around the table heartily joined him.

We then got down to the business of appeasing our hunger, and a business it was, for meals are rarely relaxed occasions drawn out for their good company and conversation. That was for after dinner, in the sitting room. About fifteen minutes into the meal, in fact, I noticed that most of the men had left to go to the mosque for their ablutions and prayers. Since I would not join them, I could take my time.

After dinner I went to the souks, always lively places but never more so than on Ramadan nights, when they stayed open much longer, brightly lit with many strands of colored lightbulbs. It was like walking along Fifth Avenue [in New York City] for Christmas shopping. And since people stayed up later, homes with beautiful windows shone like lanterns in the night sky. From some could be heard emanating the strong, clear voice of a professional chanter— well-to-do Yemenis would hire one to recite the Qur'an, verse by verse, each evening during Ramadan until the entire book was heard, and I would linger for a moment to soak up the tranquillity of the sound.

I was expected back at the hotel every night, but after about four days of this, I couldn't see the point of staying there at my own expense when there was no telling how long the investigation would take, and I decided to check out.

"Tell your friends at National Security that I am leaving your hotel." The man behind the desk was somewhat taken aback. "Here is where I can be reached. The American Institute for Yemeni Studies. Tell National Security." And I handed him a piece of paper with my name and address and bounded with my belongings out the front door.

. . . On the eleventh day after my release, the call came for me to pick up my things at National Security. Jon drove down with me, Heath coming along for company. Since it was Ramadan, it was an early evening appointment. We waited almost an hour in the reception room before I was ushered into the interior of the building.

I was taken to a room where one of the young men who had been present at the previous interview greeted me. He apologized on behalf of National Security for the inconvenience . . . and said I was free to go back to Khawlan, if I wished, or stay in Sana'a, or leave for the United States.

"Before your things are returned to you," he said, "there's just one last thing, however." [He took out a diary I had kept in Saudi Arabia.] He riffled through the pages and asked with feigned casualness, "Was there *anything* inside it?" I remembered the picture of the deposed Imam Badr that I had hidden there a long time ago. The *mudir* had asked me whether I had ever been to London and spoken to Yemenis there, meaning, no doubt, the expatriate community that grew up around the deposed imam in the 1960s and 1970s. Saudi Arabia had supported his unsuccessful efforts to thwart the revolutionaries, and no doubt National Security suspected that those efforts might be revived in the current climate of national instability, and that the picture of the former imam linked me and Saudi Arabia to a potential plot to reinstate the monarchy. I looked him in the eye and shook my head to the contrary.

"Okay," he said and handed back the diary. "Let me take you to the room where your things are." They had put everything in the same boxes, one of which was badly torn, so I gingerly carried that one while a youngster carried the other. As we proceeded down the corridor, a charismatic young man in a spotless white robe suddenly appeared in a doorway and recited a line from a famous *qasida*. Somehow, I instinctively knew that this performance was both a final test and a salute, for it was a poem I had studied and written about in my notes, so without thinking I blurted out the next few lines. He winked and smiled as I went by and then went back into the room.

Before we passed through the doors to the reception area, where Jon and Heath were waiting patiently, my interrogator said goodbye. "Well, Seif." It was the first time that any National Security officer had used my adopted name. "Take care of yourself." He smiled and handed back my passport.

Later that evening I carefully examined the contents of the two boxes. Everything had been returned—with the exception of the picture of Imam Badr. Across the flyleaves of books was written in Arabic "Translation of the Qur'an" or "Dictionary." I was amused to see that in my poetry translations someone had helpfully written alternative translations for words or phrases that seemed to suit the meaning of the text better.

Who would have thought that my brief experience as a political prisoner would have such a charming conclusion? A Yemeni friend later put the whole matter in perspective when I told him I had been imprisoned for three days. "Oh well, that's the customary number of days of hospitality." He laughed. "Consider yourself to have been the guest of the Yemeni government."

The attitude of the American community in Sana'a toward the affair was more indignant. How could such a thing have happened? Doesn't Caton have rights like any other citizen? Shouldn't a complaint be lodged? Unbeknownst to me, I became a *petite cause célèbre*, perhaps even an embarrassment to the embassy, which had not been spirited in defense of my "rights" in the first place and certainly didn't want to stir the embers now. The political timing was all off. I was not invited to speak to any auxiliary society of the embassy, perhaps because word had gotten around about my own reaction. I wouldn't have wished the experience of incarceration on anyone, but I couldn't blame the Yemeni authorities for having been suspicious—speaking of "rights," they seemed well within theirs—and, aside from my initial forceful abduction, I could not complain. They had conducted their investigation gently and with considerable dispatch, under the circumstances.

9

∾

RAMADAN NIGHTS

Walking in the streets of Sana'a one day not long after my release from prison, I happened to see Muhammad the Lion. He was in the front seat of a military jeep as it flew by, talking animatedly to a fellow passenger, a high-ranking officer, and grinning from ear to ear. He would have known the outcome of the Khawlan dispute, but I had no chance to talk to him. Even if there had been an opportunity, I wasn't in the mood. I felt betrayed by the people of the sanctuary, and for the time being I couldn't face them.

That I was able to conclude my poetry project at all was thanks to the sudden appearance in Sana'a of Muhammad the Maswari. I almost didn't recognize him at first. He looked a bit disheveled, with his hair all rumpled, his headdress draped loosely around his shoulders, one shirttail sticking out of his *futa*, and physically diminished, bowed over and shrunken, as though older and more timid. And he had no dagger at his waist, which was odd, for a tribesman is rarely seen in public without his *jambiyya*. But then Muhammad might not have wanted to be recognized as any particular tribesman and surely not a Khawlani, at least in Sana'a and at that time. Seeing him again was so unexpected that his figure, standing in my doorway, is forever framed in my memory, like a snapshot.

"How are you, Seif?" He extended his hand with a sheepish look.

"Why, I'm fine, Muhammad, I'm fine. How are *you*?" After my initial surprise, I was glad to see him. I took his hand but then pulled him toward me for an embrace and a kiss on both cheeks. He broke out in one of his shy grins, relief at this warm welcome plainly visible on his face.

I ushered him into the small *mafraj* that I used for visitors. He took off his shoes and followed me to a seat, where I made a display of fluffing the cushions and straightening the armrests. "Hey, man, relax and make yourself comfortable. I'll be right back with some tea."

When I returned, he was puffing contentedly on a cigarette. I asked him about his family. "And how's Salah al-Qiri?"

"Still sad about his brother's death, God preserve him. He sends you his greetings."

"How did you ever find me, Muhammad?"

"It was simple." He shrugged. "I went to the American Embassy. You know Ahmed the Somali? He was very nice. He told me where I could find AIYS."

"Very logical." I nodded in admiration. "As always."

There was a slight pause before he went on. "Tell me, Seif, about what happened."

I told him the whole story, and he became tentative again. "Seif, I— I hope you don't think that I—that *we* in Wadi Maswar—had anything to do with this. No, no, Seif. I have to say this. They came to Wadi Maswar, you know, wanting to take me back with them to Sana'a for questioning. But I told them, I said, 'You'll have to fight me if you do, and I won't go alive.' We argued, but in the end they gave in and left."

He seemed to want to come clean, so I thought I might as well express my own worst suspicions. "Are you sure it wasn't *you* they were after but only me they could get? I mean, maybe after you refused to go with them, they went after me instead, to see how much they could find out from me about you and your uncle. Several times on that trip from the sanctuary to Sana'a the name of al-Baradah came up. That's your uncle's, isn't it? They didn't seem to like him very much. Why is that? What's his connection to all this?"

Muhammad was shifting in his seat and seemed abject in his misery. I had to admit I savored his distress. "We in Wadi Maswar had nothing to do with your abduction," he reiterated meekly. "They came after me when you were already in prison."

I was annoyed with him for thinking I didn't deserve a fuller explanation, though I realized he was perhaps in no position to offer one. I got up and paced around the room as I thought out loud. "Was it perhaps your uncle who complained about me to the vice president? It was he, you know, who issued the order for my arrest."

Muhammad's self-possession was dissolving, and he seemed on the verge of tears. "No, believe me, Seif. My uncle would never have done that. That's unthinkable. You were his guest."

"Yeah, I know all about being a guest. Remember the guy who tangled with us at the wedding? The one who got all uptight about my taking pictures?" Muhammad nodded, looking chagrined. "He was one of the ones who abducted me. And the next day he brought National Security back to the sanctuary to get my tapes and other things. Don't tell me he was acting on his own and not the orders of someone more powerful than he in Wadi Maswar. Who more powerful than your uncle?"

Muhammad gave me a level glance that was supposed to signal a moment of truth. "Seif, what happened to you ultimately embarrassed me as well as my uncle. Maybe it was meant to. He has his enemies. Maybe they were trying to get back at him, to discredit us by imprisoning you, making it appear that there was some sort of conspiracy in which I and my uncle were implicated. But please, please believe me, I would never for the world have wished on you what happened, and I am truly sorry for it."

I said nothing, which he took to mean I had accepted his protestations of innocence. I suppose I had. We had both run afoul of forces larger than ourselves that we understood, he perhaps better than I, only dimly. I asked, "Muhammad, if they were after you and you refused to come to Sana'a, why are you here now?"

"The danger is over, Seif. Peace has been made. There's now a permanent settlement between the sanctuary and Sarkhan. There's no reason to hold you or me in suspicion any longer." He winked. "We can't do any more mischief." He chose his next words carefully. "I came because I wanted to see you again and to continue working with you on the poetry—if that's what you want."

"Okay." I grinned. "Let's get started."

Muhammad told me that the intermediaries had put forward their proposal for a final settlement at the end of June. It was still subject to negotiation, but there was tremendous pressure on all sides to agree. Abdullah the Culprit would be handed over to Sarkhan for execution. In compensation for the missing girls, the sanctuary would pay 1.6 million Yemeni riyals (about US$350,000). The son of the hotel owner Shahben would be kept in the custody of the tribes awhile longer, in case he knew the whereabouts of the girls after all and could be persuaded to talk. And another payment would be made to Hajbah for the damages he incurred when the sanctuary's supporters ransacked his convenience store in the last battle. Not all terms of this proposal were accepted. The view of the al-ʿArush tribe siding with the sanctuary was expressed in a *zamil*:

> If I once said that someone knew it [tribal law], there is no longer
>   anyone. The law has been forsaken and integrity lost.
> After the sada have given over the madman, in shackles, nothing else
>   remains for them, for they are guiltless.

"The poet is invoking the principle of revenge killing," said Muhammad, "the boy in exchange for the girls. According to tribal law, there should be no additional compensation to be paid, especially after all the expenses the sanctuary incurred hosting the sheikhs and their retainers."

Sheikh Hussein Ali al-Gadhi was also incensed by the compensation demanded for Hajbah's store.

> May God grant you insight, O intermediaries. How can Hajbah's stall
>   be the equivalent of al-Gahirah?
> Our opponent has lied to you, for truth is self-evident and the
>   evidence is in the tin cans.

" 'The evidence is in the tin cans.' " Muhammad repeated the line and chuckled. "You see, Seif, the sheikh argues that the sanctuary's loss of property cannot be compared with a few paltry tin cans." The grandest building in the sanctuary, the Citadel, had been trashed. "If anything, the *sanctuary* is owed compensation"—Muhammad cut through the air with his open hand for emphasis—"rather than the other way around."

The intermediaries conceded the sheikh's point, but they also accepted the argument, put forward in the earliest stages of the mediation, that the sanctuary was not wholly guiltless, even though Abdullah the Culprit seemed to have been acting on his own. Guilt is collective, and therefore the fine remained in place. The sanctuary would have to pay Sarkhan.

"Seif, I have a present for you." Muhammad reached into the breast pocket of his jacket and retrieved a tape cassette. "This is a *qasida* you probably haven't heard yet. Shall we listen to it?"

Muhammad realized far better than I what his coming to Sana'a meant. We could now work without interruption and for as long as we wanted, and it was working at what we enjoyed most. When other researchers came to the hostel, I introduced Muhammad to them, but then we would retire to my room to concentrate. When a spare room was available, I rented it for him, to give us both privacy, but we worked in my room together.

It did not take long for us to establish a routine. This still being Ramadan, we liked to sleep late into the morning. While Muhammad sauntered off to see his pals at the taxi stand next to the Shaʿub Gate, I would run errands, write letters, and make notes on the texts I hadn't understood the night before. Sometimes he would break the fast with me but more often he would eat with his Khawlan friends and wouldn't come by the hostel until a couple of hours after that.

I can see him now, sitting in a chair next to my desk, his feet on the seat, his knees drawn up under his chin, his hair slicked down to one side after his evening shower, wearing a new shirt I had gotten him as a present, which he buttoned all the way to the top. Of course, we were chewing *qat*. How else could we have gotten through an evening of such intense work? A pile of branches and leaves would build up; I would sweep it away in the morning. Occasionally, Muhammad might get up to go to the corner of the room and pray.

We listened to a poem by Salih Ahmed al-Radami from the Bani Bahlul tribe of Khawlan.

> O Lord, I praise you as many times as the stars revolving in the sky, as heavily as the rains that fall.

Muhammad pushed the pause button on the tape machine and dictated the words to me. Although quite conventional, this devotional beginning had renewed significance for us during Ramadan, as did the next line.

> I implore You in the name of him whom Gabriel addressed in the cave: "Keep all dangers away from Your slave."

"Of course, the person Gabriel addressed in the cave was the Prophet, blessings be upon him and his people," Muhammad said. But I knew that. "And as you know, the Qur'an was first revealed to him by Gabriel in the month of Ramadan."

I thought I knew what the rest of the line meant, but I wanted to make sure. "And what does he mean by 'Your slave'?"

"Well, you know, Seif, a devout Muslim submits to the will of God, and becomes His slave." The tape recorder went back on.

> And you, O bird, rise! Convey these poems. Convey to the poet al-Badda our copious greetings.

I knew this to be a convention of tribal *qasida*, the conceit that the poet gave his verse to a bird or some other messenger, an airplane or a taxi, to convey to his audience (often another poet). Now came the message of the poem, the gist of the matter:

> I spent Friday evening of the past month sleepless while deep in
> thought and perplexed.

Once again, the poet followed convention, imagining himself so agitated by events that he could not sleep, but the next long passage was wholly fresh in its references and powerful in its narrative, standing out from all the other poetry in the dispute:

> When the muezzin called at dawn, I was on the roof of my house,
> chatting idly. The sky was clear, and in it the moon was full.
> Lightning flashed above Mount Kanin as if there were rain, and I said,
> "Happy is he who wakes this morning to find his land wet."
> I peered into the sky as a star was streaming through the air: the lightning flashes I had seen were dangerous.

Muhammad second-guessed my perplexity. "The poet thinks he is seeing lightning and a star streaming through the sky when in fact they're flashes of cannon fire and streamer bullets." The poet then realizes his mistake:

> It was war between brothers after they grieved for the two little chaste ones.
> They, the most chaste of the group. All of us are dismayed. None of us is cut off from the rest, nor is anyone a stranger.

"Of course, he means the two girls from Sarkhan, and what he says at the end is a reminder that all of us in Khawlan, notwithstanding our disagreements, are part of the same brotherhood, and we must not carry disputes to the point of destruction."

Muhammad started the recording again. He would raise the volume a bit in certain passages and hold the speaker close to his ear when he was uncertain of the words. Sometimes what he suggested seemed unlikely to me, and I would object. "Are you sure, Muhammad? That would throw off the rhyme completely," and he would replay the passage again and again until we were both satisfied.

> The two groups of the Bani Bahlul went with the bulls to conclude the
> truce in Khawlan in the afternoon,
> Saying, "O my brothers, Khawlan, O land of the free. Help a brother
> who came to mediate, [and accept the] sacrificial bulls."
> O Bakil, sympathy is with the people of sorrow, and they will choose
> some good ones among them to conclude a truce.
> The war is between us all, a festival of evils. We shall untie our knot
> with a shazira.

"This is important, Seif. He means that in the end it wasn't only the sanctuary and Sarkhan that were fighting, but all of Khawlan—'a festival of evils,' as he puts it. But note how he insists that we can solve the problem ourselves." I was still puzzled. "What does *shazira* mean?" "I wish we were in Wadi Maswar so I could show you," he said, a little exasperated. "It's a big, thick needle"—he bunched his fingers as if to suggest its point—"that is used in sewing heavy things made of leather or burlap. If you insert it just right, you can loosen a big knot with it, for instance."

> Marib Dam was destroyed, razed because of the rat. The value of the
> rat is nothing, but its deed was immense.

Marib Dam, built by the Sabaean kings in the sixth century B.C., was one of the great engineering feats of the ancient world—measuring 680 meters long and 18 meters high, and transforming an area of just under 10,000 hectares into a fertile garden. The floodwater, whose discharge at the height of the rainy season could reach a volume of 1,000 cubic meters per second, was first contained in underground basins until its turbulence was calmed and then allowed to flow by gravity through underground canals to two main oases, where a network of smaller feeder channels directed it to adjacent fields. Though the dam was breached many times in its thousand-year history, the final bursting came in A.D. 575, when damage to the structure was so great that it was beyond repair, and large-scale irrigation in Yemen came to an end. The event is commemorated in the Qur'an, and Muhammad now recited the passage for me:

> There was for Saba, in their homeland, a Sign—two gardens, to the right and to the left. "Eat of the sustenance provided by your Lord and be grateful to him [for] a country fine and a Lord Forgiving." But they turned away [from God], and we sent against them a flood [released] from the dam. And we converted their two gardens into gardens producing bitter fruit, tamarisk and a few stunted lote-trees. That was the punishment we gave them for their disbelief . . .

Later, in the verse entitled "Saba," it says that the Sabaeans' downfall was due to their covetousness in the incense trade.

According to Yemeni legend, a rat burrowed through the dam and started the leak that led to its collapse. How does this myth function in the poem as an allegory for the events in Khawlan? "The rat is Abdullah the Culprit, who shamed the tribes by taking away the two girls," volunteered Muhammad. To me, this analogy of the Marib rat and Abdullah was too explicit, but I had to admit it had a kind of appealing symmetry, and it was compelling to think that something so weighty, essential, and even ancient as tribal honor should be compared with the great dam at Marib; that despite its monumentality it was extremely vulnerable and could be brought low by something so insignificant as a rat or a heedless young man, and that its ruin could lead to the destruction of an entire society.

> As for the one who even though he has side curls is one of our *sada;*
> maybe she was made pregnant by him when she was small.

"What on earth is this about?"

Muhammad chuckled at my helplessness. "He means that Abdullah the Culprit, who caused all these problems, is like a Jew masquerading as one of the *sada*, and that he got the older girl pregnant even before he ran away with her." "So being a Jew is something nasty and underhanded? Evil?" "Well, yes. The way you Americans sometimes refer to blacks as animals who want to fuck your women." "Well, what about this pregnancy? Does anyone in fact *know* she was pregnant?" "No, but one strongly held view is that she got pregnant by him."

"That's another thing. Even if we believe she was pregnant, why was it necessarily by him, an outsider to her tribe? Why not by someone in her own tribe or village? If we're going to speculate, why not that possibility?"

"I'll tell you why not. Because the tribes don't want to dig in their own dirt. It's more convenient to think of one of the *sada* as the culprit than another tribesman."

I was surprised by the frankness of this reply. "Okay, maybe he knew her, and that explains why she climbed into his car so trustingly, or so desperately." I compromised a bit. "All we know is what Abdullah admits to, and even that can't be taken as the truth, or at least the whole truth. He says he took them out of the village and drove them to a Taiz hotel where he had his way with them. Why do we need to invent stories about the girl being pregnant? Because it's convenient or easier to blame the girls rather than to acknowledge something more complex." I paused. I wanted to make myself clear without rankling Muhammad. "I remember what some of the younger *sada* said about Abdullah the Culprit. Yes, he was a dog for what he had done, but unlike their elders they didn't insist he was crazy. They especially complained about how hard it was to afford marriage because the elders set exorbitant bride prices. There were reasons why Abdullah acted as he did, and they go beyond his character or mental state. They have to do with Yemeni society. We don't have to agree on why Abdullah the Culprit abducted the girls and sold them into prostitution, and anyway that's not my point. My point is that one can look at the girls in the same way. Yes, they acted irresponsibly, even stupidly, but perhaps the explanation can be found in the larger context, not in their character."

Muhammad was silent. It was not that he was upset or brooding; he was simply not there. As critical as this poem was about Yemen's moral order, or the capacity of the tribes or the state to govern, or any number of other issues, it could not extend its criticism to the position or treatment of women in Yemen. One had to look to elsewhere for that . . . It was time to take a break.

We liked to listen to music, but Muhammad was not one for dancing, like the young men in the sanctuary. He found even amusements such as card games or watching television contrived. If we weren't carrying on a conversation, which was when he was in best form, he preferred to remain quietly absorbed in his own thoughts. I had grown to appreciate his reserve. Occasionally we went onto the roof of the house and took in the beauty of the city at night or ducked into a café for a late snack to sustain us until dawn, when the fast would begin all over again, but for the most part we simply, as it is said, hung out.

On one of our breaks Muhammad pulled out a stack of magazines in the corner of my room. He discovered one I had been careful to conceal but had momentarily forgotten was in the pile, a dog-eared copy of *Playboy*.

"What's *this?*" he asked with genuine perplexity. Some Yemeni men I knew in Sana'a managed to find pornographic material, but in Muhammad's milieu, it was almost nonexistent, even in private. And buxom starlets with plunging necklines on the covers of movie magazines were certainly not as raw as the photos in *Playboy*.

"It's just a magazine." I was not feigning nonchalance, nor was I trying to act sophisticated. But I was inured to explicit sexual imagery, as most people are in America, and its ordinariness, even everydayness, was banal to me.

He opened it to the centerfold. The picture is still clear in my mind: a model with long, blond hair standing full length with her back to the photographer, looking over her shoulder at the camera. I also remember a lurid red background, a velvet drape perhaps, that lent a pink, Rubenesque glow to her skin. I will never forget Muhammad's reaction either. If steam could have escaped from his ears and mouth, as with a cartoon character, it certainly would have. He grew pale and short of breath. He kept staring at the image and bringing the page closer to his face and then placing it at a distance, as though his eyes had trouble focusing.

"Amazing" was all he could say for a while. "Strange."

"Not really. These magazines are all over the United States. There are even ones with pictures of nude men."

"You must be kidding, Seif. I can't imagine it. Do you have any of those, too?"

"No, but I'd show them to you if I had. They're not prostitutes, these women. Many of them are professional actors or models—you know, women and men who pose in advertisements for clothing or cigarettes— and sometimes they are paid a lot of money or get free publicity for being photographed without their clothes on." He remained silent, the magazine trembling slightly in his hands. "And there are women and men in the United States—among them very religious people—who object to the sale of this stuff. They say it's shameful or sinful."

"Seif, this sort of thing is forbidden here. It's degrading. It shames the girl's family." Of course, it would have to be the girl's *family*. "Where are her brothers that they don't prevent this sort of thing from happening? At the very least busting up the magazine!"

I had to laugh. This was an unexpected coincidence of patriarchal anxieties and feminist concerns.

"Okay, you have a point. But don't tell me that your poetry is so innocent."

"What do you mean, Seif?" He looked up from the magazine for the first time.

I went over to my desk to read one line. " 'Maybe she was made pregnant by him when she was small.' Doesn't that strike you as a bit lewd? As if he was a child molester or she was a little slut? We've already established that there is no basis in fact for suggesting this. So it must be a sexual fantasy, no? And just as in a magazine, it circulates from poet to audience all around the country."

"May I borrow the magazine, Seif?"

I had mixed feelings about this but told him he could keep it. How could I deny him what I wouldn't a friend back in the United States?

He rolled it up and stuck it in his belt, exactly where his dagger would have been.

But Mary, the anthropologist doing fieldwork in Yemen to whom I later told this story, was furious at what I had done. "Oh please. Now he'll show his buddies the magazine, and they'll think all American women are available like pinups. Even if you told him about the professional models and actresses, he's not going to understand the fine differences. Steve, I'm a woman, and I have to deal with harassment from guys who get their images from those magazines."

"I'm sorry," I said. "I guess I wasn't thinking."

That wasn't the only reason I regretted having given the magazine to Muhammad. He did show it to his buddies, as Mary predicted, and was caught doing so by some elders, who tore the magazine to shreds and bawled him out. They didn't ask him where he had gotten it— "I never told them, Seif"—but it didn't matter much, since they presumed I was the source. I was the stereotype of the foreigner corrupting Yemeni youth who was spoken of in the poems. "Is that how you feel you've turned out under my influence, Muhammad? Turned into another Abdullah the Culprit?"

He laughed. But he didn't ask me for any more magazines, and the subject of pornography was dropped.

> The sada of the sanctuary are no longer in the wrong with the
>   neighbor, after they have handed him over for the bullet of
>   death.

"This is a silver bullet that is used to execute murderers and other criminals," Muhammad explained. "In other words, the sanctuary has handed over the criminal for execution, and that should be the end of the dispute."

> But the case has expired, grown bankrupt over a thousand dinars. The
>   vultures are hungry, and the situation is increasingly confused.
> Greed and ignorance: they are a vortex into which we have plunged.
> O President of Yemen, send teachers to exhort and inspire us.

> O stars over Yemen, there is no good in much money. Everyone knows
> to his shame what is in the deed of sale.

"Okay, Muhammad, stop the tape recorder. What money is he talking about?" I had my suspicions, of course, but wanted to know what
Muhammad thought.

"Well, there were actually several incidents involving money that he
might be referring to. The first had to do with Shahben, the hotel
owner from Taiz, and it distracted everyone for a while from the more
important matter of resolving the conflict between Sarkhan and the
sanctuary. But then, as you know, a truck was found full of Saudi riyals,
and people thought that the Saudis were paying various sheikhs to
prolong the dispute, hoping, in turn, to cause problems for the government. Of course, the poet is saying that these were shameful and
roundly condemns them."

> Solve the problem internally, and if anyone incites strife, we shall pour
> him a bitter drink.
> The wrecker in his job prevails over a thousand builders. O men of
> Yemen, everyone take stock of his conscience.
> I end the speech and pray to the best of all, the seal of the prophets
> and messengers. There is none like him.

"The end. That's it, Muhammad." Dawn was beginning to creep into
the room.

"Okay, but just one more thing. Note that he says, 'Solve the problem internally.' The solution has to come from *within* Khawlan and not
be imposed from the outside, be it from the government in Sana'a or
Riyadh or Washington or wherever."

"Right now the problem we have to solve is lack of sleep."

10

∽

FAREWELL

Before I left Yemen, I had to return to the sanctuary to get my belongings and say goodbye to some of my friends. But which ones? My
sense of betrayal ran deep. The sanctuary as a whole might not have issued the original complaint against me, but I knew it must have cooperated with National Security to have me taken in. I kept thinking back
to the night of my arrest and to various aspects of what had happened,
things that I had hardly paid attention to at the time but that now
seemed portentous.

After I chewed *qat* with Ibrahim the Beltmaker, his nephew Hamid
had asked me almost plaintively to stay on a bit longer. This seemed,
in retrospect, more than a gesture of friendship. Could it have been an
involuntary betrayal of remorse? As son-in-law of the vice president,
who issued the order for my arrest, he must have known what was
about to happen, but for him to be put in the position of knowingly
betraying a guest (whom, I had to presume, he also liked) would have
been shameful. No doubt his uncle Hussein, the shadowy figure in bitter exile in the sanctuary—the same man who had from the very beginning suspected me of being a spy—had put him up to it. I had to
console myself with the hope that he had done so grudgingly. Was
Hussein the "Abu Hashim" whom the National Security guards had re-

ferred to so disdainfully in the car that night? And had he thought he could get back into the good graces of the Sana'a regime by collaborating? It was galling to think that, of all the families in the sanctuary, it was his that had set me up. I had enjoyed some of my most relaxed and unguarded moments with them. But, of course, that was the elegance of the trap.

I pondered the complicity of others in the sanctuary. Yahya, next to whose house the vehicle containing the National Security guards had parked, had to have known what it was doing there. There was also my upstairs neighbor Ahmed, who could have let them into my apartment if I had by chance eluded them on my way home. I now fancifully spun a web of conspiracy that covered the entire village and beyond, for I knew that others in Khawlan were in on the game. I was tormenting myself with suspicions that could never be definitively laid to rest and indeed only succeeded in fueling my mounting paranoia. I had to keep reminding myself that the village had been to war, and that I'd simply had the bad luck of being in the wrong place at the wrong time. And if I had been really honest with myself, I would have had to admit, looking back to the days preceding my arrest, that friends in the sanctuary had given me ample warning, with their discreet suggestions that now was the time for me to take a vacation in Sana'a. If I'd failed to read the signs clearly, I had only my own morbid curiosity and, yes, even opportunism to blame. From blaming others, I came full circle to a morass of self-recrimination and doubt. I was disgusted with myself.

This vicious circle had to stop.

I had been explaining to Janet Mandaville my extreme reluctance about returning to the sanctuary when she had an inspired thought. Reentry might be easier if I had a companion. Wondering who that person might be, I heard her exclaim, "Heath! I'm serious. It's safe now in the sanctuary, isn't it? The fighting has stopped. National Security is letting you return, so there can't be any danger."

I began to see her point. Having an innocent, energetic child around might make me less cynical, and his happy-go-luckiness would make the situation less grim. Most important, his presence would distract me from my increasingly obsessive preoccupations.

"But would he go?"
"The question is whether you're up for him."

I was quite sure Heath would get carsick during the long, bumpy taxi ride to the sanctuary, but I couldn't have been more mistaken. He sat quietly, even pensively, next to me, dreaming whatever ten-year-olds dream as he watched the moonlike volcanic landscapes slip by the car window. I had learned to love them, and I wondered whether he would, too.

I didn't know what shape my apartment would be in, if Ahmed and his brothers had amused themselves inside, but my fears were unwarranted. A quick inspection revealed nothing amiss or missing. I suggested that Health might want to put his backpack in the *mafraj* and to consider that space his own. Only one thing was of interest to him, however, a bullet hole in one of my bedroom shutters. I explained how it got there. We then made a brief tour of the village, where I introduced him to Muhammad the Hunchback and some of the other denizens of the souk. Predictably, the fact that he spoke Arabic so well immediately led to speculations about his possible Yemeni origins. Heath's unexpected appearance, and the sensation it caused, momentarily diverted us from the embarrassment of my sudden reappearance in the *hijra*.

Only moments after Heath and I had finished lunch, there was a loud knock on the door. I knew it couldn't be Ahmed, for I had learned that he was away on a job. Like many others in the village who had been thrown out of work over the last few months, he was desperate to earn cash, and in his absence Fatimah had moved in with her parents. Perhaps she had come to give me some freshly baked bread, as she had kindly done in the past. And after the Citadel had been ransacked, the old man Ali had never moved back to it with his daughter-in-law and little grandson, and who could blame him? I missed him.

"Could He-e-e-th come out and play soccer?" asked the boy at the door, whom I recognized as a neighbor. Before I had a chance to relay the request, Heath was out the door. I shouted instructions in Arabic

and English as to when he should return for dinner, but it was clear
that he was no longer mine to control.

I sat on the front steps and gave in once more to brooding thoughts.
The village was more than usually quiet for this time of day, no doubt
because most people, even the wretched schoolteachers, were still
away. There was something haunting in its aspect—or perhaps it was
the air of exhaustion one encounters in places recently ravaged by catastrophe—that accentuated my feeling of abandonment. Heath had
helped to break the ice, but my resentments now congealed into an-
tipathy. I retreated into the interior of the house to decide what to
pack and what to give away. I would leave my hiking boots to Ahmed,
who could use them. I doubted that Fatimah had the money to buy the
furnishings, so I would pile them in the corner for her to find.

Heath returned sooner than I had expected. Nothing was wrong, he
assured me. He had enjoyed playing ball, but then he decided it was
time to come home. I was touched to realize that in his own way he
felt responsible for me.

"Would you like to take a walk to see where the tribesmen fired on
the *hijra?*" I asked.

I hadn't actually been to the top of the mountains since the war had
begun, so this prospect was as interesting to me as it was exciting for
Heath. In the crisp air of a late September afternoon, the village's outlines were sharply visible below us. I tried to describe the fierce battle
that had raged that night, though the only view I had of it had been
from the slit in my bathroom window. Stirring our feet in the pebbles,
we found some shell casings. I had expected a more boisterous, boyish
fascination with the detritus of war, but except for an uncomfortable,
high-pitched titter now and then, Heath uttered hardly a sound.

That night I was suddenly awakened by moaning. At first I thought
it was my own. Then I realized that it was coming from the *mafraj.*
Heath's head was damp with sweat, and he was shivering with fright.
Perhaps he had been having nightmares about the fighting in the sanctuary. I confessed to him that I, too, had slept poorly and suggested
that we spend the night in the *mafraj* together. I offered to take him

back to Sana'a the next day if he liked, for it had always been our agreement that we could return anytime he wanted to, but he bravely decided to wait and see.

As the novelty of Heath's presence wore off in the village, various of my friends and acquaintances started to welcome me back in earnest. "You're innocent, you're innocent," Muhammad the Hunchback cried almost exultantly. "Now I and everyone else knows that you hadn't done anything wrong." I had to laugh at how he was betraying his own initial misgivings.

"What are you going to do, Muhammad, now that hostilities have ceased?"

"I? I'd like to make the Hajj before it's too late in my life. But we have so much to pay back in damages and fines that I won't have the money to do it."

"How much do you think it would cost you?" I asked.

"About five thousand riyals."

I looked at his *jambiyya*, the beautiful carved knife that every Yemeni tribesman carries, which I had long admired. "What if I were to give you five thousand riyals for your *jihaz*?" The *jihaz* is the whole kit of belt, scabbard, and knife.

We shook hands on the deal. It now hangs in my apartment in Boston.

Ibrahim the Beltmaker was looking after various mosque properties in Khawlan al-Tiyal, and while he was away, it was unlikely that his son and nephew would be home. As it turned out, I was not in the *hijra* long enough for our paths to cross, so I never saw them again. It was probably just as well.

People I bumped into said it was good that I was out of prison, though not without also an embarrassed little laugh. Muhammad the Lame, alone of all the *sada*, invited Heath and me to lunch with him and his family. This was the closest I got to an apology from anyone in the sanctuary.

"It turns out that you're the chronicler of our dispute," he said.

"What do you mean?"

"You've been taking careful notes of our troubles from start to finish." He gave me a wry smile. "Now we can come to you to find out what actually happened," he added sarcastically.

I pondered the implications of his statement. "It's a chronicle now, Muhammad, but someday I may want to turn it into a story. If I can. Does that worry you?"

He laughed. "You mean that will be your revenge? To tell Americans how you were mistreated?" Then he abruptly changed his tone and became more philosophical. "Such a strange story, isn't it, Seif? I hardly understand it myself . . . You will have your hands full."

I left Yemen in October 1981. Muhammad the Maswari came to Sana'a to see me off and to give me a series of *zamils* he had collected on a recent dispute between two tribes in Khawlan. It was the last I saw of him.

11

∿

TRAVEL ADVISORY

Twenty years elapsed before I went back to Yemen. Why it took so long is a question I have puzzled over many times. Even more perverse than the long delay in my return was the ostensible reason for it: to *end* my personal and intellectual attachments to Yemen. But why should I do that, when I had invested three years of my youth in the country and been so richly rewarded for them? How could I explain these strange feelings, to myself as much as to my Yemeni friends and American colleagues who had continued to work there? And if I wanted to break off relations, why go back at all?

"Finding closure" is what I told my incredulous friends and family concerned about my safety—determining whether the "event" of 1980 had ended when I thought it had, then catching up with the lives of its participants and seeing how Yemen had changed in the interim. Perhaps I could find out what had happened to my friend Muhammad before his death and to other people who had experienced the "troubles" in Khawlan. Perhaps I could finish the book about them that I had started twenty years before and never had the heart to complete?

But what would such a return and such a work signify: an act of turning away and bidding farewell, or one of reconnection and renewal? If one wants to end an affair, one should *end* it, or risk falling in love all over again. Perhaps that is what I secretly hoped would happen when I went back.

The day after my arrival in mid-June 2001, I went to the Old City's Sha'ub Gate, expecting to find the Khawlan taxi stand, but it was no longer there. What had been the outer edge of Sana'a in 1981 was now densely packed with ugly cement buildings as far as the eye could see. I was told to go about a kilometer and a half to the other side of the city to find what I was looking for. There I was greeted by a more familiar sight of Land Rovers set over greasy pits and jeeps being serviced by oil-smeared mechanics. A knot of suspicious onlookers formed around me. Any westerner in that part of town created a stir, especially after kidnappings of foreigners that had recently become common, but particularly when, like me, he wore a Yemeni headdress in the Khawlan style. I had not forgotten Muhammad the Maswari's instructions: fold the square piece of cloth once on its diagonal to form an equilateral triangle and drape this over the head so that the apex falls down the back and the two other angles frame the sides of the face. Then wind the right one tightly around the head, tucking the tip under one of the folds, and do the same with the left or let it hang like a drape on the side of the face or pull it over the mouth for protection against the dust or flip it over the head to give—well, a flippant appearance.

I bought a Pepsi at a hole-in-the-wall store and explained my errand. "I'd like to deliver this letter to Ahmed Muhammad Qasim of Wadi Maswar." A curious onlooker kindly took me by the hand and walked me to a large one-room structure, where a tall, distinguished-looking man greeted me and said *he* was Ahmed Muhammad Qasim. Though I had a feeling he was familiar, I couldn't quite place him.

"There must be some mistake," I said politely. "I knew Muhammad Qasim, and he would have been your age. His son Ahmed would be much younger."

"How did you know Muhammad?" the man asked. "In any case, he's dead, God preserve his soul. What do you want with his son?"

"I would like to visit his father's grave and pay my respects to his widow and children."

"Very well, I'll give Ahmed your letter. How can he get in touch with you?"

Experience had taught me not to expect a message to get through in Yemen with any alacrity, so it was a pleasant surprise to pick up the phone the next morning and hear a young man's voice on the other end saying he was Ahmed, the son of my friend from Wadi Maswar.

"Truly?"

"Ah-h-h," he replied.

"In Sana'a? At this very moment?"

"Ah-h-h-h."

I suggested we meet by the cannon outside the Military Museum on bustling Abdul-Jamal Street (named after the Egyptian president), a landmark that a Yemeni tribesman with a cultural interest in weaponry would know. As soon as I laid eyes on him, I discerned the likeness to his father and, even more, to his grandfather. Tall and thin, with a long, craggy face, he also possessed the latter's intimidating reserve and regal bearing. He made me think of a young Abraham Lincoln. I would soon discover that, though he lacked his father's oratorical flare, he possessed the full measure of his tenacity.

Dodging cars and pedestrians in the traffic-clogged streets, we made our way back to the American Institute for Yemeni Studies, still the home for American scholars doing research in Yemen, though it had changed location numerous times and was now in a neighborhood known as al-Qa, which had been inhabited predominantly by Jews before they emigrated en masse to Israel in 1952. One of the routes (as a precautionary measure, Americans were asked by the embassy to take different ones to their residences each day) brought us to a building, the sight of which always gave me a shiver of fright.

"Did your father tell you that I was incarcerated there? They call it the nail-puller prison. National Security wanted to haul him in for questioning, too, but he told them he would never go alive. That was your father to a tee."

I introduced Ahmed to the Institute guards—another security precaution since my earlier days in Yemen—and then escorted him to the *mafraj* of the main building, one of the loveliest old homes in this part of Sana'a. "Your father and I used to stay at the Institute and work on poetry day and night. Now that's no longer possible." I didn't tell him it was for security reasons. I was embarrassed that I was unable to extend to the son the same hospitality I had to the father. "Let's have some refreshments."

While we sipped our tea loudly, I presented some mementos.

"This is a tape of your father reciting poetry. I don't know if you remember what he sounded like, but his enunciation was so clear and his voice so powerful that I thought you might like it." We listened for a while.

"And here are some photos."

One of them Ahmed had already seen in my book on Yemeni tribal poetry, the product of my earlier fieldwork, which Flagg Miller, then a graduate student and now a professor of anthropology, had given to him a few years earlier. It showed his father squatting on the ground next to two little boys. I pointed to the one on Muhammad's right and said, "This is Muhammad Hussein, your cousin, I believe." Ahmed nodded. "He was such a good boy," I said. "He'd go with me everywhere in the village to make sure I had everything I needed. Is he still around? Is he in good health?" Ahmed nodded.

"And this is you!" I pointed to the other boy, not much older than a toddler, on Muhammad's left. The father glanced shyly at the camera, and this look in combination with the crouching posture made him endearingly vulnerable. One arm was around his tiny son, the hand tenderly clasping his shoulder in a gesture of paternal affection.

"That's not me," Ahmed demurred. "That's one of my cousins, also called Ahmed."

"But I'm sure it's you. Your father would take you out to the fields, and while he was cutting alfalfa for the cows, I'd play with you. You'd stand on a little stone wall and bravely jump into my arms and then we'd whirl around like dervishes. You laughed and laughed and begged me to do it again. We would spend the whole morning like that while your father would occasionally look back at us over his shoulder and smile."

"It's possible" was the only crumb Ahmed would offer.

"You might have been too young to remember."

"You came to Wadi Maswar in 1980, right, Mr. Steven? I was just born then. I couldn't have done the things you describe."

"But, Ahmed, I'm sure your father told me that the little child I played with was his son by the name of Ahmed. The infant your mother was nursing at the time—which you say was you—was your sister, Fatimah."

He retrieved an identity card that gave his year of birth as 1980. This evidence was hardly conclusive, however. Yemenis, especially the older generation, because birthdays were rarely recorded, are hazy about their exact ages. The mandatory identity card did not come into existence until well after I left Yemen, and it is conceivable that when Ahmed applied for one and was asked to fill in his birthday, his mother and uncles said, "Around 1980." There was much at stake for us to believe our respective stories or, more accurately, to not disbelieve them. If my book was wrong about something so crucial as the infant in the picture, where else, I wondered, could it be in error, and what did this say about my anthropological expertise? I had come to Yemen to reconstruct a narrative about an event, and this was my first inkling of how difficult it might be to do. For Ahmed it must have been equally disturbing to have this stranger claim his age to be other than what he all along had thought it be, impugning the memories of his mother and older relatives to boot. Is cultural memory any less trustworthy than scientific knowledge? Each of us clung to his certainty as to a raft in a turbulent river.

Another photograph shows Muhammad standing next to a relative and friend who was building a new house in the village. They are grinning from ear to ear, their cheeks bulging with *qat*. I had caught them in a relaxed, jovial mood, as though they are enjoying a good joke. Gazing at the young man next to Muhammad, I suddenly realized why the person I had met at the Khawlan taxi stand looked familiar; a younger version of him was staring back at me. Ahmed hinted that something had caused a falling-out between his father and this man, and he warned me to stay away from him.

"As I said in my letter, Ahmed, I'd like to see your father's grave. Do you think it's possible?"

278 ~ *Steven C. Caton*

"Ah-h-h," he said. "We can take you back to Wadi Maswar under cover of darkness and no one will be the wiser." I liked the bravura with which he dismissed government regulations, the way one might swat a fly, but it was hard to imagine keeping my appearance in Khawlan a secret when an American was forbidden to go there without official permission. What had happened since 1980 to cause this region to be off-limits to foreigners and particularly Americans?

A word I added to my working vocabulary in 2001, which I did not even know twenty years earlier was *mukhtataf*, "kidnapped." There had been at least a hundred kidnappings in the 1990s, mostly of prosperous-looking tourists; employees of development, banking, and health organizations; oil workers; diplomatic personnel; and occasionally members of their families. Preposterous though it may sound, they were treated like "guests" in the kidnappers' households—there being a thin line between being a hostage and being a guest anyway—and in all but one case they were returned after a few days unharmed, if a little unkempt and weary. A folklore had even arisen around kidnapping in Yemen, and one story was about a Chinese worker taken from a crew that was laying the asphalt road between Sana'a and Marib. When his abductors approached the Chinese government for a ransom, their demands were rebuffed, and after a couple of months the worker was quietly dropped off in Sana'a without further ado. The erstwhile victim, by contrast, supposedly begged his kidnappers to take him back to Khawlan because he had been treated more kindly there than he was in his own country. The one kidnapping that ended badly, making U.S. news headlines (and lingering to this day in the public imagination), involved Islamic militants who threatened to harm or kill their sixteen hostages if their political demands were not met by the Yemeni government. The latter responded with armed force, and several people, including four of the hostages, were killed, two execution-style and two in the cross fire. The rebel ringleader was put on trial, sentenced to death, and executed.

While my friends in Khawlan admitted that their region had been involved in some of these kidnappings, they also were adamant that the primary culprit was "one crazy sheikh." He had pulled off his latest stunt just a few weeks before, in early June, when he and his accomplices snatched a young German tourist from the middle of the capital's main square in broad daylight *and* under the noses of the police. The deed's sheer audacity embarrassed the state, as it was surely intended to, and amused the tribes with its derring-do. Two weeks later the foreign community was relieved to see the young man's unshaven and haggard face on the front page of the *Yemen Times*. No details were provided as to the kidnappers' conditions or the ransom the German government paid in the form of money or the promise of development projects. What caused this rash of kidnappings? Khawlan—including al-Jawf in the east and Saʿdah in the north, where other kidnappings took place—realized that, by comparison to the rest of the country, it lagged behind in badly needed development. Highways were yet to be paved, schools and clinics built, rural electrification—not to speak of telephone service—installed, and water pumps replaced or repaired. The government had not been forthcoming in channeling such resources to Khawlan because of its uneasy political relationship with the region, and pork-barrel politics being what it is, these monies were earmarked for more loyal clients. The cynical adage of twenty years ago still applied: "Yemen is the Republic of the Sinhan [the president's tribe]."

By 2000 the threats against foreigners had gone beyond kidnapping and came from a different source. The wake-up call was the October terrorist attack in Aden harbor on the U.S. naval ship *Cole*, an attack that was linked to al-Qaeda operatives in Yemen. One week before my planned trip, the State Department, responding to "credible evidence" of a bomb threat against its embassy in Sana'a, had issued a travel advisory to Americans. The continued presence in Yemen of FBI men investigating the *Cole* incident might have prompted this threat, but another reason may have been that it was the anniversary of the devastating 1998 bombings of U.S. embassies in East Africa. Though these threats were real for U.S. personnel and matériel, their seriousness for ordinary citizens like myself was harder to gauge. I recalled that when I was in Yemen for the first time in 1979–81, when North and South Yemen were at each other's throats, and I received a telegram from my sister urging my return, I imagined that U.S. press reports had exaggerated the dangers. Sitting in my Boston apartment in late spring 2001 and reading similar stories about political violence in Yemen, I wondered whether they were doing so again. The only way to find out was to contact people "on the ground," like then resident director of the American Institute for Yemeni Studies, Christopher Edens. He was the latest but arguably also the most academically distinguished in a long line of successors to Jon Mandaville, the Institute's founding resident director. He had a Ph.D. in archaeology from Harvard and had been doing surveying and excavation work in Yemen for several years. Chris reassured me that everyday interactions of ordinary American citizens and Yemenis remained calm. What the situation was like in Khawlan he would not venture to say, and he conceded that getting permission to go there might be impossible.

"Would you like to chew *qat* with the governor of Sana'a Province?" I now asked Ahmed. Khawlan al-Tiyal came under his jurisdiction.

The governor happened to be a good friend of a friend of mine, a man I had known many years ago by the name of Sabri Salim. In Yemen, what gets done usually depends on whom one knows, as well as on good timing and good luck. Sabri was the founder and director of a successful Arabic language school in Sana'a and knew everybody of any importance. When I told him about my hopes of visiting Khawlan, he suggested I bring the matter up with the governor at a *qat* chew he hosted every Thursday afternoon. "Bring Ahmed along," he advised.

Sabri's house is one of the tallest and grandest in Sana'a, and in keeping with all such edifices, the *mafraj*, where the chew was held, was at the top. "We've always joked that all it lacks is an elevator," the governor said. He was about my height, bald, with a round face and twinkling eyes. Somehow I expected someone more fearsome looking to be governor of arguably the most important political region of the country. His unpretentious, easygoing manner disarmed me, as perhaps it was intended to, and belied his toughness and efficiency, of which I would learn in due course.

"Yes, I nearly wore myself out getting up here. But it was worth it." I was alluding not just to this opportunity of meeting the governor but also to the spectacular views of the city on three sides of the room.

The governor was surrounded by a small entourage and phones that kept ringing all afternoon. When he took a call, there would be a lull in the conversation as everyone strained to pick up a stray hint or two about mysterious affairs of state.

I had brought along a copy of my book and at an opportune moment opened it up to the picture of Muhammad. "This is the father of the young man next to me. He helped me a great deal with the research and saved my life when there was a war where I was doing the fieldwork. Unfortunately, he died some years ago."

This was Ahmed's cue. "Mr. Steven would like to visit my father's grave. I would escort him to Wadi Maswar, where he'd be my guest. I would make certain he did not venture beyond the wadi. Do we have your permission?"

"And you're from which village in Wadi Maswar?" the governor asked. "Okay, Ahmed Muhammad Qasim al-Hajjam from al-Hijla. If you get permission from your sheikh for Mr. Steven's visit, have him write a letter to that effect and take it to the administrative director of Wadi Maswar in Jihana for his approval and signature. Then come to my office in Sana'a on Saturday, and if the papers are in order, I'll issue the permit."

"I'll be there on Saturday morning, *inshallah,*" Ahmed said.

I was dumbfounded. Most bureaucrats would have told us to go away until they'd had a chance to sleep on it and then would have pushed the request up the chain of command to avoid making the decision themselves. The governor had everything to lose and little, if anything, to gain by granting my request. Were a U.S. citizen kidnapped under his watch, his head would be on the chopping block. I could not account for his magnanimity other than that he was moved by appeals of friendship with Muhammad the Maswari—something a Yemeni, though probably not an American, bureaucrat would understand.

"But I'm curious about one thing, Mr. Seif," the governor said. "Why have you waited twenty years to come back?"

How was I to answer him?

When I completed my dissertation in 1984, the U.S. economy had stalled, and the effect was felt at colleges and universities across the country. Only a series of part-time and visiting appointments awaited me. Summers were when I could move to the new jobs and also when I might have gone back to Yemen, but I could not manage both. Then, when my life stabilized after I got tenure, something was invariably happening in the Middle East to deter me: the Iran–Iraq war (1980–1987), the first Palestinian Intifada (1983–1990), the first Gulf War (1991), the Yemeni war between the regime in Sana'a and southern secessionists (1994), and so on. This much I told the governor. What I couldn't express, because I only half understood them myself, were the deeper psychological and political reasons for my reluctance to return. It was not just that three uninterrupted years of fieldwork had taxed my reserves of emotional strength. Throughout the 1980s and 1990s Middle Eastern studies were embroiled in political feuds that mirrored the region's turmoil—Palestinians versus Israelis, Iranians versus Iraqis, Turks versus Kurds, Lebanese Christians versus Muslims—and I was not the only scholar dispirited by these events. At the same time, the salutary but severe criticism of "orientalist" knowledge launched in 1978 by Edward Said in his book *Orientalism* was taken up by others in what came to be known as postcolonial theory, which left many, including myself, questioning the politics of their scholarship on the Middle East. Disheartened, I told myself I was an anthropologist first, a sociolinguist second, and an Arabist and Middle Eastern specialist last; I was preparing to switch my area of specialization to Europe, where I was born and had been raised until the age of ten, or to the United States, where I came of age. But above all, like other anthropologists in a world increasingly torn by violence, afflicted by pestilence, and ground down by poverty, I was crippled by despair over the situation in the Middle East. This came home to me most poignantly during the 1991 Gulf War, when I received news that my friend Muhammad had died and left behind a widow and seven children: Ahmed, Fatimah, Haliya, Amina, Salih, Baqla, and As'ad. The two events—one world historical, the other not even qualifying as a historical footnote—

blended in my mind, and a part of me that was committed to working in this region, with its peoples, and its problems, died. Or so I thought.

Two unexpected developments made me reconsider. In 1998 I was unexpectedly offered a chair in contemporary Arab studies at Harvard University, which boosted my self-confidence; if I accepted it, I would have to recommit to a definition of myself as a Middle East specialist, though not necessarily one with a focus on Yemen. The second impetus came from younger anthropologists working in Yemen—Engseng Ho (my colleague at Harvard), Flagg Miller (University of Wisconsin), and Lucine Tamamian (Jordan)—whose research reignited my passion for Yemen and quickened my desire to return to the country.

"Very well," said the governor. "Do as instructed, Ahmed from Wadi Maswar, and see me in my office on Saturday. If everything's in order, Mr. Seif can go to Khawlan."

As we left Sabri's place that evening, I said to Ahmed, "Well, that was a useful chew."

"*Very useful,*" he replied with his typical laconism

Still, he faced an uphill climb. It was too late to go back to Khawlan that evening to persuade the sheikh of Wadi Maswar to go along with the plan, so he would have to wait until the following day, Friday (the Muslim Sabbath), and then on Saturday he would have to see the regional administrative director in his Jihana office *and* be back in Sana'a to see the governor again. But he was not his father's son for nothing. On Saturday morning I got a call.

"Did you get the permissions?"

"Ah-h-h. I even got an additional one the governor did not mention, a permit from the Khawlan head of National Security, whose office is also in Jihana." I was jubilant.

Sabri made his car and chauffeur available for our drive to Rawdha, where the governor presided. Once a beautiful garden spot to which the imams retreated from the summer's heat, it was now a crowded, well-healed suburb of Sana'a, where the nouveaux riches of the boom 1990s economy had their massive cinder-block walled compound built in one or two square stories, Gulf Arab style. Rawdha was not the only affluent community that had sprung up in and around Sana'a since the

1980s, marking the rise of a new upper class. But the dark side to this prosperity was the mass of unemployed and beggars, many of them veiled women cradling infants who flopped on the city sidewalks like stricken, exhausted birds, and the sick, the old, the homeless. Never had I seen so many poor people in Yemen and in such wretched conditions. The division of prosperity and poverty had become extreme.

I thought the rap music blaring from the car stereo might be for my benefit.

"Sabri's son," explained the driver, a man of Iraqi descent who had come with his family to Yemen after the Gulf War. "He likes American music."

"I guess you do, too," I teased him.

"See that monument over there?" asked Abdul Wahid, a cousin of Ahmed's who had come along for moral support. He and I would become friends in the next few days. He pointed to a large sculpture outside the Ministry of Justice. "One day a tribesman from Khawlan asked his companions what it was. The Scales of Justice, he was informed. With that he took out his gun and shot at it, causing the scales to tip. 'Now it looks right,' he declared."

"Where's your name in the appointment book?" drawled the *qat*-chewing soldier outside the governor's office. "Unless your name's there, I can't admit you."

"But we just got off the phone with the governor," Ahmed said. "He told us to come right over."

"Well, he hasn't told *me*."

"Can't you call him to confirm?" Ahmed pleaded.

A half hour passed before someone let us into the stately building that had once been one of the ruling imam's palaces. When we got to the top story, a burly man with a Kalashnikov ushered us into a large, well-appointed chamber at one end of which the governor was seated behind a massive wooden desk. He was dressed in a beautiful robe with a mandarin collar and an elegant dark blue jacket. Like every successful bureaucrat, he understood the theater of administration, not looking up as we approached but keeping his eyes on his stack of papers to let us know he was busy with important matters. He finally looked up.

"Well, Mr. Steven, it's nice to see you again." We shook hands, and he invited us to sit in leather-upholstered chairs in front of the desk.

Coming right to the point, he asked Ahmed, "Do you have the signed letters, al-Hajjam?" He read them over carefully. Would he bring up an objection to make him change his mind, I wondered. The suspense felt interminable, though it probably took him less than a minute to go over the documents. At last he scribbled a note at the top and signed underneath.

"Very well, you have five days for your sojourn, starting tomorrow," he instructed me, "and you are not permitted to venture outside Wadi Maswar during this period. Al-Hajjam or one of his relatives will accompany you at all times."

I nodded and thanked him profusely.

"Now, take these to the head of National Security for authorization," he said to Ahmed. "He'll alert the Khawlan checkpoint to allow Mr. Steven into Wadi Maswar."

Yet another obstacle thrown in our way. My heart sank. Perhaps what the governor did not do the head of National Security now would, refuse me entry into Khawlan. He was just about the most powerful man in the country after the president. Would he even have time for us? Would there be a file at National Security with a record of my former arrest and detention, reviving past suspicions and raising questions as to the ostensible purpose of my visit?

"Where would we find the director?" Ahmed asked, undeterred.

We entered a huge, two-story, concrete complex across the street from the governor's office. It was as ugly and nondescript as the former was handsome and distinguished, and menacing not because of massive gates or barbed wire but because of a shocking, seemingly inexplicable squalor. The furniture was broken, the walls dingy, the carpeting dirty and threadbare, the windows cracked, and the place hadn't been swept in ages. But then, whatever transpired within its walls did not require the niceties of civilized life. The men on "duty" looked more like street thugs or hired killers than disciplined police, a far cry from my jailers of twenty years ago.

The man in charge that afternoon was seated on the *qat*-littered floor

286 Steven C. Caton

of a bare room. It looked to me as if he was wearing pajamas under his army jacket. With his pockmarked face, distended jaws, *qat* pouches for cheeks, and heavily lidded eyes, he resembled a crocodile idly floating on a bed of reeds. Like that creature, too, he seemed falsely languid, waiting to snap at the nearest passing prey. He was holding forth with some cronies, laughing so broadly at his own jokes that his eyes disappeared in the folds of his face. He never once looked at us. Not being the center of attention was gratifying until I realized his inattention was studied: a foreigner in his midst meant he might have to rouse himself from his torpor and do something.

The director was not in, we were told. No one knew when he would return. Come back tomorrow. Ahmed was not to be fobbed off. He squatted so as to be eye level with the Crocodile. But the governor just spoke with the director. Well, in the meantime he's gone out, the Crocodile replied smugly and smiled at his cronies, who chortled on cue. Ahmed persisted. You can see from the papers that the governor has given his approval for Mr. Steven to travel to Khawlan. He has to leave tomorrow, and he can't do that without the director's permission. Well, then, come back tomorrow. The director will be in tomorrow morning. Ahmed decided that discretion was the better part of valor, and we silently followed him out of the building.

It was now dark outside. Abdul Wahid said with evident disgust, "That lowlife gave me the creeps!"

"Well, that's it," I said glumly. "We'll have to come back tomorrow. There's no other solution."

"Yes, there *is!*" I was taken aback by the vehemence of Ahmed's rejoinder. He went up to another officer, this one better dressed than the last, and inquired whether the head of National Security was in. What did we want him for? the officer asked brusquely. He seemed intrigued when he looked over the papers. Ahmed added that the officer inside had not been helpful, which seemed to soften and galvanize him. He ushered us back into the building, where Abdul Wahid, the driver, and I were told to sit in a dingy waiting room while he led Ahmed down a dimly lit hallway.

After a while, a good-looking man dressed in a white robe (a *thob*) appeared with his lackeys in tow, the officer and Ahmed bringing up the rear. He could not have been much over thirty and seemed surprisingly young to be head of National Security. His face registered irritation as he passed swiftly in front of us and went into the office, but Ahmed seemed hopeful as he followed him inside. The door shut behind them. "Now we're getting somewhere," Abdul Wahid whispered in my ear.

Suddenly, the Crocodile came into the waiting room, looking a tad flustered. No longer wearing nightclothes, he was stuffed into a uniform that was at least one size too small. He had been transformed into Porky Pig, I thought. He again avoided eye contact but now for a different reason: he was apparently being summoned to explain his lackadaisical conduct. He made a vain attempt to adjust his ill-fitting uniform before knocking on the door and entering the office. There was some shouting behind the closed door, and after about five minutes the Crocodile came out, looking thoroughly deflated as he waddled out of sight. Abdul Wahid and I exchanged gleeful looks. Seconds later Ahmed emerged, triumphantly waving a signed order.

"I'm happy for you," Abdul Wahid said, shaking my hand.

DAY 1

We got an early start on Sunday morning. Ahmed was taking his exams at the Teacher Training College, a branch of the University of Sana'a in Jihana, and we had to be there by eleven o'clock. I looked smart in a gray-green *thob* with matching sports jacket, this outfit having been purchased the night before with the aid of Ahmed and Abdul Wahid. I also wore new sandals and wound a checkered cloth around my head in the Khawlan style. But there was something missing in my attire. Suddenly Ahmed realized what it was and took off his *jambiyya* for me to wear. His was a young man's waist, so we had to stop at a *jambiyya* store to have the belt lengthened before it would fit around mine, but then I was deemed presentable and we were on our way.

Another individual joined us. "Do you recognize me?" he asked. I didn't, not even after he mentioned the picture in my book. Muhammad Hussein had grown into a tall, athletic man, but what was mesmerizing was his face. It might have been the carved head of an Aztec ruler: high cheekbones, prominent nose, dark, deep-set eyes. From such features, even a subtle physiognomist might have failed to deduce his kind, sweet nature.

"No," I confessed, "but I remember you as a boy. You went with me everywhere in the village. You were my constant companion and faithful guide. I'm so glad you can be with me now. It's only fitting. I shall call you Muhammad the Guide. But do you remember me?"

"A little." He paused. "I remember your saying it was healthy to eat apples and you bought me some."

"Unfortunately, I also remember buying you candy."

Thanks to a new road, the trip to Wadi Maswar lasted about forty minutes and not the nearly three hours it took twenty years earlier. The narrow, two-lane highway was asphalted nearly to Marib. Why the Chinese hadn't completed the last stretch of ten kilometers or so was unclear to me, but it may have had to do with tensions between eastern Yemen and the central government. In 1984 oil was discovered by the Hunt Company about sixty kilometers east of Marib. Though the state claimed it for the nation, powerful tribes in the region had other ideas. An agreement was eventually reached between the tribes and the state for a pipeline to extend from Marib through Khawlan all the way to Sana'a. But if the tribes felt cheated in their oil revenues or otherwise disgruntled with government policies, they threatened to wreck the pipeline or kidnap the oil workers. The state responded by extending its authority over these regions, which it could now do because of increased revenues from oil sales that paid for arms and patronage, but its control was far from absolute.

The landscape was as austerely beautiful as I remembered. Aeons ago these cone-shaped hills had been active volcanoes; now they were only wind-blasted peaks standing in a row like the battered teeth of a comb. Here and there, a pencil-thin line of green fields stretched across dusty earth that, because of a five-year drought, depended on artesian wells for irrigation.

"See those mountains over there, Mr. Steven?" Muhammad the

Guide pointed in the direction of hills with a narrow valley where once a village had stood. A dam had been built there, he told me, but the water catchment behind it was bone dry because the hoped-for rains never came. A nearby abandoned pump had not been able to draw groundwater from far below the earth's surface. "Where did the villagers go?" I asked. "To relatives in other areas or to Sana'a" was Muhammad the Guide's reply.

Suddenly we were at the checkpoint on the Khawlan border. So absorbed was I by the alarming water situation that I had not paid attention to it.

During my first stint of fieldwork, there had been hardly any checkpoints in Yemen, and they were not then—nor are they now—the cinder-block, barbed-wire, barking-dog affairs that I imagine existed in Eastern Europe during the cold war. They usually were no more than ragged tents or at best a makeshift building outside of which scraggly soldiers lounged in the shade and relieved themselves against any available barrier. But their greater number and wider extent in the Yemen countryside in the new century were symbolic of the extension of state power. The soldiers searched for hidden weapons, collected the papers they probably could not read, and waved the cars on. This checkpoint was different from the rest, however. Its ramshackle air notwithstanding, it had a reputation in Yemen as fierce as Checkpoint Charlie's had been in once-divided Berlin. The officer in charge was a gruff, taciturn tribesman from Khawlan, specifically the Bani Jabr, and as his legend grew, he was simply known as al-Jabri. One might have thought that al-Jabri's heart would be softened by his confederates' entreaties, but the opposite was true: he was at once hated for his obduracy and grudgingly respected for his evenhandedness. He might turn a powerful person away even if his traveling papers were in order, unless a phone call from National Security had given clearance ahead of time. Naturally, I was less than sanguine about my prospects of getting into Khawlan under al-Jabri's watch. One look at my American passport and his suspicion that a political fiasco was in the making would be aroused.

We were told to pull over, and al-Jabri appeared. He was as impres-

sive as his reputation led one to expect, though less arrogant or inso-
lent perhaps, certainly not a ludicrous figure like the Crocodile. Once
again I was ignored. Was this part of the training of security officers, I
wondered. Ahmed presented the papers. He and Muhammad the
Guide got out of the car and wandered off the side of the road to discuss the matter with al-Jabri. A heated conversation ensued, but being
in the car, I couldn't hear the words. Curious soldiers with Kalash-
nikovs slung casually from their shoulders came to gaze at me. One
of them smiled coyly and muttered to himself, "Dressed just like a
tribesman!"

"There's no order in this country," Ahmed fumed as he threw himself
back into the vehicle and slammed the door. It was the only time I
had seen him angry, and the display was all the more impressive for
that. "Here we have letters from the sheikh, from the regional director
of National Security in Khawlan, from the administrative head of
Khawlan, from the governor of the whole province, and from the head
of National Security of the whole country, and that bastard still won't
let us through." The problem was that al-Jabri hadn't gotten word of
our arrival from headquarters in Sana'a.

"Then it's no good," I said dejectedly. "We have to turn back."

Once again Ahmed had an idea. We went just a little way back on
the main road and stopped at a convenience store where there was a
phone. We sipped orange squashes while Ahmed got on the line with
Sabri, and before we had finished our drinks, the governor's call came
through. It was nothing short of miraculous that the telephone lines all
happened to be working in those few minutes, not to mention that the
governor had been reachable in that exact interval. We were told to go
back to the checkpoint.

"Yes," al-Jabri said to the governor on the other end of the line, "the
papers are all in order, but I wanted to speak to you in person before I
let the American through . . . All right, sir, I'll let him pass."

We cheered as we lurched back onto the highway and headed for
Khawlan, but it was a bittersweet victory for Ahmed. It was eleven
o'clock—too late for him to make it to his exams. He would have to
take them next year.

Villages I knew from before but barely recognized now flew past. Job, Asnaf, Jihana. Muhammad the Guide turned around in the front seat and said to me, "Now it's only thirty kilometers to Wadi Maswar and the village of al-Hijla, where you stayed twenty years ago." He had hardly finished saying this when the road descended into a broad valley and a sense of recognition came over me.

"But *this* is al-Hijla," I said.

"You've not forgotten after all, Mr. Steven."

Seeing the house in which I had stayed was like stepping back in time. It had changed very little, which made it sadder for me that my old friend was no longer there to welcome me. It was a three-story mud-brick building with a tiny garden outside, where Ahmed had planted a pathetic flower or two. From there one entered a dirt court-yard and approached the front door. There still was no electricity, and in the dark stairwell I stumbled on the uneven steps, just as I had twenty years earlier. Except for some beehives Ahmed had installed on the roof with his cousin Nasir's help, all was nearly as it used to be. He boasted that his honey was as good as any in Yemen, rivaling even what I might taste from the Hadhramawt, but he sadly admitted that not much honey had been produced in the combs lately. The drought had drastically reduced what the bees could eat of the wadi's delicious flowers.

"Oh, stop your whining!" Ahmed chided Nasir, whose foot was swollen and red from a recent bee sting. I got a couple of aspirin out of my backpack for the pain.

We entered the *mafraj*. I declined to sit in the place of honor. "This was your grandfather's spot. I sat on the opposite side and would listen to the radio with him. That's where I'll sit now."

"Had the room been plastered and whitewashed then?" someone asked. I said I thought it had, but the photographs on the wall were new. One was a head shot of Abdul Wahid dressed in a suit and look-ing far less handsome than in his tribal headdress, which he liked to set at a rakish angle. Another was a more touristic photo of Ahmed, Nasir, and me, taken in Sana'a's Tahrir Square a few days earlier. The rest were of my friend Muhammad.

One showed him as a young man. Judging from his age, it must have been taken not long after I left Yemen. He's standing in front of a painted backdrop of the sort one sees in nineteenth-century studio portraits, holding the hand of a good-looking young man roughly his age, his eyes brimming with energy. No one seemed to know where the picture was taken or who the other young man was. I thought that Muhammad might have been in Saudi Arabia at the time and that his companion, a Yemeni in appearance, was a coworker. The other photograph was of Muhammad, shortly before his death. Shot by an amateur, it was more candid and gritty than the carefully composed studio portrait. He's alone, a fact that adds to his solitary, even isolated air. His hair has thinned, he's grown a scraggly beard, and the forthright gaze of the earlier portrait has given way to a more fugitive, haunted, even haggard look. By the time that picture was taken, something—or, sadder to say, perhaps everything—had gone wrong in Muhammad's life. My gaze would compulsively drift back and stay riveted on that picture.

The screenless windows were open, and the flies were as bad a scourge as I remembered. Muhammad's youngest son, Asʿad, and the much younger brother of Muhammad the Guide had a technique to get rid of them that was as effective as it was amusing. With the closed *mafraj* doors at their backs, they slowly walked toward the open windows at the other end of the room, twirling towels before them with a wrist action as vigorous as that of a chef beating an egg, creating currents of air that swept the flies out the windows like a broom. There would be a frantic moment at the end when they tried to shut the windows before the flies had a chance to rush back in.

A person who has been away for a long period is expected to take a walk, or *dowra*, in the village, on which he is welcomed back by relatives and friends. And so I sauntered forth to be treated like a long-lost kinsman—a simple but very moving experience. It became more like a royal procession than a walk, however, and I was accompanied by what seemed like half the village, though in fact it was only the boys and younger men, for whom this outing was a great diversion. And I was constantly being "handled," which was exasperating, with someone deciding to carry my bottle of drinking water, another my backpack, a third my camera. We headed up a scree-strewn path to a tall building called the Fortress, which afforded panoramic views of the wadi. My sandals weren't sturdy enough for the terrain, and I kept walking out of them and losing my balance, which of course, only reinforced the impression that I was doddering and in need of close tending. Soon I was being supported under both arms, which occasioned the remark "Poor guy! He's already an old man." And from their perspective, at the age of fifty-one, I clearly was. Few men in Yemen live much beyond that age.

The Fortress, a five-story stone building built as a tourist hotel, was not completed, which came as no surprise. Khawlan was not exactly a tourist attraction, given its kidnapping spree. I had gone to the top of it with Muhammad in 1980 and taken his picture as he crouched in one of the window frames, with Wadi Maswar for a splendid backdrop. I asked young Salih to pose in what I thought was the identical spot.

Next on our itinerary was the main village mosque. Some of the older men reminded me of the time I was there last, when Muhammad and his friend Naji had mischievously invited me to go inside and I had adamantly refused. This time I dared to go as far as the interior courtyard, which housed a large water tank used for ablution before the prayer, its algae-covered surface a none-too-inviting lurid green.

What was new in al-Hijla was a religious institute located up the wadi a ways, built by the Islah (officially known as the Yemeni Reform Grouping), a conservative religious party in Yemen. These strict interpreters of Shariʿa law had gotten their start in the late 1970s under the leadership of a religious sheikh, Zindani, who was later joined by the paramount sheikh of the Hashid, Abdullah al-Ahmar, the one who had helped to mediate the final stages of the dispute between the sanctuary and Sarkhan. Their combination made the party appear religio-tribal, which appealed to a large segment of Yemeni society, but it did not become a political force for President Ali Abdullah Salih to reckon with until the mid-1980s when he developed his own political party, the General Popular Congress. A third party, the Yemeni Socialist Party, had been the ruling party of South Yemen and entered into the fray of national politics when the two countries united in May 1990. In protest over northern domination of political and economic life in the south, the Yemeni Socialist Party seceded from the union in 1994, precipitating the second bitterly fought civil war. The northern army won decisively, symbolizing more than perhaps anything else could the dramatic reversal of fortune and power between north and south Yemen. Though the south still chafes at the north's hegemony, its leaders have participated in the national government as high up as the prime minister's office, and reconciliation seems to be occurring.

A group of zealous religious students approached, wanting to persuade me of Islam's superiority over Christianity. "The Wahhabis have arrived," Muhammad the Guide clucked disapprovingly, a not-so-veiled reference to the fact that much of the money the Islah party raised for its schools, clinics, banks, and other public works came from the country where Wahhabism originated: Saudi Arabia. "They're *mutatawwi*," someone else complained, referring to self-appointed religious police who patrol the streets in Saudi Arabia to make sure Islam is practiced according to their own narrow, intolerant dictates. I told the students that I wasn't a religious person and that their lesson would be lost on me. Embarrassed by their overbearing manner, my Yemeni friends whisked me away.

Not far from the Islah institute was something else new, a government school covering grades all the way up to high school. It was a much more modest affair, but Muhammad the Guide proudly exclaimed, "We built this with our own money. The government provided some help, but most of it we did on our own." Since now most of the male children and some of the girls went to school, the literacy rate had risen, which was definitely an improvement. Ahmed's younger sister Baqla, for example, was always first or second in her class, which prompted me to ask Ahmed whether she would go on to high school and perhaps even university. That would depend on when and whom she would marry, he said. I was determined to bring the matter up again when the time was right. A couple of high school students could be observed huddled over their books, cramming for their final exams. They rose to greet me and immediately wanted to practice their English, though only one of them was much beyond the level of "What's your name? Where are you from?" Not only had he not heard of my university but he wondered why, if Har-f-a-a-rd was so distinguished, it didn't have an English dictionary named after it, as Oxford did.

Our tour's last stop was the house of Muhammad's friend Naji. Though grand in design, it was unfinished, its owner having run out of money; his large family—two sons and several daughters from different marriages—occupied the completed first story.

Shortly after I left Yemen in 1981, Naji and Muhammad had gone to Saudi Arabia, where Naji owned a metal workshop. Their specialty was doors, which entailed more than just soldering pieces of metal: they made doors with decorative motifs resembling the great mosque in Jerusalem or the Ka'ba in Mecca or, if the homeowner were more secularly inclined, the crossed swords and palm tree, which is the national emblem of Saudi Arabia. More arcane and fanciful designs were possible in bright, hand-painted colors, depending on the client's tastes and the workman's skills. No wonder that Yemenis, who are among the world's best craftsmen, excelled in this work, and Muhammad found it both fun and profitable. But within a few years, Naji and Muhammad became disillusioned with Saudi Arabia. It was difficult for me to imagine a proud, hot-tempered man like Muhammad lasting very long in a country where Yemenis are condescended to and insulted.

Naji sold the workshop and decided to start a car dealership in Sana'a, precisely at a time in the 1980s when a consumerist middle class was emerging in Yemen. At first, everything went well. The economy was expanding, a wealthy class was growing, and there was demand for both utility and luxury vehicles. One of Muhammad's jobs was to drive new cars from the Red Sea port city of Hodeida to the capital, and from Naji's recounting, at least, he seemed to relish it. But on one of his trips, he caused a bad accident and incurred hundreds of thousands of riyals in fines and damages. Naji had no insurance, and the business never fully recovered.

A year or so after that, Muhammad was killed in a tribal war, and Naji was so brokenhearted that he couldn't bear living in Yemen anymore. He sold the struggling car dealership and with his money emigrated to the United States. He was the only man from Wadi Maswar to have made this epic journey, which is more common among affluent Yemenis from the central towns like Ibb. Most ordinary people from Khawlan could not afford the visas and the costs of passage to the United States, much less find a sponsor among kinsmen in the Yemeni community in America. Muhammad told people that I'd gotten him a visa but that he had turned it down. Was it true? they asked me. I lied and said it was, thinking that it was more important to make Muhammad appear truthful than to be truthful myself. It was not a response I had much time to think about, and I have repented of it.

We found Naji lounging outside his house with his son Ali attending him. I was shocked by his appearance. The strong and vigorous man of twenty years ago was infirm and almost blind, stricken by a mysterious (at least to me) debilitating disease that left him tired, sweating profusely most of the time, and with crippling neurological pain shooting down his legs. His thinking was also sometimes confused and his speech slurred. Ali showed me a Saudi Arabian doctor's diagnosis of his condition, but I didn't know the meanings of the medical terms, which I meant to write down and look up later but never did. I was fairly certain, however, that it was not syphilis or AIDS. Whatever the ailment, the ravages of alcoholism had contributed to his physical and mental decline. Even when I knew him in 1980, he would ask me whether I would care to take a nip with him and Muhammad, a common enough practice among *qat* habitués to bring down the high. He would make this offer in front of everyone, for he had no pretense of concealing his vices or excesses, in which, after all, others indulged as well. That he was not the least bit hypocritical was one of his endearing characteristics.

A ruin may have faced me that morning, but Naji was far from dispirited. Another of his likable traits was his gift for laughing at himself, and in his colloquially accented if ungrammatical English he regaled me with stories about his adventures in America. He said he had arrived in New York on a tourist visa in the late 1980s, speaking not a word of the language and not knowing anyone. This did not jibe with his assertion that he had emigrated after Muhammad's death, which I had established to be in 1990, but maybe his memory, like much else in him, was faulty. The first thing he did was to put his thirty thousand dollars in a bank account and a prepaid return ticket to Yemen in a vault. This was about the only prudent thing he did in the States, he commented. Then he decided to see the country—Washington, Philadelphia, Miami, Chicago—by train. On his travels he met a Hispanic woman, Maria, who became the great love of his life. He called her Disney because she made him feel so good in bed. By the time they reached Las Vegas, they had gambled nearly all his money away, though they kept enough aside to get back to New York, where he slaved away for the next several years as an illegal, undocumented laborer. In the boom years of the 1990s, he had no trouble finding jobs in the many Yemeni-owned groceries in Harlem, the Bronx, Brooklyn, and Manhattan, but it was still a hard life. People would leave the store without paying, yelling "Fuck you, towel head!" over his feeble protests. Several times he was threatened at gun- or knife-point and beaten up. This dark side of his immigrant saga was lightened by occasional flashes of absurd humor, one of which he recounted with such hilarity I thought my sides would split. One day shortly after he had arrived in New York from Yemen, he was sipping tea in a café with a new Yemeni friend. When they got up to leave, Naji took the paper cup with him and then pitched it in a large container on the street corner into which he had observed people tossing things. It turned out to be a mailbox, which in Yemen would be found at the post office, not on a street corner.

The sheer drudgery and penny-pinching of the poor immigrant's life finally got to Maria, and when an older man of means proposed to her (Naji referred to him as "the Jew," without apparent bigotry or jealousy), she left Naji. (His last words to me were "Tell Maria in Brooklyn—I'll tell you how to contact her—tell her to come to Yemen. I miss her.") Meanwhile, Naji got ill and became too weak and tired to work. Without insurance, he could not afford medical treatment, so he retrieved his return ticket from the bank vault and flew back to Yemen and then Riyadh, where he sought treatment in one of its great hospitals. Medicine was prescribed along with daily doses of vitamin D, both of which Naji asked me to bring back from the United States in the near future; he had run out of them and could not get the prescriptions refilled in Yemen.

Naji was more than what people sometimes condescendingly call a character. Because of his unique status as someone who had spent years abroad and seen something of America, he was looked up to in his village. However, the fact that all he had to show for his hard work and trouble was broken English meant that people's respect was tinged with pity and not a little disdain. Would he come to the *qat* chew that afternoon? I asked. I wanted to learn more about Muhammad's life after I had left Yemen. He would like to, he replied, but he was afraid that the heat and stuffiness of the *qat* chew would be too much for him.

On our way back to Ahmed's house, an impromptu *barac* dance was held in my honor under the shade of a large acacia tree. I danced a little bit with the younger men, all the time trying hard to keep my sandals on, but when the older men joined us and the tempo accelerated, I could not keep up. Watching from the sidelines with me was a young man who remarked, "Now you're really seeing the *deep* traditions of the tribe. We younger ones can't dance like that anymore, and when they die, the dance will die with them." Another one pointed to a house about twenty yards away. "Do you remember the old man, Ali [al-Fagih] whom you featured in your book, the one who competed with the poet Ahmed al-Sharegi?" he asked me. He was referring to one of the best *bala* poets in Khawlan at the time. "He died last year. He would have wanted to see you again." I wondered whether *bala* poetry, like *barac* dancing, was in danger of disappearing, for with the spread of literacy came prejudice against oral and colloquial forms of expression, but since there were no weddings scheduled during my brief visit in the wadi, I could not find out.

Among the people who started to straggle in for lunch at Ahmed's house was Dahhan, Ahmed's grand-uncle, a man now in his late seventies. He was still handsome, with high cheekbones and square-cut features, and in reasonably good health for a man of his age. When

I asked him if he was going to chew *qat* later, he said he probably wouldn't, because he had lost his molars. I was touched to see him anyway, carrying his *qat* in powdery form. I reminded Dahhan that he had taught me how to till a field by steadying the plow and shouting verbal commands to the bull. He said he was too old to work in the fields now. When we rested, he would recite *zamil* poems in his resonant voice (and I now realized where Muhammad must have gotten his). I told Dahhan that he had taught me one of the best poems in my book, and he smiled in recognition when I recited the lines.

With the help of his wife, Miriam, Ahmed had prepared a magnificent lunch. His brothers helped serve the meal, and one of them set a knife and fork in front of me.

"What is this?" I said in mock indignation. "Take them away!"

As we rolled up our sleeves and prepared to dig in, a tall man entered the room. "Hail to the great scholar from America," he declaimed, "a thousand thousand greetings to him. He has come to Yemen to pay his respects to his friend whom he has not forgotten, God's blessings upon him. How honored we are today to have him as our guest, and great has been the generosity of this house toward him and all the village . . ." He was the wadi's *doshan*, or town crier, who, alerted to my presence in the village, had come to sing my praises. For money, of course, and I quietly slipped Abdul Wahid a couple of thousand riyals to give him. A Yemeni proverb says, "Cut off the *doshan's* tongue with giving."

The afternoon *qat* chew was held in the largest assembly room of the village, which was already filled by the time I arrived. "See," said one of the youngsters, "the whole village has turned out for you." I made the rounds, greeting each person individually.

A whole generation had died since I had left Yemen, and those who had been middle-aged then were old men now. "Gosh, we remember you as having been so slender," one of them said. I was no longer a spring chicken.

"We've all aged, haven't we?" I shot back, stroking his iron-gray hair.

In the audience were two poets, one of them a member of the *sada* by the name of Hussein al-Qumaisi, whom I had not met before. Unprepossessing in appearance, he nevertheless had a forceful personality and a deep baritone voice. He could neither read nor write but was renowned for his tribal *qasida* and reputed to perform the *bala* outstandingly as well. He would have been interesting to work with twenty years ago, for I did not know many *sada* then who were adept at an art form considered "quintessentially" tribal and rather beneath them. People were urging him to recite, but I could tell that he was too tired. To recite from memory a *qasida* dozens of lines long is quite taxing; perhaps after he had rested a bit he would be up to it.

"Please," I told him, "relax. It's such an honor and pleasure to have you in our company."

He had just come back from the sanctuary, where he knew I had lived two decades ago. It had been having "troubles" of late: a dispute over land boundaries with the local tribe. That was why he was tired, for he had been spending many days and nights helping to mediate. When I discovered that the tribe in question was the Bani Dhubyan, I inadvertently blurted, "By God, things haven't changed. They were fighting the sanctuary twenty years ago."

"Exactly," said al-Qumaisi. "The wound never healed. They've been at odds ever since. Small things up till now."

"Would it be possible for me to visit?"

He shook his head. "One dead from the sanctuary, two from the tribe, and the headman of the sanctuary in a Sana'a jail. Better if you waited a couple of months." I kept to myself that I didn't have two months. I inquired after my old friends Muhammad the Hunchback, Ibrahim the Beltmaker, Muhammad the Lame. All passed away, alas. He didn't know Ali the Bird. I didn't ask after Ahmed, my irritating upstairs neighbor.

"There is no point in seeing it again," I remarked sadly.

"Oh, but you should!" al-Qumaisi said. "It has changed. You wouldn't recognize it. Electricity. Telephones. And many more houses than twenty years ago. The asphalt road has made it easier for people to work in the capital and commute every day." So it may have had its "troubles," but in other respects fortune had smiled on it, unlike Wadi Maswar.

The other poet at the *qat* chew was Salih bin Salih al-Baradah, son of the old sheikh. We had met when my friend Muhammad came to my house in the sanctuary for the first time to chew *qat*, and he had given me several *zamils* for my collection. Though I remembered the scene, I did not recognize him now, a confession he received graciously enough. Shortly after that visit, he had emigrated to Saudi Arabia, but the kingdom, angered by Yemen's support of Iraq during the 1991 Gulf War, had expelled its Yemeni expatriate or noncitizen workers, and Salih had returned to Wadi Maswar.

"I want to recite a *zamil* of welcome," he announced. He read from a slip of paper.

> Welcome, Seif. You've come to our land a guest after prolonged
> absence.
> Welcome, to strains of music and delight, to *zamils* and the ever-
> recurring *bala*.

I inscribed the words in one of my pocket-sized spiral notebooks. It wasn't easy at first, for I hadn't heard this poetry in a long while and was no longer fluent in colloquial Yemeni Arabic. But there was another reason why the experience was strange: in the past Muhammad would have been at my side to help me understand the poem, and his absence now made me realize more than ever how much I missed him. When Ahmed started to make corrections and offer explanations, an uncanny feeling stole over me, as of the past magically slipping back into view.

The poet al-Qumaisi now roused himself to compose a *zamil*. "What's his name?" I heard him whisper to a neighbor.

> Welcome, Steven, from the land and bosom of this place, welcome
> from my tongue that bestows special honors on the dear guest.
> Like a drink of pure water, he makes a person smile from atop the
> camel. He plays the bala with the children and the aged.

This translation hardly does justice to this *zamil's* sonorities and grammatical intricacies, which made al-Qumaisi's gifts instantly clear. The image of a person atop a camel in the desert who smiles at the sight of pure drinking water was a particularly fine metaphor for a guest like myself.

Now it was Abdul Wahid's turn, in honor of his dear friend and cousin, Ahmed.

> Welcome, hero of Maswar. Welcome, Ahmed, hero of an ancient
>   house, who acted as the intermediary between the government and
>   Dr. Seif.
> How many problems did we face alongside Sabri Salim! But he
>   overcame them with incomparable style and grace.

More poems followed in quick succession. Some were from men who couldn't be present at the gathering and had sent them for Ahmed to read.

> Welcome, Steve, [a welcome that extends] from Paris to London, and
>   from America to Sweden.
> Let fill our Yemen and the Gulf, especially Aden, a greeting that is
>   torrid, not one that is tepid.

> Welcome and hello to you, Seif, in the land of Yemen, [a welcome]
>   that fills Aden and leaves its echo in Hadhramawt.
> Maswar welcomes him who came from America the nation, who came
>   in the year two thousand and two, a million voices welcome.

The poet could not resist the prettiness of the internal rhyme in Arabic *alf-ayn w-ithn-ayn,* "two thousand and two," even though the date was off by a year. If this *zamil* is remembered, the year 2002 will wrongly be remembered as the date of my return.

By six o'clock, attendance had thinned as people went to the mosque for sunset prayers. Someone turned on the large television mounted on the ceiling. Television had been uncommon in Khawlan twenty years before; now many in Wadi Maswar even had satellite dishes. We watched the local news as well as cable networks such as the Qatar-based al-Jazirah. Not surprisingly, most of the coverage was devoted to the Middle East and the second Palestinian Intifada, which, like Vietnam for a generation of Americans, was powerfully mediated by televised images.

"Do you see this kind of stuff in the United States?" I was asked.

"Not really. We see far more coverage of the Israeli side. Do you see much of that?"

"Not really."

It had been a long day, but before retiring that night, I asked to see Muhammad's widow, to whom I wanted to pay my respects. She appeared with her daughter Fatimah. The widow's stout figure and crow's-feet that became more pronounced when she smiled gave her age away.

"Your parents, are they still alive?" she asked. This was the standard question asked of the arrival, and I informed her of their deaths. "God preserve them," she said.

After a pause, I said, "I miss Muhammad. I think of him often. Life must not have been easy for you after he died." She reflected for a moment and then said simply, "No, it wasn't easy." I felt guilty, remembering that I had done nothing materially to help her and the family.

"I think of Ahmed as my son," I found myself saying. I was as astonished as she by this remark. It had not occurred to me before, but it was true, and I was glad I had said it. "You must be especially proud of him. He has a lot of responsibilities."

She nodded, and I could tell that she was smiling under her veil. Then she and Fatimah were called away to attend to a domestic squabble before I had the chance to speak with her about her husband, and I was not to talk to her again. The conversation was all too brief, but I'm not sure she would have said much about Muhammad anyway.

After the widow left, Salih, As'ad, and a few of their cousins kept me company. I taught them to arm- and thumb-wrestle in exchange for learning some of their games. Then a final guest made his appearance. He was in his late forties, a handsome man with, I thought, a hard face.

"Ah, you don't remember me, do you?" he said bitterly. That was true. From the pocket of his green army jacket the man retrieved a piece of paper, tattered and greasy from being handled so many times. In shock I recognized the Arabic handwriting to be my own. In addition to letters, there were some self-addressed envelopes—artifacts from my stay in Khawlan. Seeing them was like unexpectedly coming across one's own belongings in an archaeological dig, or like a detective discovering evidence of his own crime. For that, I would now learn, was what I was accused of. Drowsiness left me, and I was instantly alert.

"Why didn't you write, Seif?" The man spoke in a tone mingling recrimination, hurt, and confusion.

"But I *did* write," I said defensively. "And in those instructions I told Muhammad to keep in touch by sending me letters in those envelopes. I never received a word."

"Muhammad and I called America once at the number you gave. But the person who answered the phone—was it your father?—didn't understand." I vaguely remembered my father telling me someone had phoned and asked for Seif, but of course he had no idea what the person was talking about and thought it was a wrong number. We were both upset about the missed connections and misunderstood communications.

"Was it you who wrote me of Muhammad's death? There was no date or signature. But it was sent to my parents' address in America, and I thought only Muhammad knew it." He shook his head. Perhaps it had been Naji, I thought, and made a note to ask him about it.

"You said you would help us come to America."

"Yes, I did say that. But I wasn't in a position to help then, and because I didn't hear from Muhammad, I assumed he didn't want to emigrate." This was a lame excuse, and I knew it. The photograph of Muhammad as he appeared at the end of his life—exhausted, dispirited, a little hardened—was haunting me.

"How could you think that Muhammad wouldn't want to come? Every Yemeni does."

"But why did he tell people that I had gotten him a visa?"

"Why have you told them now that you did?"

After a pause, I asked, "Is there no way for you to go to the United States on your own?"

"Yes," he replied proudly. "I know of a Yemeni in Michigan who owns a supermarket who said he would sponsor me for a green card . . . but I haven't decided yet."

Who knows whether this story was apocryphal? But it spoke to the power of the myth of migration to the United States and the desperate need to believe in it. What could Yemeni men like him do to support families of five, six, eight, or more? Joining the army meant an annual salary of little more than a thousand dollars, and even at that paltry sum, the ratio of applicants to acceptances was over a hundred to one. The continuing drought made farming precarious. Ahmed was getting a degree in secondary-school teaching, but there would be no jobs when he graduated. Young men increasingly went to find work in the big cities, where they had to compete with thousands of others who had left the countryside. With no special credentials or connections, the options were few and bleak: driving battered taxis in Sana'a's congested streets, serving as private security guards on the estates of the rich, clerking in a store or government office. The man grew disgusted with me, and after a while he left.

It was late, but now I was too shaken to sleep. Alone at last—or nearly so, for Muhammad's second oldest son, Salih, and one of his numerous cousins were curled up under the blankets like two pups keeping each other warm—I kept thinking about Muhammad and what had become of him. The evidence was circumstantial—when is it not in such highly personal affairs?—but his marriage had been troubled when I knew him and had probably remained so because of his restless nature and his frustrating home life. Words spoken to me earlier in the day came back with renewed force: "You know, Muhammad was never one for staying around the house. He was always away." His wife may have resigned herself to his absence with equanimity and perhaps even relief, given his moody temperament, but how had the children, especially Ahmed, the oldest, borne it? It was no wonder that he came to resemble his laconic but more dependable grandfather rather than his mercurial father.

If living in his father's house and working his father's lands had irritated Muhammad when I knew him at the tender age of twentysomething, how he must have chafed even more over the years. What outlets existed in Wadi Maswar for his talent, energy, and ambition? Becoming a common bricklayer? Selling Pepsi and cigarettes in a hole-in-the-wall store in Jihana? Peddling *qat* from the back of a car, or driving a taxi between Khawlan and Sana'a? These were dull, dead-end jobs. Muhammad would have made a fine tribal sheikh, given his mediating skills, fierce courage, charisma, wisdom, and the deep respect of his peers, but Wadi Maswar already had two sheikhs and didn't need another. Because he could neither read nor write, teaching was out of the question, though I had benefited from his pedagogical skills and knew he would have made an inspiring instructor.

According to Ahmed, his father had died in 1987, but this didn't make sense. Muhammad's youngest child, As'ad, was ten years old, which meant that his father had to have been alive in 1990. And I had been informed of Muhammad's death in August of that year. Little had I thought, when last I laid eyes on him, that he would have only ten years of life left. I suppose I had kept on postponing my return to Yemen because I complacently thought that time was on our side. The desperateness with which Muhammad lived the last years of his life deepened the sadness of his end for me. He became a drinker, thanks to Naji. Someone confided that Muhammad had been in his cups when he'd gotten into a heated argument with a neighbor over land. My hunch was that the neighbor was the man I had met at the Khawlan taxi stand, and the fact that he had once been one of Muhammad's dearest friends made the incident even more tragic. I was shocked to learn that Muhammad had drawn his *jambiyya* and wounded the neighbor, though not mortally. My interlocutor, misunderstanding my reaction, agreed that drinking alcohol was reprehensible. A hefty fine was levied, but how Muhammad was to pay it when his job prospects were so bleak, only God knew. Leaving the wadi to find work was not only politic under the circumstances but a financial imperative. Might this have been when he tried to contact me in America for a visa? And when it became clear that I was not to be his lifeline, what choice did

Muhammad have but to work for Naji? Not long after joining the business—say, one or two years—he had his car accident and then had to pay off blood money for two offenses. Whatever dreams he may have had to start over would have faded.

Dawn. The photograph of a tired, grim, and scraggly Muhammad became visible. *Damn picture Picture of the damned Damning picture.* I pulled the sheet over my head as much to block out the photograph as to hide the soft morning light. Cocks crowed. There were stirrings in the household. I could hear the diesel engine for the water pump being primed and started. As the village awakened, I finally drifted off to sleep.

DAY 2

It was not until late in the morning that I woke up. I was to have lunch with al-Baradah, the same who had been sheikh of Wadi Maswar when I visited twenty years before. He was an old man now, who barely left his house, let alone the village. Too weak to be more than a figurehead, he consigned his duties to a much younger and vigorous deputy. Had Muhammad lived, he might have become that deputy.

"Yes," said the sheikh, when I raised that possibility with him. "It's what I wanted. But it wasn't God's will." Because he had hardly any teeth left, it was difficult to understand him, so his nephew Abdul Wahid served as his spokesman.

"Whenever there was trouble, Muhammad was at my side. He'd drop whatever he was doing, even if it meant coming in from Sana'a, to help. He always knew what to say to people. And, by God, could he ever listen, I mean *listen*, to discern the deeper truth or the clever lie or the unspoken intent. I also never knew a more perceptive person, or a greater analytical mind. He could untie the knot of an argument. And if in the end the only way was war, he was the first to grab the rifle and rush into battle. I still miss him after all these years." The sheikh was tired with the talking and sat quietly in his time-honored place in the *mafraj* chewing his *qat*.

"Do you want to hear the two elegies that were composed for Muhammad?" asked Salih, the sheikh's son. "Here's the poem by Hussein al-Qumaisi, the poet you met yesterday. He sent it to me while I was still in Saudi Arabia." He retrieved a piece of paper from his jacket's inside breast pocket, unfolded it, and began to read, interrupting only to interject explanations for things I didn't understand. (That evening and through the next day, Muhammad the Guide inscribed the poem into my field notebook in his beautiful hand, and we went over the texts together, adding definitions to words or interpretations of allusions.)

> In the name of Allah, I begin [the poem], Creator of the World and its
>   Protector. Allah, who apportions everyone's livelihood, Provider of
>   life for every creature.
> Praise be to Allah [as many times as] the Qur'an is chanted from [the
>   verses] "The Roman Empire" to "The Dawn," praise
>   plentiful, with intention truthful, from a heart sincere.
> On the Prophet may Allah heap His blessings, [as many times] as the
>   tree has branches and the branches leaves, [the Prophet] who
>   founded Islam and destroyed the sinners
>   [worshipers of the idols in Mecca].
> And now al-Qumaisi says, "In my heart despair has swelled. The world
>   has become too narrow: my mind wanders, my soul drowns. My
>   worry and distress were compounded the
>   moment the hero of Khawlan was felled—al-Hajjam, the attacker of
>   the barricades with bullets blazing."

"See how clever al-Qumaisi is in the last lines," said Muhammad the Guide. "Al-Hajjam is Muhammad's ancestral name, but it also has the meaning in Arabic of attacker. The phrase 'Hajjam, Hajjam' intertwines Muhammad's name with the meaning of someone who is always ready for war."

> When he died, like a prisoner in shackles, I sighed, or in the airport,
>   the [shriek of the] Mirage and the MiG at takeoff. For the hero
>   kept his word and never lied. No one who met him doubted his
>   character and nobility.

In every battle he showed his mettle: he pounced on the enemies and
  they retreated. Of this, Madad is witness, the sanctuary and the
  mountain spired.

"Madad," explained Muhammad, "is another name for al-Qumaisi. The
sanctuary is, of course, the same that you know, and 'the mountain
spired' is a metaphor for the sheikhs of Khawlan."

[He scaled] a towering redoubt or burrowed a tunnel to the enemies.
  The warriors he exhorted and left the earth scorched.
No opponent could withstand the hero, even were he made of stone.
  Of Hajjam everyone heard in bygone days.
O messenger, rise and carry my writing without delay to the land of
  al-Khumaisi, once my country in a better day.

"By al-Khumaisi he means ᶜAsir," Muhammad explained. This is a province in southwestern Saudi Arabia that once belonged to Yemen and
was ceded to the kingdom.

Ask for Salih and tell him, "My heart has shrunk and cleaved in two,
  over your uncle of sterling qualities I have grieved.
At the hour of his death, I thought God's Creation would tremble and
  shake, the world would sway and the earth would quake.
The mortal pains he suffered, our comrades in arms avenged. Not even
  the worms in the grapes did their gunfire spare.
Against the doors they hurled themselves, not with knocking opened
  them. As the rooster does the grain, they gobbled the enemy.
Together they aimed their guns, not a soul said a word. But they failed
  and were attacked, God curse the infamy!

I wasn't sure I understood the image, and Muhammad the Guide explained that the attackers tried to surprise the enemy by quietly aiming
their guns and shooting at the same time. But it didn't work, and they
were counterattacked.

"We could not rest after the dying one had a bullet in his heart, for like
the hawk after prey, he would have circled the battlefield.
But I cannot go on, son of Salih, the muse is exhausted. I can no longer
explain or express.
The event has wounded my heart and frightened sleep away. My hair
has grown white, my knees have stiffened."
This is the truth, and Hussein [al-Qumaisi] cannot add to it. Khawlan's
men bear witness to the son of Qasim, as does his Creator.
God's paradise welcomes the pure of heart, for the noble one flashes
His lightning.
He is the Lion who pounces on the sinner and hangs him. God's
Mercy upon him who is overtaken by decrepitude and old age.
I pray to the Prophet [as many times as] there are branches and leaves
on the tree, he who established Islam and extinguished the people
of sin.

"How did he die?" I asked him as we worked on the poems.

"Khawlan was attacked by the Nihm in a border dispute. Muhammad was in Sana'a when he heard the news and came rushing back to
help Wadi Maswar. 'Come on,' he said. 'There's no time to lose.' Some
of us had just returned from the fighting and were exhausted. The exchange of fire had been very intense: rifle fire at close range, hand-to-
hand combat. There were many wounded on both sides and some
dead. 'Better wait until things have cooled down a bit,' we urged him,
but he wouldn't hear of it. Grabbed his gun and challenged us to join
him. As the poet al-Qumaisi says, he was always the first into battle.

"By the time we got to the front, Khawlan had pushed deep into
Nihm territory, but as I said, the enemy put up a stiff fight. Muhammad
was with a group of us making our way toward a village. We hid in the
vineyards, taking aim at the houses in front of us and trying to find
shelter behind the stones supporting the grape trellises. But the enemy
was firing so hard that it was all but impossible to advance. Suddenly,
Salih, the son of Sheikh Muhammad al-Qiri—you remember him,
don't you, Seif? Salih was one of Muhammad's closest friends and

fought with him in the war between the sanctuary and the Bani Dhubyan—Salih was shot and fell. Muhammad picked him up and tried to carry him, but after a few feet he was shot, too. Salih died instantly, Muhammad on the way to the hospital in Sana'a. He was hit in the chest and was bleeding badly but still conscious when we put him in the car and drove off. But he lost a lot of blood and then just stopped breathing and died."

How like him, dying to save a friend. And yet, was this self-sacrifice a suicide of sorts? Suicide, of course, is forbidden in Islam. I don't mean that Muhammad consciously entertained such a thought when he put his life in danger to save his wounded friend, which he probably did unthinkingly, in the way of all heroes. But he was, as the cliché goes, courting death, throwing himself in the breach both because doing so was expected of him and because he had come to the end of his tether. Perhaps the only promise life held for him was redemptive martyrdom.

Now Salih read his own poem commemorating Muhammad's death, echoing the rhyme and meter of al-Qumaisi's. It was much briefer, but what it may have lacked in fullness it more than made up in compactness, and an internal rhyme, thrown in the first hemistich of every line, elevated the technical difficulty, like an added twist in a gymnast's routine. Salih dispensed with the invocations of God and the Prophet, a convention that al-Qumaisi had observed. Nor did he summon the stock figure of a messenger carrying the poem to its recipient, another traditional device used by al-Qumaisi, so the poem came more abruptly to its point. After the briefest of welcomes to his interlocutor, "who grieved to me in worthy letters," he described his own response to the news of his cousin's death with a stirring and emotionally convincing immediacy:

> My reason has been locked up, Hussein, while my soul is shredded by
> anger. Despair wells up in my breast, and my heart is consumed
> by anguish.
> Your brother grieves for the fallen warriors of Khawlan. Because of my
> cousin, my soul is in pieces and my eye overflows.

> I have been wounded as if by a thorn driven into my heart, or like a
>> body pierced by bullets that have burned holes through it . . .
> War begets war, until it overtakes the army. You see it before the army
>> like lightning in the sky.

This novel and salutary comment on Muhammad's death brings us back to the problem of violence in tribal Arab society. In Salih's view, it is like a cyclone that overtakes everything in its path and sucks it up in its vortex. But what is producing this violence? Is it an inherent destructive quality? The mechanisms of mediation do exist, and peaceful resolution of conflicts can occur, though peace is fragile and mediations can break down. Are there other causes encouraging armed violence? The machinations of national and international agents, as in the conflict between the sanctuary and the Bani Dhubyan, or the sale of increasingly deadly armaments to Yemen by foreign powers such as the United States and Russia? Salih opted for a different explanation that had to do with the weakness of political forces within Yemen.

> The parliament has convened and created divisions among the people,
>> while the officer trades in goods and leaves the tribes fighting each
>> other.
> The house of the adversary who tells the truth is demolished by an
>> army that acts as it has in histories of centuries past.

The problem was the weak and divided legislature, which reflected rather than overcame society's rifts. And as for the armed forces, though still the most powerful element in the country, they were interested more in enriching themselves than in acting as peacemakers between the tribes. Indeed, though the poet does not says so, the government's neglect of tribal problems might even be strategic, weakening the tribal opponents to its rule by letting them bleed to death in factional feuding. Understood in that sense, Muhammad was a "martyr," a tragic victim of forces not of his own making. When I later asked Salih, as I had asked my companions from Khawlan in 1980, why the tribes didn't submit to the rule of Yemeni state law, I was answered by a question: Would you submit to a state that is unjust?

By evening I was exhausted but could not retire before the rest of the household, so until the lights went out around eleven o'clock, the kids kept me company. I suggested they might help me compile a genealogy of the people in al-Hijla—the anthropologist's stock-in-trade—and they quickly became engrossed in the exercise, as though they were doing a crossword puzzle. Starting with the reputed ancestor as the trunk of the tree, the various houses he founded as the branches, and so on, we had in a few hours filled in a crown as broad as a chestnut tree, with Muhammad Qasim no larger than a twig and his seven children its leaves. I had happily become a fieldworker again.

Day 3

As if to probe clinically the thorny question of tribal violence and its causes, we went the next morning to Jihana, ostensibly to visit Ahmed's college, but our first stop was the souk where Muhammad the Guide wanted to show me something. Twenty years earlier people had boasted that any weapon imaginable—even a tank—could be purchased on the black market but that souk was in the north, outside the city of Saʿdah and near the border with Saudi Arabia, not in Jihana. There were dozens of arms emporiums open for business.

"Almost any kind of weapon you might want, Seif," said Muhammad the Guide, not without a hint of sarcasm, extending his arm in a sweeping gesture like that of a tour guide unveiling the town's showcase. There were the old standbys, of course, the M-1 rifle and the Kalashnikov, and also state-of-the-art handguns, assault rifles, automatic machine guns, bazookas, even antiaircraft missiles. A novice in the world of military hardware, I didn't recognize most of the weapons, but the place would have been heaven for the NRA. "And you should see what's in underground storage, Seif. That's where they keep the heavy stuff."

"Are there are other markets like this one?" I asked.

"Everywhere in Yemen," Muhammad the Guide told me. "Tourists might not see them, but they're there. Your country makes the best ones."

"True," I admitted shamefacedly. "We are the biggest manufacturer of weapons in the world, and we sell most of them to middlemen who then export them to Third World countries. We are exporters of death, no doubt about it. But why do you buy them? Why do you smoke that cigarette, which probably also comes from America?"

I regretted this asinine question as soon as I had asked it. As if the problem could be handled by a public relations effort like the "war on drugs." I could just see Muhammad the Guide as Khawlan's poster boy: "Just say no to guns!" with a big red circle and a diagonal across it over a picture of him exchanging money for arms in a Yemeni souk, while Uncle Sam and the Russian Bear look on with disappointment.

In a teasing tone he said, "I know. I know. That's what you mean by a free market. You Americans are simply supplying a demand you've done nothing to create. It seems as though we crave guns the way a smoker like me does cigarettes. But wars, our wars, are good for your business. And with these weapons, there's no limit to the wars we can have. The weapons feed the wars, which in turn create a demand for more weapons, in a vicious circle. Look, Seif, what choice do I have? I see my enemy arming to the teeth, and the state, which is no friend either, is getting arms from the Americans. In my situation, what would you do?"

"Where does it end? How many people have to be left fatherless like Ahmed over there? And will Ahmed too be killed in a tribal war?"

"It's revenge killing that's the problem behind our wars, Seif." This was an important point, and I'd heard it expressed by people across a broad spectrum of Yemeni society. "Just yesterday a young man was shot to death in Rawdha. In fact, right where you'd been standing in front of the governor's office. He was the son of the most powerful sheikh in Wadi Maswar, al-Dahmish, a nice, sweet guy. The intended victim was badly wounded and hospitalized, but the murderer got away. Now the leaders of Khawlan have to decide how to solve the problem."

"Oh, God, does this mean war?"

"No," Muhammad the Guide said, patting me reassuringly on the shoulder. "We'll settle it peacefully. It's the terms of the settlement the sheikhs have to agree on."

Before leaving the souk, Ahmed wanted to call Sabri Salim on the cell phone of one of the merchants to confirm that he would be coming to have lunch in al-Hijla on my last day in Khawlan. When he passed the phone to me, I said to Sabri, "Well, I've been kidnapped." My friends laughed at hearing this. "Good," was his response, "I'll come rescue you on Thursday."

Our next stop was the College of Education, University of Sana'a, Khawlan Branch, which was housed in a brand-new, two-story campus on the outskirts of Jihana. We pulled up in our jeep next to a large metal gate. It was against the rules to bear arms on campus except for the *jambiyya*, so Naji and his son stayed in the car with our weapons while we went inside.

Several students who had just finished their exams crowded around me. "What is your name? My name Yahya. You from America? What you do—what *do* you do? In what—*which* university? No, I don't know it. Where do you live? Where is Boston? Boston in which—*is in which* district—*state*? Maa-ssa, Maa-sa-chuu, Maa-ssa-chuu-setts. I study English since three years. But it—*it's* no good. We do not learn English we can use! ChaucerShakespeareMilton. Tragedycomedysatireelegy-dramanovelshortstorysonnet. Yes, yes, beautiful lit-liter-literature, but *old*. You not speak like that in your country now, correct? Then we learn grammar rules. Nounverbregularirregularactivepassiverelativesub-ordinateprepositionconjunction. What good knowing rules and we not speak good—*well*?"

It was ironic that they knew more *about* English and its literature and grammar than many American students. Would that I could presume they knew the difference, say, between active and passive verbs. Still, their point was well taken.

"Your students, they speak English since little boys. *And* girls. After that is when they *should* learn ChaucerShakespeareMilton. It is like with us in Arabic. First we learn to speak, then we learn ʿUmr al-Qays's poetry and *faaʿilmufaaʿil*. No, that not problem, Mr. Steven. No need to go America or England to learn good English. I have friend in Sana'a. He take English course in *Yali*. You know *Yali?* He speak good—*well.* He learn *American* English, not Oxford. Our teachers from—*are* from Hind, most of them. They not speak Oxford, but they *say* they speak Oxford. I know because I listen BBC. *They* speak Oxford. *Indian* English? Who want to speak Indian English? . . . You want to meet director of college? He want to meet professor from America." I had feared this might be the case. I would be welcomed with great fanfare, sip tea for an hour or more, and be harangued about the stupidity of American foreign policy. "I wish to see the college, not the director," I replied.

The classrooms were clean, light, and airy, with lots of blackboard space. In one, young men and some fully veiled women were seated at desks, hunched over exam papers. I worried that my sudden presence might distract them. An exam monitor, a teacher, sat at the front, looking bored. A sari-clad woman made an occasional appearance, collecting the finished exams and retreating with them into another room, presumably to grade them. Neither acknowledged my presence.

"Yesterday was Arab history," explained Ahmed. "The day before that Arabic language and grammar. Today, English."

"Is the exam hard?" I asked a student.

"Easy," he replied. "But I wasn't sure about one question. Is *The Tempest* a comedy or a tragedy? Or a tragicomedy?"

"I don't think it's any of these. Or maybe all of them. To tell you the truth, I don't even remember the exact literary categories used by critics to classify Shakespeare's plays. The important thing is, what is the play about and did you like it?"

"Yes, I liked it, but the story is confusing. During a bad storm a ship comes to an island, ruled by a very smart but frightening old man with great powers, like Imam Yahya, who was feared by everyone. His servant is a creature who is something between a beast and a human being. The old man is also assisted by a *jinn*. Like the ancient Romans who invaded Yemen and then were led into the desert and got confused and died of thirst, or like the Ethiopians after them who were driven out by our king Seif bin Dhi Yazin; the evil men see and do things because of the imam's magic that drive them crazy and leave them weak and defeated." I had to think of the anthropologist Laura Bohannon's marvelous essay "Shakespeare in the Bush" or the Merchant-Ivory film *Shakespeare Wallah* while this young man was talking.

"You remember the play better than I do," I said. "I remember only a few lines that I was made to memorize in school. 'Our revels now are ended. These our actors, as I foretold you, were all spirits and are melted into air, into thin air, blah blah blah. We are such stuff as dreams are made of, and our little life is rounded with a sleep.'" It was pathetic that I could not remember more. This young man could probably recite hundreds of lines of Arabic poetry.

Someone suggested we go to the roof of the building, where we could see the whole campus. We were joined by more young men eager for a diversion and an older caretaker, who was very proud of his college.

"There was nothing here five years ago," he explained. "Now we have three large buildings. Tomorrow maybe more will be built."

"Yes," I replied. "It's like a city." The young men laughed at the metaphor, and the caretaker smiled approvingly.

"And what do you hope to teach?" I asked one of them.

"History. I like history. But we're trained to teach any subject. Arabic. Religion. Mathematics. Science. All grades from elementary through high school."

"But not everyone will get to teach," someone said solemnly. "Not enough positions."

"I don't understand," I said. "There are many in this country who don't know how to read or write. How can there not be enough positions?"

"You saw the school in the village, Mr. Steven," said Muhammad the Guide. "We built that ourselves. But we need many more, and we need school supplies like books and chalk."

"Then why are you getting a teacher's certificate?" I asked Ahmed.

"Because it's better than not. Things might improve, *inshallah*. It's a skill I might use later."

They were young and full of hope. Who was I to gainsay their optimism?

Back in the village, I was told that Sheikh al-Baradah wanted to speak to me, so I went to chew *qat* with him that afternoon. Only Abdul Wahid, Nasir, and Ahmed were present. Muhammad the Guide had gone to Sana'a to help deal with the aftermath of the revenge killing he'd told me about.

Abdul Wahid once again served as his uncle's intermediary. "He's wanted to tell you this ever since your return. We owe you an explanation." I could barely believe this moment had come. I was finally to learn his story of what happened twenty years earlier.

"Do you remember, Seif, the disappearance of the two girls? Yes, the boy from the sanctuary was accused of having abducted them. His recklessness started the dispute between the sanctuary and its neighbor who belonged to the Bani Dhubyan, and I came with the other sheikhs from Khawlan to mediate it, assisted by Muhammad Qasim. As you know, the boy was found but not the girls. It was presumed that they had either been killed or sold into prostitution somewhere in Saudi Arabia or the Gulf. We shall now let you in on a secret. They were found by some of the sheikhs from Khawlan and were handed over to me and another to keep in hiding. In fact, when you came to our village, they were staying here, but no one told you, not even Muhammad."

Seeing the astonished look on my face, Nasir laughed. "Most people didn't know, Seif. As a boy of ten, I wasn't supposed to know either, except that I came across one of them by accident. I happened to be in the sheikh's house one day and opened the door to a room, where I saw a girl turn her head and glower at me. She was beautiful, and I could tell by her defiant air that she had a commanding personality. Suddenly I realized who she was, and I slammed the door and scurried down the stairs, all excited about my discovery. Someone in the house grabbed me and asked what I had seen in the women's quarters. The veiled face in front of me said that I mustn't tell anyone and shook me until I promised to keep the secret. Later the sheikh"—and Nasir nodded his head to the old man—"made me repeat the promise."

I was only half comprehending what he said. "Why Wadi Maswar?"

"Wadi Maswar was chosen by the other sheikhs for the hiding place because we were discreet and would not be suspected by the sanctuary or its allies, at least not in the early stage of the conflict."

"Why did she seek protection if she had nothing to fear? Could she help it if the boy abducted her against her will?"

"It was more complicated than that," said Abdul Wahid. "The boy hadn't really abducted the two girls. The older one went willingly, and the younger one they took along because they didn't know what else to do with her. You see, the boy and the older girl were in love. They had been seeing each other secretly and wanted to marry, but her father, the sheikh of Sarkhan, refused, saying that the tribes didn't marry *sada*."

"That isn't true!" I burst out.

"Of course. The sheikh said that only because he had other plans for his beautiful daughter. He wanted her to marry one of the sons of Khawlan's great sheikhs. Together they pleaded with him to change his mind, but he remained adamant. At first, they thought that they could live apart, that their love for each other would fade. But it proved too great—and not a little mad, for in the end they defied the sheikh and eloped. We call it the love of wolves, an all-consuming passion heedless of social responsibility or consequences. The plan was for her to wander on the hillside searching for firewood while Abdullah the Culprit waited in his car in a nearby wadi. But their secret rendezvous was discovered by the girl's cousin, and afraid that she would go back and tell on them, they took her along. At the time of her disappearance, the sheikh suspected that his willful daughter might have acted rashly, but to admit this would have been shameful, and so he accused the young man of having abducted her and her companion against their will."

"But how did they expect to get away with their plan?"

"The girl told us that they were going to throw themselves upon the mercy of a distant sheikh, one over whom Khawlan had no power, hoping he would let them marry and live incognito within his tribe. Indeed, the hotel in Taiz to which she and her cousin were taken by Abdullah the Culprit was owned by a man with connections to a very powerful sheikh in the southern part of the country."

"Let me see if I understand. You came across the young man while he was running an errand in Taiz, and it was he who told you of the girls' whereabouts. You then found them in the hotel. The older pleaded for protection, and it was granted, after which she and her cousin were transplanted secretly to Wadi Maswar. But the boy knew you had found the girls, isn't that right?"

"Perhaps he suspected, but he never knew."

"But so many parts of this story are confusing! Why didn't Abdullah say that he and his lover had decided to elope? You tortured him—and he said the girl was pregnant and asked him to take her away from Sarkhan. That was his confession. Was it a lie?"

"No, he did confess it."

"Then he was *lying* in his confession! You just told me that the boy and the older girl had decided to elope."

"Ah, that is what *she* told us, and that's what he *led* the older girl to believe. But when he left her and her cousin in the hotel room, we think it was because the hotel owner and his son were going to sell them into prostitution."

"So there are two versions of the event: his, which is that he abducted the two girls with the most evil of intentions; hers, which is that she innocently believed they were going to elope. And you chose to believe *her* version. Why is that?"

"No, you still don't understand, Seif. We believed both versions. She really did believe he was in love with her and meant for them to elope, once it was clear that the sheikh would not permit them to marry. But then he began to have other ideas."

"And the girl? Was she pregnant?"

"No."

"Well, what about the hotel owner and his son and their assistant?

Why did you believe the boy's story that they were running a prostitution ring in the hotel?"

"We discovered that they *had* been running illegal sex activities and wanted to punish them for it."

"But why were the girls kept secretly?"

"It's the custom, Seif. If a fugitive throws himself on a sheikh's protection, he is honor-bound to hide him and keep him safe."

Everyone—the sheikh of Sarkhan above all—had said that the continued absence of the girls was the reason for war. If the real story had come out, much trouble, not to mention bloodshed, might have been avoided.

"Yes, it was the reason for war, though we kept trying to talk the Bani Dhubyan out of it. How could we tell them? That would have betrayed an ancient custom. We had to persuade them to negotiate as if the girls would never be found, but they refused. What could we do? We defended the sanctuary with our own blood."

"And did my arrest by National Security have anything to do with the secret?"

"No. Something else was behind that. The government wondered whether you were a spy and were helping to turn Khawlan against it. And they were after Muhammad for what he might have known about the girls. As it was, of course, they never managed to get their hands on him, and even if they had, he never would have talked."

Such a mix of feelings was swirling within me as I thought about the sheikh's story. I had been little more than a patsy, and yet the sheikh had protected me. "That was why Muhammad wanted me to stay in Wadi Maswar, wasn't it?" I said. "Why he hoped I wouldn't return to the sanctuary? He feared he was delivering me into the hands of National Security."

"I told him to persuade you to stay or to go to Sana'a, but he said you were adamant about returning to the sanctuary. He said he was sure you knew nothing about the girls' whereabouts. To have kept you against your will would have created more problems, so we decided to let you go."

"And do you know who *did* turn me over to National Security?"

"Someone complained to the vice president about you."

"I already know that. But who set me up that night?"

"Ah, that you will have to sort out with your friends in the sanctuary" was all the sheikh would say. But of course I wasn't going to have that opportunity. Besides, who was still alive from that time who would know and would talk to me frankly? I suppose the point was that what had happened to me was a foregone conclusion once I returned to the sanctuary, and that Muhammad knew it. Indeed, perhaps the wily sheikh had himself agreed to turn me over to National Security, to make it appear that he was cooperating with the government and thereby divert suspicion from himself. What better way than to have my arrest occur in the sanctuary, where I would suspect the *sada* but not him? If actual evidence of my spying had turned up, he could always have claimed to have helped uncover a meddlesome foreign agent. And as for Muhammad, had he allowed our friendship to be used for the sheikh's political machinations, had he simply been caught in the middle, rather as I had been, or had he been duped?

"What finally happened to the girls?" This, at least, would be clear, I thought.

"After the dispute was settled, the older one was married off to the son of the Bani Dhubyan. It was determined that the younger one was innocent, so she was allowed to return to her village, where she eventually married." The older girl's fate could hardly have been easy, as trophy bride of the powerful Dhubyan sheikh's son, like Helen at the end of the Trojan War. Suddenly it occurred to me that this denouement to the crazy drama could have been made up, that the girls had never been found after all. If they had been sold into prostitution, not only was their fate abhorrent to contemplate, but it unutterably shamed their tribe's honor; claiming that they'd been brought back to the tribe, by contrast, meant that patriarchal control was reasserted. Might the ending of the *Iliad* also have been contrived? Had Helen vanished or died before the Greeks could reclaim her?

"Well," I said to the sheikh, "if that's the case, then the people of the sanctuary eventually found out about the secret. Did they renounce the settlement? After all, it had cost them a fortune. Did they ask to have the fines reduced?"

"The sanctuary didn't challenge the settlement," he said. What he had done—to give asylum to the two girls and keep it secret—was within his rights, and the sanctuary was thankful to have the dispute settled. I remembered how exhausted everyone had been, how determined to pick up the pieces and get on with their lives. Yet al-Qumaisi's words of the day before haunted me, for he had made it clear that the conflict with the Bani Dhubyan wasn't over "once and for all." The wound hadn't healed, and resentment had continued to fester through the years. The sheikh added, "What the boy did was wrong, and the *sada* were responsible for him, no matter the complicity of the older girl."

"But the boy was shot with a silver bullet!" I burst out. "That was because it was assumed he had abducted and then raped them. No one ever contradicted that story."

"But he wasn't shot, Seif." The old man's eyes betrayed a gleam of satisfaction at my surprise. "The tribes decided to turn him over to the state, saying they wanted nothing more to do with him, and he languished in prison for seventeen years. He was released only a few years ago—a broken man. And he died shortly thereafter. His father had already gone mad before that, and the family went bankrupt."

"I don't understand. Why did the state keep him in prison for so long?"

"He had confessed his evil intentions toward the girls and deserved to be punished. Had we not found the girls when we did, they might very well have had a terrible end in that hotel we destroyed."

After this long conversation with al-Baradah, I didn't want to attend another large assembly, but Ahmed said that as guest of honor I had no choice, and he dragged me to another chew. Suddenly there was a surprise guest, and I realized why Ahmed had been so insistent. He was Ahmed al-Sharegi, the great *bala* poet whom I had recorded during the dispute between the sanctuary and Sarkhan. I was overjoyed to see him again. His entirely white garb announced him as a member of the Islah party, whereas I remembered him leaning toward socialism. He, too, had a poem in honor of my return:

> Welcome, Seif, from the Arabian Peninsula, which belongs to the
>   Arabs.
> As for Palestine, it is in a large hand, which overcomes power.

I had known it would be only a matter of time before the topic of U.S. politics in the Middle East came up. The first line alluded to the sizable American military base in Saudi Arabia established during the 1991 Gulf War, to which many, not only Osama bin Laden, strenuously objected. The second line I interpreted as being about the help the Palestinians were receiving in the Intifada from Hamas. Huge pro-Palestinian demonstrations had taken place in Yemen's major cities in April and May, some of them purportedly supported by the Yemeni government, which called Arab regimens everywhere to war against Israel.

But for the time being, I was spared another withering interrogation about U.S. Middle Eastern foreign policy, and instead, somewhat to my surprise, it was Ahmed al-Sharegi who was put in the hot seat. He was running on the Islah ticket in the upcoming parliamentary elections. Electoral politics had barely begun when I was in Yemen twenty years before, but after numerous delays, the first parliamentary elections had been held in 1993. The Yemeni Socialists gained a few seats in the north and lost some in the south to Islah, with the president's General Party Congress gaining the majority. The polling, which was monitored by international organizations, had been conducted fairly for the most part. Civil society had also opened up, with one of the freest and most vigorous presses in the Middle East, representing a broad spectrum of views. A women's rights movement started in Sana'a. But with the outbreak of civil war a year later, the government clamped down and options for political expression receded. By the next parliamentary elections, in 1997, people had become more jaded, because in the end the political process didn't seem to alter realities. There were widespread complaints of government corruption, and people wondered whether Ali Abdullah Salih would ever step down to let others besides his own family members exercise power. It was disheartening to see how quickly attitudes had shifted, and ironic that they mirrored the cynicism and disillusionment many in the United States had felt for some time about their own electoral politics.

Ahmed al-Sharegi had come not only to say hello and to honor me but also to canvass support at what was sure to be a large turnout of potential voters. Thus, it was local, not international, politics that people were interested in debating, and they proceeded to grill him on all kinds of issues. Why did the Islah do things only for people who subscribed to its religious beliefs? If it was a national party, as it was supposed to be, why didn't it work for the good of everyone? Building new schools was great, but what was being taught in them besides religious subjects? What about clinics? What about electricity and water? Al-Sharegi had rather formulaic answers to these questions, but he offered them with charm and a sense of humor. Still, I felt a little sorry for him and intervened to change the topic.

"Do you still compose poetry?" I asked. I feared his newfound religious ardor and political conservatism had dampened his enthusiasm for the art, but he said he found no contradiction between religion and poetry. "Poetry between men and women," he clarified, "that is not permissible. Otherwise, there's no harm in it."

"But what about you? Didn't you want to compose *qasida*?"

"Poetry in Khawlan is no longer what it once was, Seif. Al-Sufi, al-Gharsi, al-Bowra⁽ᶜ⁾i—they've all passed away or stopped composing poetry. If you were to do your research today, you'd have to go to the south—to Yafi⁽ᶜ⁾. There's where the action is." A vision of my colleague Flagg Miller came to mind: he had worked there on poetry. "And twenty years from now, it will be somewhere else. It goes in cycles." This interesting observation was new to me. We carried on in this fashion for a few minutes, but at the first available opportunity, al-Sharegi excused himself. It had not been an auspicious campaign stop.

DAY 4

"Do you know what today is?" I asked Ahmed the next morning, when he brought breakfast. "It's my country's birthday. Like your September 26, we had a revolution on this day over two hundred years ago."

"Well, then, maybe you should have a bath to celebrate." He laughed. "We're going to take you on an outing to a lovely spring called Hababuth."

The route lay along a wadi floor that, I was told, one could follow all the way to Marib. According to legend, the Himyarites and Sabaeans had plied it centuries ago on their trading expeditions. We drove through a spectacular canyon with dramatic cliffs soaring a thousand feet above the wadi floor, and there were rock formations that looked suspiciously like ancient ruins. "Natural or man-made?" Ahmed asked Nasir, who was in the backseat. "Natural." The swelling from the bee sting on his foot had gone down, so he had decided to join us.

I was in the front seat, wedged between Ahmed and the driver, a beautiful youth of fifteen. He was hardly an inexperienced driver, demonstrating considerable skill in the way he navigated the rugged watercourse. The kid ought to work as a driver and tour guide for one of the travel agencies in Sana'a, I thought.

Ahmed decided to start an impromptu jamboree. A chant was stuck up, based on the *zamil* poems from the day before, with boys delivering one line of the poem and the older men the other. This was a moving experience—to hear those words composed in my honor being repeated by hearty, raucous voices echoing off the sheer cliff faces around us. Ahmed winked with delight and urged me to get it all on tape, which I did. I listen to that tape from time to time and grin at the exuberance, as brilliant as a bright, clear day in a Boston winter.

We finally arrived at the spring, hot and dusty and ready for our baths, but others had come before us. A group of Bedouin women had just finished their laundry and left it out to dry, spread on the cliffs like a giant, colorful patchwork. The ladies were taking a break in the shade of an acacia tree, sipping their tea. They waved us on to enjoy the spring while they chatted away, oblivious to our presence.

Rather than the mad dash I had expected, our advance was more tentative.

"The last time I came, about two years ago," Nasir said, "the water was up to my hip." But all we could see ahead were a few puddles that widened into a shallow stream as we approached the foot of the mountain from where the spring issued. He was obviously concerned.

"What do you suppose caused the water level to decline?" I asked.

"I think it's the artesian wells in Wadi Maswar," he replied without hesitation. Since the time of the Himyars, over a thousand years ago, this place had been a watering hole, but the unthinkable had happened and the spring was drying up. Water use made possible by artesian wells now exceeded the recharge by rain. My younger companions must have wondered how much longer they could come here and frolic.

Men and boys shed their clothing, leaving on only their knee-length underpants. This was not out of politeness to the women nearby, who couldn't have cared less in any case, but out of respect for one another, for it is considered shameful for men to expose their genitals to other men.

The spring bubbled up from a cleft at the bottom of the huge mountain and issued into a pool just deep enough for the smaller boys to wade in over their heads. The older ones climbed up the cliff face and then did cannonballs into the water. "C'mon!" they shouted to me. I was badly in need of a bath and sorely tempted to jump in, but I feared contracting bilharzia. Inspecting the pool for snails, I found none but still thought it best to be cautious, and I declined.

"I'll keep guard over your clothing while you swim," I jested, and grabbing Ahmed's Kalashnikov, stood in a sentry's pose. AMERICA OCCUPIES YEMEN flashed like a headline through my mind. Ahmed took my picture and then tore off his clothes to join his confederates.

We returned as we had come, except that our car, with shorts hanging from door handles and the luggage rack, looked like a circus truck with pennants fluttering in the breeze. I couldn't recall a Fourth of July on which I had had so much fun.

DAY 5

I woke up tired and felt a cold coming on. I was saddened by the thought that I had to go but also relieved, frankly, that my taxing visit had come to an end.

"We've worn you out," said Ahmed when he came in with tea, "rest now." I coughed and poked around for some cough medicine in my backpack, which Abdul Wahid had jokingly dubbed my pharmacy. When he left I retrieved my notebook and fountain pen and began writing down the story about the two girls and Abdullah the Culprit.

"You're not resting," Ahmed admonished me when he returned with breakfast. As soon as he left again, I started writing.

I should have known that the peace and quiet would not last. Suddenly, Muhammad the Guide came into the room. I didn't begrudge him the interruption and expressed my pleasure at seeing him again. From the rifle over his shoulder, I could tell something important was up.

"Remember the revenge killing I told you about? They're bringing the body back to Wadi Maswar this morning to bury it. You've seen our wedding celebrations and our religious festivals but never, I think, a funeral. Would you like to come with us?"

He was right that I hadn't seen a funeral, but I was of two minds about the proposition, given my deteriorating health. Hearing a commotion outside, I looked out the window and saw men congregating along the asphalt road.

"What are they doing out there?" I asked.

"They've come to greet the funeral cortege," Muhammad explained, "and pay their respects to the dead man's father, the great sheikh al-Dahmish. Let's go." Suddenly, my mind was made up for me.

I grabbed my headdress and *jambiyya* and put them on as we headed out. I had not forgotten my backpack with my gear in it, for I figured this would be an ethnographic event just as Muhammad the Guide predicted.

Honking could be heard from the direction of Sana'a, and suddenly the first cars of the funeral procession came into view. This must have been what my friend Muhammad's funeral was like when his body was brought back from Sana'a. There were dozens of vehicles—jeeps, pickup trucks, vans called saloons—all racing to Dahmish's village. This was not a slow, stately cortege but a rushed, noisy, chaotic affair, more like traffic on one of Sana'a's busy streets or the final push on a military holdout. Everyone but me saluted with rifle fire as the cars went by. Suddenly, Muhammad the Guide pointed to a van. "It's carrying the body, and the father is in the front seat." I could barely see the grim-looking man wearing sunglasses behind the dusty windshield. Sunglasses are rare for Yemenis; perhaps he was wearing them to hide his tears. Muhammad pointed his weapon to the sky and discharged several rounds of ammunition. Had I been the father, I could not have endured this sound that reminded me of the way my son had died.

We got in our vehicles and followed at the same breakneck speed, and before I knew it, we had arrived at Sheikh Dahmish's house. It was large, built in the "modern" boxlike style but with expensive dressed stone instead of cement blocks, perched on a hill overlooking a prosperous little village that belonged to the sheikh's clan. Besides the many cars parked in front and on the road leading up to it, we could see dozens of sheep and bulls in the backs of trucks or tethered to them, munching on fodder—their last meal.

Taking my hand, Muhammad the Guide stepped gingerly through the graveyard, where one large hole had been freshly dug. Muhammad told me that the dead man's body had been washed in Sana'a and wrapped in the traditional white shroud for burial, which according to Islamic law must take place within twenty-four hours of death or as soon thereafter as possible. It was now in the house, where the mother and sisters would pay their last respects. My presence excited attention and drew not a few raised eyebrows—precisely what I had feared. Sensing my anxiety, Muhammad pressed his body close to mine as if to protect me. We headed toward a rocky outcrop from which we could observe the proceedings without being noticed.

"Who is he?" Muhammad the Guide was asked.

"One of our people," he replied enigmatically.

My level of discomfort rose. I might as well have been a celebrity spotted in the bleachers of a baseball game. People started arguing with Muhammad the Guide. I should not be there, someone said. Who had brought me? another wanted to know. Muhammad seemed unfazed. "Take pictures if you like," he urged me, almost defiantly. I took my camera out of my backpack. It was one of the small snap-and-shoot models that had recently become popular in the United States, and I hoped it would be inconspicuous, but it had the opposite effect. My neighbors were used to the Canons with big barrel lenses that they'd seen tourists sling over their shoulders like rifles but not this miniaturized equipment, which looked to them like a spy camera.

Suddenly, all attention switched to the center of the graveyard, and the crowd grew still. The body had been brought from the house on the shoulders of the dead man's kinsmen. Somehow the corpse seemed more vulnerable in the white cocoon than if it had been in a coffin. The body was gently lowered into the grave, and some words were said that I could not hear. Dirt was swiftly piled on top and smoothed over, and the service was over almost before it had begun. Visitations to the grave would continue all day, I was told, especially by the women, who would pay their respects when the men were not around.

An imposing individual strode purposefully toward me. He was small, even for a Yemeni, but had extraordinarily expressive eyes that could narrow into slits of alarming portent or widen with mischievous mirth. As he saw him approach, Muhammad the Guide grew uneasy, and I suspected that he was questioning the wisdom of having brought me here. He was Abdullah Hentish, one of the biggest sheikhs of Khawlan, who hailed from the Bani Jabr tribe. He accosted me, but not in an unfriendly manner, wanting to know who I was and what I was doing here.

I explained the reason for my presence in Khawlan, and Muhammad showed him the documents to back up what I said. Yes, he had known Muhammad Qasim well, the sheikh said. A great hero.

"The governor is right over there." Hentish chuckled. "You can say hello to him if you want." Sure enough, a bald man dressed in immaculate tribal robes was standing on the outskirts of the crowd, directly opposite us.

"He seems busy with people, and I don't want to bother him," I said. "But if you'd like me to leave, I will immediately."

"No, no. You're welcome, most welcome, Seif from America." Pointing to my camera, he added, "You can even take pictures."

"Well, maybe one or two of you and your companions," I suggested. Seeing him pose before the camera was like a signal to the men watching us to get back to business. I'd been a magnet, and tension had run like an invisible current in the air, but Hentish managed to dispel it.

Now a new anxiety seized me as he dragged me by the hand to the knot of assembled tribesmen in the middle of the graveyard. I felt like matter being sucked into a black hole. I looked over my shoulder at Muhammad the Guide, who waved me on with a sheepish grin. I was under the sheikh's protection and there was little he could do to help.

From being in a backseat to this spectacle, I was suddenly being thrust onto center stage.

I joined a rank of formidable-looking men who, besides Hentish, included Sheikh Muhammad al-Qiri, one of the defenders of the sanctuary years ago and father of the Salih who had died with Muhammad in battle; and the great sheikh al-Royshan, the Ulysses among them, who had played a more duplicitous behind-the-scenes role in the conflict between Khawlan and the Bani Dhubyan. (Sadly, the one sheikh I had met and liked was not present; Hussein Ali al-Gadhi had died in battle several years before.) The charisma of these sheikhs was apparent in their faces, in their bearing, in the circumspect way their followers approached or disengaged from them, all of which I had noticed about them twenty years before; what was different was their newfound wealth, resulting from government subsidy and capital accumulations, evident in their big cars, expensive guns, and many retainers.

How long tribal leaders in Yemen would continue to be primus inter pares and deal with their constituents in direct, face-to-face communication was an intriguing question. A powerful figure like Hentish obviously relished the drama of public life and still possessed a common touch with his people, but he could get government-sponsored projects for them only if he had influence with key officials, and that would require a residence in Sana'a, no doubt, and hours and hours of hobnobbing with the capital's political and business elite. A good sheikh has to perform a delicate balancing act between his obligations to his followers and the demands of the state, which put a strain on him that might have always been there but never in so acute a form.

A tall, rugged man in his late twenties said to me in perfect English, "Hi. I'm from the Royshan family. I studied computer engineering at a university in Tennessee. Have you come to help us solve the dispute?"

"Not unless it can be done over the Internet. I leave for America soon."

"Ah, the Internet hasn't arrived in Khawlan yet. But wouldn't you like to join us for lunch and then listen to our negotiations?"

I was torn mightily by this proposal. I had always wanted to witness such a high-level negotiation, yet Ahmed was expecting me for lunch with Sabri Salim, and it would be horribly impolite to skip it. The irony did not escape me that now, when I was ostensibly not doing fieldwork and was identifying myself as a tourist, I was being handed the fieldwork opportunity of a lifetime. Reluctantly I passed up the invitation. I didn't get very far with my explanation, however, before angry voices drowned out the conversation.

The sheikh of the killer's tribe stood before us, his retainers on their haunches behind him, listening hard to his oratory. He made his case, gesticulating angrily, it seemed to me, or perhaps just heatedly. At one point he came within a foot of Hentish, close enough for me to see the antimony lining his eyes like an actor's eye shadow. The tribe wanted to negotiate, he affirmed, and they had arrived with many guns as their pledges. This was the signal for his men to bring out dozens of automatic rifles and pile them in a circle. He backed away from Hentish and gestured toward the stack of military hardware on the ground and then beyond, to the bulls and sheep about to be sacrificed. The meat would be eaten for lunch in the following days.

Next to speak was the dead boy's father, al-Dahmish. Behind him stood a small entourage of his people. He looked worn out and was still wearing sunglasses. Grief and rage had rendered him nearly incoherent, it seemed to me, but I did make out his warning that the terms of peace would be dear and war inevitable if the price were not paid.

Now it was the turn of the mediators to speak, and they were represented by Hentish, the most powerful sheikh. In measured but forceful tones, he told the sheikh of the killer's tribe that the mediators would refuse to guarantee the truce unless they doubled the number of guns. The gravity of the crime as well as the amount of work it would take to redress it required this amount. There were clamors and furious gesticulations, but soon an agreement was reached: everyone wanted to solve the problem peacefully. As if a curtain had come down, the spectacle ended. Everyone broke ranks and smiled, filled with goodwill and optimism. Muhammad the Guide later told me the killer's tribe would probably not be held responsible for the boy's death, because it had been an accident.

"The governor knows about you and says hello, Seif," Hentish said. Someone had apparently gone over to check up on me—no doubt at the sheikh's behest—and the governor had confirmed my story. "Won't you join us for lunch?"

I politely declined. "Well, then, let me at least drive you back. I knew Muhammad Qasim and know his son Ahmed. I've been to his village many times." I happily agreed to this compromise, and we headed toward his car. Muhammad the Guide and others from al-Hijla were to follow us. They were a bit awestruck in front of the sheikh, the closest thing Khawlan has to a celebrity.

I got into the passenger seat while Hentish drove, with guards sitting in the back as well as standing on the footboards and clinging to the baggage rack. No sooner had we gotten to the village exit than some men threw themselves in front of the car to make us stop. They were furious. How could Hentish leave, they demanded to know, when he had been invited to lunch by Sheikh Dahmish? He was dishonoring them. Yes, yes, replied the sheikh, leaning out the window to talk to them, he was only going to drop the American off and then come right back. But the demonstrators refused to let us go, one of them actually lying down in the road. Bring the American with you to lunch, they insisted.

Wouldn't it be better, I suggested to the sheikh, if we said goodbye here and I left with my companions? He agreed, and we exchanged telephone numbers and addresses.

"I hope to visit America someday. Would you be my guide?"

"Gladly," I said.

"Then go in peace." We shook hands.

When I got out of the sheikh's car, however, Dahmish's tribesmen stopped me and insisted in no uncertain terms that I join their dignitaries for lunch. I had to forestall this possibility, so I addressed myself to the most adamant of the men and began an explanation. I knew my delivery had to be dramatic but sincere, so I looked him squarely in the eye and raised my voice for all to hear. It would not do for me to break a promise to lunch with the son of a dear friend of mine, Muhammad Qasim, God preserve him. Nor would it be prudent for me to stay in Khawlan beyond the time allotted by the Yemeni government, for then I would be declared a missing person and Yemen would be in trouble with the United States. They wouldn't want that, would they? We all laughed at this suggestion. I would be back in Yemen in six months and promised to lunch with them then. Very well, the fierce one said, and we shook hands. I turned around and said to my companions from al-Hijla, "Let's get out of here, quick!" They needed no prompting. One of them extended his hand to me so that I could hop onto the back of the pickup truck, and away we flew.

It was wonderful to see Sabri's smiling face when we got back, and I was relieved that now he, and not I, was the center of attention at the lunch and *qat* chew. I would finally relax.

When the time came for me to say goodbye, I went around the room and shook hands with each person, singling out three men— Naji, Abdul Wahid, and Nasir—for special farewells. My memory is that I patted Asᶜad on the head and grasped Salih's hand in mine through the open car window before we took off.

"Well, how do you feel?" asked Sabri in English as he drove the jeep onto the tarmac road. Ahmed and Muhammad the Guide were in the back, serving as my escorts and fulfilling their final obligations in accordance with the governor's instructions. From the dark clouds mass-ing on the horizon, it looked as if Sana'a had had rain. There were shadows on Khawlan, too, but not dark enough, I feared, to bring desperately needed relief.

"Like weeping," I said.

In the few days left to me in Yemen, I saw Ahmed several more times, though since I was frantically trying to complete my errands before my departure, I didn't have time to luxuriate in the bonhomie of a *qat* chew. He understood and did not take my abruptness as an affront, but then he wasn't one for extended conversation in any case.

On one of our last visits, he brought a videotape that he had just fixed at one of the local stereo stores. It was a home movie of his father, taken toward the end of Muhammad's life when he went to Marib to see the tourist attractions, both ancient and modern, like the great dam, the Temple of the Sun, the Throne Room of the Queen of Sheba, and so forth. But when we put the tape in the VCR, it turned out to be blank. At first Ahmed thought the stereo store had made a mistake and given him the wrong tape, but he examined it carefully and concluded that it was indeed the same one that had been in his possession all these years. Apparently someone had borrowed the original tape and kept it, returning the blank in its place.

"Oh, well, perhaps it will turn up," I tried to reassure him, but my heart went out to this young man who had been robbed of this sentimental reminiscence of a father he had hardly known, much less remembered.

Suddenly I reached out and held his hands. "You know I'll never forget you, Ahmed. I'll see what I can do to get you a visa to the United States. It won't be easy, but I'll try. Maybe you can find work in Boston or New York. I have money to get you started, and you can pay me back once you have a steady job. But no matter what, I'll be back." A smile played on his lips, the more beautiful for being so rare.

Epilogue: Hope

I should have known that I would not get to the bottom of the 1980 events by going back to Khawlan and interviewing people there, but my need for narrative closure overcame my common sense and theoretical judgment. When I left Yemen the first time, the strange events in Khawlan struck me uncannily like an enactment of the *Iliad*: females abducted; a war of honor over them; justice corrupted by greed and secret political wranglings. All I needed, or so I thought when I returned, was to tie up the loose ends of the story and catch up with people's lives. Learning not only that the two girls had been found, but that the older one had fallen in love with the young man and that they had planned to run away together deepened the parallel with Homer's epic. But could I believe this account for which I had no evidence or testimony from the main protagonists?

Just as disquieting was to learn that the dispute between tribe and sanctuary, though it was supposed to have been "settled" long ago, continued to fester—a bitter lesson of how events not only echo the past but reverberate ominously in the future. Why did the hostilities between sanctuary and tribe persist? Was it due to the sanctuary's lingering bitterness over the 1980 settlement, which, it turned out, was predicated on a secret—the hiding of the two girls—and in the sanctuary's eyes might be tantamount to betrayal? Or was it that national and international political forces continued to swirl in the region, dragging sanctuary and tribe into a vortex of mutual recrimination? If that was the case, the dynamics of such confrontations would only sharpen and become more dangerous as the Yemeni state gained in strength, popular opposition mounted to its policies, and Yemen's arms markets proliferated. Would that I could return to the sanctuary and ask those who remember the events of 1980 to explain them if they can! But I know better than to expect the mysteries to be dispelled rather than deepened. So long as the conflict continues, memories of it will be contested.

Most painful of all was to find out, or *try* to find out, what happened to Muhammad and to grasp the downward spiral of his life and his mounting desperation. My sense of responsibility toward his family springs not only from my guilt over not having done enough to "save" him but from a deep well of gratitude for all that he did to make my fieldwork a success, and from my growing affection for his family.

But the plan to bring Ahmed to the United States came to naught. Shortly after the events of September 11, 2001, Ahmed left a message on my voice mail in Boston saying he hoped neither I nor "my people" had been hurt by the attacks on the World Trade towers. He could not have imagined then how this event would dash his hopes of coming to America: it became almost impossible for Arabs, especially Yemenis, to emigrate to the United States, and travel to Yemen wasn't easy for Americans either. At the request of the U.S. government, the Yemeni embassy did not issue visas until new security arrangements were in place. I had to delay my return.

Important as it might be for Americans to be involved in countries like Yemen, I could not describe my own motives in politically strategic terms, however. I wasn't going back to win the hearts and minds of people so that Americans could be safer. Nor, when I finally was able to get back to Yemen in the summer of 2003, could I believe in the fiction stamped on my visa: "object of travel—tourism." I longed for a deeper connection with the country—to stay in touch with Ahmed and his family and friends, and then to do fieldwork again, that desire having been awakened by my memories of Muhammad and quickened by my friendships with his son, Muhammad the Guide, Abdul Wahid, and the little boys of al-Hijla who taught me their genealogy.

I was returning for another reason, too: to plan fieldwork on water, a topic I'd started thinking about during my trip in 2001, with an ethnography to follow. No one knows for certain what can be done to alleviate the dire water shortages in Yemen, and I'm not sure that anthropology can help, but I feel compelled to try. With luck, I can train Yemeni students to work on issues of water scarcity and degradation, and perhaps a couple of them will be good enough to go abroad to get a Ph.D. and return to teach in Yemen.

Yet the political situation in the Middle East—which we know deeply affects all work there—has been the most volatile and depressing in a half century, and also the most dangerous for Americans. How events affect the lives and works of people and the anthropologist who studies them has been a principal theme of this book; and the U.S. invasion and subsequent occupation of Iraq in that same year of 2003 was another world-historical event, as shattering in its own way as those of 9/11.

Heralded by the Bush administration and its supporters as an opportunity for "regime change," not to mention for remaking the political map of the Middle East, the Iraq war has been guided by a top-down, mostly go-it-alone strategy (inflated by arrogance the likes of which we have not seen since the days of nineteenth-century imperialism) and it has badly faltered. Americans may now be in the mood to reflect on what went wrong, though so far reflection has been about only logistical concerns, such as the need for better planning or an "exit strategy" for the U.S. military. There has been little or no reflection of a philosophical or existential kind, asking whether the U.S. attitude to its encounters in the Middle East is not fundamentally flawed. I would hope that the very different encounter this book describes betweeen an American and a beautiful but troubled Arab-Muslim land has lessons to impart.

Everyone agrees that things must change, but Americans have learned at immense cost to their nation and to the Iraqi people that change cannot be dictated but must be negotiated. Otherwise, the agent of change comes across as a bully and tyrant to be resisted at all cost. Force, or rather the threat of force, should always be in a dialectical relationship with mediation or negotiation. The point is not that force should never be exercised, but that it should be a means toward mediated settlements, not the end dictating the final result. Understanding the use of force in this way entails working patiently with partners in highly complex situations, accepting the vulnerability that comes with such partnerships, and, perhaps most important of all, the negative possibility of uncertainty and contingency. Such are not attitudes conventionally associated with a super-power like the United States, since some Americans view them as a weakness, not a strength, as a cause for failure, not success.

Yet one might ask whether it would not be wiser to embark on world-historical endeavors with humility and a degree of tentativeness. Hubris usually brings with it a simplified view of reality that can do real harm. Steadfast decisiveness may have succeeded in mobilizing the United States behind a highly dubious military project, but it also blinded us to possibilities and potentials that we need to explore, now more than ever. The failure is due not only to poor political leadership (though that, too, is greatly to blame) but to a cultural habit: Americans prefer simple narratives and easily comprehended choices, which then make them susceptible to specious rhetoric that the administration has used to defend the war in Iraq. I hope that this book will inspire readers to rethink American assumptions about how to "deal" with the Middle East: if so, there may be hope not only for us but also for people like Ahmed and his family.

Why on earth, my friends and relatives ask, do I still want to go back to Yemen? It will always be difficult, I say, the time will never be opportune, the conditions never ideal to work and live in the Middle East. One has to accept the dangers and tragedies along with the joys and fascinations or not live and work there at all.

At least there is a glimmer of hope for Yemen. When U.S. Special Forces went there to combat al-Qaeda terrorists, President Salih cooperated with the efforts and shut down Islamic institutes that preached anti-American propaganda. Islah's influence seems to be waning. Animosity toward Americans has abated, though it has hardly been replaced by friendliness. To date, the U.S. government's predominant strategy for dealing with terrorism has been through force, and it has not addressed the underlying conditions that lead to despair and the self-destructive behavior it spawns. Had my friend Muhammad the Maswari been a religious man, it's not unthinkable that he might have ended up in an al-Qaeda training camp.

If the U.S. government has been helping Yemen to eliminate terrorist elements within the country, it has been much slower to give aid and create development projects that might help its people. This can partly be explained by Yemen's poor security, of course, but that has improved, and much, much more could be done to stimulate the economy. Or will America cynically turn its back on Yemen now that elements that had threatened its personnel seem to have been neutralized?

In al-Hijla things have gotten better even without that intervention. For over a decade Naji, Muhammad's old friend, had been working very hard to get the government to help the village build a water project, which involves pumping water from new wells, holding it in above-ground cisterns, and letting it flow by gravity from a network of pipes to people's homes. When I returned in 2004, it was just being completed. No longer do women have to lug water for long distances. It seems that Naji had one last burst of energy in him after all. Presidential elections were held in 2004, and as I was leaving al-Hijla, electricity and telephone were being installed, thanks to government assistance. Is it any wonder that Ali Abdullah Salih's poster was on many *mafraj* walls?

Now that Ahmed can't emigrate to the United States, he has to figure out how to provide for his family. There is little future in farming as long as the drought lasts. As for off-farm work, that too is limited by the deteriorating national and global economies. He's passed his teacher certificate exam, but the nagging question remains: What can he do with it? Why not upgrade his skills, I suggested, by taking English lessons in Sana'a? Because he has several mouths to feed and the lessons are costly, I've offered to help out, and he's now completed his first year. Nasir still searches for occasional construction work, but little building is being done in Sana'a, so Ahmed, with some of the money he has saved, has hired him to help out with home improvement projects, like replastering the *mafraj* and installing tile in the bathroom. Salih is learning to drive, and I have promised to help pay for a pickup truck in which he hopes to ferry people and goods back and forth from Sana'a. I am working on them to let Baqla attend high school, even if that means she has to postpone her marriage.

Limited goals, small victories, but they give us hope.

Acknowledgments

I thank the Institute for Advanced Study at Princeton for providing a fellowship in 1998–99, during which time I wrote a major portion of this manuscript. Without Elisabeth Sifton's unstinting editorial help, it would never have seen the light of day, however. That our friendship has not only survived but deepened in the process, I count as a miracle and a blessing.

Printed in the USA
CPSIA information can be obtained
at www.ICGtesting.com
LVHW091129150724
785511LV00001B/40

9 780809 098828